To Jane & Risa,
With heartfelt thanks for
trusting me ... your
great treasu... ...ible
support have ma... in
for my work to be done, & in
some measure, for this book
to be written.

Love,

Patti ...

# The
# Secret Language

SUMMIT BOOKS
New York • London • Toronto • Sydney • Tokyo • Singapore

*of Dolphins*

*Patricia St.John*

SUMMIT BOOKS
Simon & Schuster Building
Rockefeller Center
1230 Avenue of the Americas
New York, New York 10020

Designed by Edith Fowler
Manufactured in the United States of America

10   9   8   7   6   5   4   3   2   1

Library of Congress Cataloging in Publication Data

St.John, Patricia, date
   The secret language of dolphins/Patricia St.John.
      p.   cm.
      1. Autistic children—United States—Language
—Case studies.   2. Language disorders in
children—Treatment—United States—Case
studies.   3. Human-animal communication—
Case studies.   4. Dolphins—United States—
Behavior—Case Studies.   5. St.John, Patricia,
date.   I. Title.
RJ506.A9S7   1991
618.92'8982—dc20                                   91-29022
                                                          CIP

ISBN 0-671-70979-8

*To CSJ—who made it all right for me to do my work.*

*To HAK—who made it possible for my work to expand and be seen by the world.*

*To ALL—who is all I'll ever want and knew from the very beginning that he would have to share.*

*1*F THE EYES are the windows of the soul, then our friends are the mirrors of our selves. My research would never have been possible without the people who have been there beside me through the long journey of discovery.

The scuba people who hung in there all these years deserve particular recognition in this book. They were the very first to understand the depth (no joke intended,) breadth, and scope of my efforts.

I say a special thank you to Armand "Ziggy" Zigahn, who loaned me his precious laptop for my first trek to Russia and his endless, tireless support of my work over the years; and to his wife JoAnn, to Chris Kenney, and to all the generous people who volunteer to make the New York–area, Westchester dive show "Beneath The Sea" such a success. By donating booth space and—thank God—money to MID★POINT Foundation over the years they have made it possible for us to continue our work.

To Walter "Butch" Hendrick, Jr., a legend in dive rescue training, who made us truly professional at slide shows and gave more than we could ever give in return.

To Boston Sea Rovers for giving me my start on the dive show circuit and making me feel that I had a family; to Our World-Underwater and the many scholarship "kids" who have helped me with my research; to SEAS, New Jersey Council of Divers, and Houston Seaspace for their eager endorsement of my research.

To Ronnie Segars, a brave and wonderful woman, and Herb Segars, whose underwater photographs have opened the eyes of thousands to the pleasures of cold-water diving, for their endless generosity and his superb color title slides.

To my certifying agency, the Professional Association for Diving Instructors (P.A.D.I.) for their enthusiasm and willingness to publish my articles; to Bob Chaplin, who made certain we received drysuits and then taught us how to use them; to Ned Taber and Viking America for their donation of the suits that have made it possible for four of us to never freeze in the water again; to Frank Fennell and Nikon for loaning us equipment when we needed it; to Dave Stancil and U.S. Divers Corporation for opening their treasure chest and completely outfitting us all; to Jim Fulton for the fabulous Delphi Orca Dive computers that brought us into the space age; to Marian Rivman of the Divers Equipment Manufacturer's Association (DEMA) for providing equipment for use by autistic children.

My heartfelt appreciation goes to Robert "Seal" Limes, owner of South Side Scuba and Grotto Bay Scuba in Bermuda, for his generosity of self and anything relating to scuba diving; and to Chris Wachholz of Diver's Alert Network for never giving up on that free trip to Belize, Cancun, and Cozumel. (Hang in there, Chris. Who knows, anything is possible given enough time and enough tries.)

I owe so much to the following: my dear friend Leena Muukki, former head inspector at Kolmarden Dolphinarium in Kolmardens, Sweden, a legendary teacher of trainers and an absolute fanatic on good water quality; Dr. Wolfgang Gewalt of Duisburg Zoo in Duisburg, Germany; Martin Huyguen of Munster Zoo in Munster, Germany; Leandro Stanzani and Guiseppe Caniglia of Delphinarium Riccione Adriatic Sea World in Riccione, Italy; Cees Kamminga of Delft University of Technology for his faith and support and hundreds of EMail letters which kept me going when times were particularly difficult; Dr. Margaret Klinowska of Cambridge University, a very special woman indeed, who always takes the time to make certain my papers are correct; Victor Manton, past editor of *Aquatic Mammals,* who encouraged me to publish; and the European Association for Aquatic Mammals for their willingness to listen to and explore my findings where others wouldn't. Randy Goodlett of Pittsburgh Aqua Zoo provided me with the rarest experience anyone could have with a dolphin and I am forever grateful to him for making it possible.

I have a gigantic thank-you for my agent, Mel Berger of William Morris Agency. He saw the importance of what I was doing when others were blind, knew from the start that it would all wind up in a book, and never gave up working to make it possible. A man of mostly nouns and verbs, his support enabled me to write this book filled with adverbs and adjectives.

Without the vision and enthusiasm of my editor, Dominick Anfuso, this book would still be nothing but a goal unachieved. His continued support and delicate hand at editing changed me from an aspiring writer into an author.

I could never have continued my research or lived a reasonably normal life without the help of those dedicated volunteers at MID★POINT—Nancy Gulash, Cynthia Butts, Tracey

Mahon, Nicole Smith, Marilyn Travinski, and the many others who were there when we needed help. Allison Kritzstein, an especially courageous young woman, stands out not only as MID★POINT's first intern, but as a special friend, and a super sushi spotter.

To Cindy Cornett-Stendig, who guided my efforts chapter by chapter, Dan Stendig, Norma Andes, and Llyn Fulghum— all of whom happen to be from the beautiful state of Virginia— I owe great debts of gratitude. They read this book and freely gave their praise and constructive comments. When they said it was worth reading, I knew it was. Their interest and feedback kept me going during the slow times and gave me hope that I actually might be a writer. And an extra thanks to Norma, who provided a haven away from insanity and the worst pullout bed in the United States. (Perhaps that's the secret to being sure friends come for a short, but happy stay.)

To Mandy, Molly, Sean, Alex, Jam, Honey, Farley, Zach, and Teddy goes the credit for keeping me sane. They are more than dogs and cats, they are friends and loved ones. June Kavanek, babysitter at sixteen, dear friend at eighteen and for life, singer par excellence, and surrogate mother to all the animals that I've ever had, never said no when I needed her most.

I save my deepest thanks for Hedy Kinney and her love, support, friendship, and patience in the face of all the awful and wonderful things we've endured together.

My dear son, Christopher, with whom I've traveled three lifetimes and more, all since he was born, always provided a reason to come home. I've been his stay-at-home mom, his traveling mom, and now his writing mom.

Although JoJo, resident dolphin of the waters of the Caribbean, is another story for another book, I must acknowledge him for bringing me the greatest treasure of my life. Were it not for his love of humans, I'd never have met my extraordinary husband, Allison Lee Lake.

While Alli labored in the treetops of New York State tweaking amplifiers for rabid television viewers, I tapped the black off the letter *N* on his computer, which he selflessly taught me how to use and then let me appropriate. He never gave up on me, always supplied life and love support, sensitivity, understanding, and humor. Together we've fended off five foreclosure attempts and things much worse than that. He is one "finest kind a man" and this book belongs as much to him as it does to me.

It's no wonder that Alli is so remarkable. He learned how to be special from his equally incredible mother, Harriette Hill. It's a measure of her greatness that she not only took me and Chris into her heart, but supplied the means for the three of us to exist throughout the years of hardship. More than money, she was always there with faith, encouragement, and endless prayers. Anyone fortunate enough to have her on their side can never lose.

I don't know how I was lucky enough to have become friends with these people, but I respect and love them all. They became my far-flung, worldwide community, my surrogate family, and they made it possible for me to always move forward, to push ahead a little further, to work a bit harder, and to ask the right questions.

*It is better to know some of the questions than all of the answers.*

—JAMES THURBER

# Preface

$O$ F COURSE it was the eyes. There they were, staring across at me in the dark, dirty, frigid saltwater tank. The stare, direct and aggressive, was from Spray, an Atlantic Bottlenose dolphin. She was no mystical creature, like so many people had claimed, or had hoped. But she also wasn't like any other animal I'd ever met.

The drama of being in the water with this creature turned the tables on my life. I'd never expected to feel like an outsider, almost an alien, on my own planet, yet I was immediately aware of how much a stranger I was in this pool of hers.

Never a graceful person, I now found myself face-to-face with the most sinuous creature I'd ever seen. I watched as she moved through the water effortlessly, more assured in her movements than any prima ballerina. There was no doubt. This was Spray's world, and I was a stone in it.

As her left eye widened and sought to make contact with mine through my diving mask, I realized I'd never known such a powerful, intellectual gaze in my life. I found myself not breathing, trapping the air still held in my lungs, hoping that the moment would last forever.

This dreamlike reality seemed out of place with the rest of my life, with my experiences. I had no way of placing it in comparison to anything else I'd ever done or felt. I had taught myself to become so structured, so in control of my responses that I'd almost lost the ability to live spontaneously. Since I'd been a child I was told I was too emotional, that I had to downplay my tendency to reveal my innermost feelings and thoughts. They were undesirable, embarrassing, even threatening to other people. My life had become a series of veils and filters that I had created in order to survive.

By the time I was thirty-eight I had mastered a skill

most people aren't even aware they possess. I'd learned to control the physical and emotional energies that strained to be released whenever I felt good, bad, happy or angry about a situation. I'd become more like other people but muted, almost as if a self-imposed lobotomy had been performed.

The veils hid the exuberance but allowed the humor through. The filters strained out all the excessive feelings that might be too difficult for others to relate to. I had become what I wanted, yet feared the most.

I'd been brought up in a very dysfunctional family and had longed for a "community" that I could call mine. To do that, I was constantly told through words, glances, and subtle hints that I would have to change myself in order to fit in. I would have to become less of an individual, more like others. Now, at this point in my life, I was beginning to fit in, to be "normal." But not quite.

My desire to be different, the enthusiastic way I approached life, and my creativity in solving problems were still causing me to be not quite "acceptable." Somehow I always managed to find and befriend people who felt it was their duty to correct my behavior, my sense of humor, my responses. They wanted me to meet their needs, to direct my energies toward them in such a way that they felt fulfilled. The problem was getting larger and harder to surmount. My family wanted and needed me to be one way, my friends and acquaintances another. I was too busy trying to be accepted to see that I had no clear image of myself.

Now, as I faced Spray I felt as if she was probing deeply into the center of my being, of my essence. I could actually "feel" her seeking out the inner me, the one I had hidden even from myself.

As the probing intensified, I began to sense an inner burst of emotion, as if she had touched a deeply buried button, pressed it, and then released the contents of my most inner self for her to examine. She "knew" me— whatever that might have meant. Somehow she had sought, found, and touched this self, this soul or spirit I'd concealed over all those years. For the first time in my life

I felt a quiet affirmation that I was just fine with her, warts and all.

Of this I was sure, am sure, will always be sure: This animal, by taking a moment to look at me, looked into me. I could feel it. A sensation of thousands of tiny bubbles whirled around inside my brain and my being, bounced off my consciousness, and spun through the core of my body.

I'll never know what she did or how she did it, but she touched and freed the person that lay encrusted beneath all that guarded self.

This moment was so intense for me that even though I've since met and worked with countless dolphins, the encounter stays in my mind, fresh as the day that it first happened. I only have to close my eyes for it to return intact, thrilling and wondrous. I never sought to repeat that experience, and in fact I never have.

When I left the pool that first day, I had no way of knowing I was taking the first steps toward breaking the barriers of dolphin-human communication. I only knew that I'd touched and been touched by an experience too large for me to comprehend. It was a drug and I was to become a willing addict.

I wanted, at all cost, to pursue further what had just happened. I needed it, my soul needed it, and most of all my mind needed it. It wasn't the emotional jolt I wanted to examine, rather the fact that this "animal" had the ability, the capacity, even the desire to perform such feats of magic.

I would do whatever I had to do to continue to learn from my watery teachers, learn how to behave correctly, how to interact with different species of dolphins, both captive and wild, how to create a mind-set that would dissolve the distance that had held the two species apart since we shared the planet together.

Most importantly, I would go on to find a way to use what I'd learned to improve the condition of other humans. At that first meeting, I had no idea how this information would enable me to eventually free autistic children to communicate with those who cared for them and about them.

In that first contact with Spray, I had an all-too-brief glimpse into a mind and a form of socialization that were more ancient than humankind's. The inner knowledge that this even existed in some form on the planet was what I had unknowingly sought all my life—a community built upon basic social and survival needs, primitive at its core, complex in its creation, with rules to be revealed and used to help humans.

It was a totally unexpected benefit of my original purpose for having begun this project. All I had hoped to do was to find a way to expand the use of the brain as a trainable muscle, perhaps to learn how to do this from these remarkable marine mammals. What I was to eventually uncover was far ahead of my original theories. In fact, by the end of that first session with Spray and her tank-mate Scotty, I had vowed to put aside any and all theories and just try to learn whatever it was that these dolphins felt I needed to learn.

I had expected nothing, looked for nothing when I first slid into the pool. The shock of Spray's intellect never let up throughout the entire session. More than through her movements and her chattering, she conveyed her intentions and questions through her eyes.

Once she had settled upon my acceptability, she moved on to the next level of interaction.

I became aware of a subtle change as I saw her right eye narrow and intensify in its purpose. Her unspoken appraisal seemed to indicate that she'd been rating me on a scale unknown to me but important to dolphins. Her continued stare and gentle high-pitched runs of sonar sound seemed to say that I'd been accepted. It was as simple and easy as that. I suddenly understood that all I had do was be me. There was no rating as to whether or not I was a good or bad person. I was me, and for her and for Scotty, that was enough.

In that microsecond I became aware of yet another change. Spray seemed to indicate her willingness to adopt the role of being my teacher, and I hoped I would be able to live up to her faith in my ability to learn from her. I had never experienced such a sense of vibrancy, of importance, to what I was learning and might be taught, and I dearly wanted to be able to take advantage of what she was offering me.

She moved away with a backward glance in my direction, then turned and slid toward me, insinuated her broad gray flank across my extended palm, and pressed her flesh to my thick glove. The invitation to accompany her was unmistakable. Perhaps there was hope for me yet. If I could correctly assign her values to her movements, then I might be a student she would want to continue to work with.

Through her acceptance, my life took a ninety-degree turn, and I was forever to become impassioned, imprisoned by the promises that lay behind her eyelock.

How did I come to be in a pool of March-chilled water with Scotty and Spray, two dolphins, two animals that were clearly far more than I had bargained for?

For all the years I'd spent preparing myself, I was totally unprepared for this moment. A product of the late fifties and early sixties, I had been taught by my parents to respect authority, to follow the rules, to carry on the heritage and tradition of a strong German Jewish–American past which allotted a certain percentage of altruistic return to their fellow man. My desire to question and learn was held in check by my need to be loved and cared about. It was an uneasy truce, for me a no-win situation.

I was taught to ask few, if any, questions, to do as I was told and taught, to explore no further than whatever it took to protect what was already mine.

By the time I was nineteen it had become so bad that although I knew how to be admitted into college, I only knew that you could get out through graduating or flunking out. I hated the too-large university I'd entered and so set about failing every course I could. It was only afterward that I learned about being able to transfer to another school. I still shake my head in amazement at how ingenuous I'd been. Like the animal who gnaws off its leg to escape a trap, I did what I thought was the correct thing to do to get away from that hated school.

But I eventually learned not only how to survive and prevail, but how to ask probing questions which would open the world around me and to me. I didn't have to go the course alone, I could learn from others. And this change in approach grew alongside my research.

I'd been a schoolteacher, a wife, a mother. I'd been active in the library of my small, cozy Connecticut town, a singer in a local amateur chorus, a baker of pies and sugary delights which brought out the child in even the most adult person, eventually a tough competitor in the local state fair and the winner of over 150 ribbons, most of them blue.

But as if in a dream, after that first encounter in Cape Cod, I would put that life aside. I knew I couldn't do it all, and what I wanted most was to collect the clues and solve the mystery of these remarkable animals.

Since my teens I had loved to work crossword puzzles and avidly read books about real-life mysteries. I always preferred nonfiction to fiction. To me the intricacies of life around me were always to be looked at, measured, tasted, tested, evaluated, then placed within the overall scheme, like a puzzle pieced together. Everything that happened to me, everything I had done and would ever do held the means to better understand myself and the world.

A logical mind lay within an emotional personality and the older I grew, the more I valued the logic and wanted to apply it to other areas of my existence.

I had somehow stumbled across both a puzzle and a mystery. If I could use the pieces of my own life and experiences, perhaps I could uncover other pieces and treat them as if they were clues to solve a mystery. It was the first time I was to put two concepts and disciplines together in order to create the means to solve a problem.

I would become a detective and my mystery would carry me around the world, put my life in real danger, and eventually open up an entirely new frontier in communication. The lines of my life's division became clearly drawn. To Spray would go the credit for this change. Of all the dolphins I was ever to meet, she was the one who opened the world to me.

## One

*T*HE MORE I forged ahead to learn from Spray, Scotty, and all the other dolphins that have followed since then, the more I had to seek the reasons for my slightly skewed approach to thinking about and perceiving the world around me. I also had to look more closely at how my opinions were formed. It isn't easy to understand why I saw, felt, understood, and thought just a little differently from others around me. I was always comfortable with the dissimilarities, but I was also curious as to why they existed and why they sometimes seemed to separate me from the very people I wanted to be close to. Even as a young child, they didn't seem to match those of my family and my friends.

I've always loved parables and anecdotes. They convey ideas and concepts through the actions, feelings, ideas, and behavior of other people and enable me to look at myself with greater clarity. I decided to review my own past as if it were being shared with me by a person other than myself. The stories would unfold and allow me to examine the motives, thoughts, and background of the little girl who had begun life as Patricia Marie Unger in Brooklyn, New York, in September of 1945.

I was conceived in war and born in peace. My mother had given birth to my sister in 1939 and then had miscarried four times in the following years. I was unexpected and I came with some unexpected problems. Soldiers returning from the Pacific Theater of World War II brought home many souvenirs. Some of them were contagious tropical diseases. One of the worst was called paratyphoid, a form of salmonella, a dysentery which ravaged infants and the elderly.

By the time my thirty-two-year-old mother went to the hospital to deliver me, she'd had to change the place of arrival three times. Newborns in the other hospitals had contracted the disease and had died in large numbers.

I came home from the hospital a healthy and happy baby and contracted the disease thirteen months later. In those days, new mothers had help with their infants. It was common to have a baby nurse. Ours came highly recommended, and with a boyfriend in the service. The friend returned from the Pacific and brought the disease with him, which he passed on to me.

It was this illness, and the resulting events that followed, that forever changed the way I was to interpret my environment and those who shared it with me. My parents were never too clear as to whether I contracted paratyphoid or salmonella, or both. Even now, I'm not certain myself.

Timing is everything in this world. In those thirteen months of my early life, a young pediatrician had come back from the service. He'd been involved with the development and testing of a new "wonder drug" called Streptomycin. Somehow my mother heard about him, found him, and begged him to help save my life. He agreed to do so, but warned her that the drug was experimental, had never been tried out on infants, and might fail.

This didn't stop her and in the end they were able to secure the precious medicine. The five bottles of liquid were doled out to me in such a manner that they saved my life. But they also had serious and lasting side effects because the dosage was too high. My legs, arms, and especially my eye muscles began to weaken and malfunction. I had begun to walk and talk at an early age. Now I had to learn all over again.

Photographs of me at age two show a slim little girl holding a doll in her arms, looking at the camera through painfully crossed eyes. The dark irises can hardly be detected. There were days when I had no sight, others when I saw double. I went through two operations to correct the problem but neither worked. The diagnosis was for double vision with a decline to permanent blindness. Only a miracle could change my sight.

When I was eight my mother learned of an eye surgeon in New York City, Dr. Conrad Behrans, who had unsuccessfully attempted to save his son's sight with an eye muscle transplant. She called him and told him about my problem, and they made an appointment for me for the next week.

I'd had some horrifying experiences during my other operations. One of them left me with a lifelong aversion to needles. Dr. Behrans and my mother agreed that it was important that I be the one to make the final decision whether or not to operate. They presented all aspects, pro and con, of the possibilities surrounding the procedure.

I don't know why I elected to do it, but I said yes. I knew I would have to be more than a patient. They had stressed that I'd have to be reliable about doing certain exercises afterward. This would strengthen the new muscles and make them work well with the others.

The operation took nine hours. In those dark ages of eye surgery, this was a delicate and heroic event.

I remained swathed in bandages for a week, lying quietly in a bed, sharing a room with three others who were adults. I was told that I shouldn't move too much in order to protect the stitches. I suspect that part of the reason I'm such a ravenous reader today is because of being deprived of any stimulation other than a radio during that time. But though I was very young, I learned a lesson which has remained with me ever since.

I had a favorite nurse. She would spend more time with me, and she seemed to care about me and my needs just a little bit more than the other nurses. Behind my heavily bandaged eyes I envisioned her to be young and slim, with shining blond hair and bright blue eyes. I asked her to describe herself to me but she always teased and said I'd have to wait until the bandages were unveiled and I could see again.

The evening arrived when the doctor decided to see if the operation had been a success. He chose to do the unveiling at night so my eyes wouldn't have to deal with too much light all at once.

It was like a scene out of a bad B movie, the little girl lying in the hospital bed, small and frail. Gathered around me were the nurses, doctors, and my parents. The bandages were slowly unwrapped and lifted from my eyes. I remember hoping I'd be able to see again. With delicate motions they gingerly removed the last gauze pads and then stepped back expectantly.

I slowly opened my eyes and told them that I could see a thin light. It shone from the slim flashlight held in Dr. Behrans's hand. My blurry vision began to clear. Yes. The right eye was good, but what about the critical left one?

Oh! Yes! I could see!

The nurses hugged each other. My mother turned and moved into my father's arms and began to cry soft sounds of relief. The doctor was congratulated by all those present.

But where was my friend, the special nurse? I looked around but couldn't see my golden angel. Time was running out for me to see her.

I was only allowed to use my eyes for a short period. The doctor was afraid I might put too much strain on my new muscles. All too quickly the nurses once again began to make a little mummy out of me and the room faded to black.

Where had she been? She had sworn that she would be there for me. When she came in to see me the next morning I asked her why she'd failed to show up. She told me she had been there, standing next to me the entire time.

"But," I said, "the nurse there was old and had brown eyes and gray hair."

"Yes, my little friend," she said. "That was me."

I was stunned. How could I have been so wrong about that beautiful voice? How could she not fit my mental picture? Her voice had been sweet, tender, young, and lovely. How could her appearance be so totally different than what I'd expected?

I have never forgotten that moment. It was a major discovery for me. I had created an entirely false set of ideas based solely around what I had heard. I had learned that the impressions I'd gathered from my other senses could be subjective and misleading.

Making decisions about people and the events in my life now seemed to be more than just the random gathering of information. There was a process going on and I wanted to figure out exactly what that process was and how it worked. I decided to examine other moments in my life and search for inconsistencies in how I had chosen to define them.

My mother's uncle was mentally unstable. His greatest pleasure in an otherwise sedentary existence was to call my mother up in the evenings and provoke arguments. He always found a way to get to her and badgered her until she was exhausted, crying and yelling.

It came as no surprise that she eventually had a nervous breakdown. Whenever she was on the phone with him, I could feel the thick tension, as well as hear her end of things. When she would finally conclude the conversation and come out of her bedroom, I would always approach her.

"Mommy, do you love me?" was the question I constantly put to her. I was too young to connect her calls from her uncle with her distress. Somehow, even though I was so young, I was always able to accept and understand what I eventually later recognized as rational leaps of understanding.

She was with me. She was tense. She had worked in my father's office all day. She was tired. I could literally feel her anger inside of me, running through my inner self. It would rush at me like a wall of water and wash over me.

"Mommy, do you love me?"

She would finally turn after I'd asked once too often and shout the answer back.

"Yes! I love you! Now stop bothering me!"

It was all too confusing. If she loved me, why did I feel that she was angry? If she wasn't angry with me, then I would have to trust her enough to believe that she would speak the truth about her feelings. Her tone of voice was totally hostile. Her response, in anorexic words, spoke love. Which was the right choice for me to believe?

I always chose her words over her voice, over her obvious distress, and the intense signals her body was emitting. It was a contradiction of realities for me.

At a time in a child's life when affection and comfort are necessary for emotional security, I was learning to

survive by weaving my way through the maze of conflicting information my mother was offering. If soft, embrac-
ing feelings and tender words were not evident, but only
the sterile declaration of love, then I would take whatever
I could get.

It was then that I began to create the veils and filters that
served me so well for much of my later life. Because I had
become overly sensitized to all the emotions I was unwittingly gathering, I had to develop a way to separate out
what I was receiving and not take everything so personally. I would have to discern whether or not it was actually
directed toward me or just being emitted from those
around me, and what to do with all of the information.

Eventually I came to wonder whether some forms of
paranoia don't actually stem from a heightened ability to
sense the inner attitudes of those who surround us. But
that idea was to come many years later, after I'd worked
with both dolphins and autistic children.

Again, from my adult perspective, I reexamined my
childhood experiences, particularly the months I'd spent
recovering from my last and final surgery. Dr. Behrans
taught me how to do two crucial eye exercises. They were
designed to force my left eye to work with my right one.
It became a matter of training my brain as much as training my eyes. I recall many moments of frustration when I
couldn't get it right. I would close my eyes, relax, speak
to myself, and then just do the work.

I have no memory of the day my eyes were pronounced
strong enough for me to stop having to do the exercises. I
just remember a strange by-product of the training. It
showed me what I could do with my other, less practiced
voluntary muscles, if I were to activate my brain to control them.

One day I looked in the mirror at my hairline. As a
youngster I wore my hair long and pulled back in a pony-
tail, revealing a dramatic widow's peak. I stared at my
hairline and watched as it suddenly moved forward on its
own. This was interesting. Then again, there are many
irrational things that are interesting to eight-year-olds.

I recall thinking hard, as I had when I was training my

eyes to work together, and then seeing my hairline travel forward. To my unsophisticated mind, this was pretty neat. Not too usable as a career choice, but so what?

With some effort, I perfected the movable hairline maneuver. Later, I also taught myself to flex my ears, individually and then together. I was amazed to find that my mind could help me control my brain and ultimately muscles I hadn't known existed. I had begun to develop the means to use both my mind and brain. I had unknowingly discovered, for myself, the line that divides the two.

The brain was the muscle, to be developed and used like any other muscle in the body. The only difference was in the training regimen.

The mind was that elusive entity, perhaps coupled with what we call the soul, or the spirit—maybe even both. It was free and independent of the brain, making, even urging it to work harder. Yet alone as it might be in "personality," the mind was as dependent upon the brain as more obvious symbiotic animals are upon each other. In other words, the brain was no more than another muscle without the mind's presence to exercise it. Conversely, the mind could do nothing without the brain's ability to control and drive the body. It was a breakthrough which lay at the heart and core of my future research.

My second major discovery came from looking at my environment. I eventually came to believe that some good can come from living in a dysfunctional family. I certainly wouldn't recommend that people choose dysfunction as a way of life, but it can teach you how to survive. I never lived a miserable life, but it also never quite fit in with the patterns of the times. That was fine with me; after all, children accept their own families as the norm. It's everyone else's that is strange.

My father came from a family that showed little emotion. My mother came from one that couldn't keep their feelings under control. She loved to smother us with kisses and then walk away to do something else. She needed those kisses throughout her life; her emotional self was so riddled with holes that she hardly seemed to feel the kisses she got, was always looking for the next ones to come.

My sister, more like my father, could never abide being overwhelmed with affection. My father needed children to be adults. His mother would greet us with a kiss to the side of the face, saying, "Kisses spread germs."

When she died in 1970, at eighty-eight, I threw away years of accumulated Christmas gifts. They'd all been the same: monogrammed hankies. Tomboy that I was, this was not the best present to get me. Besides, I'd become a dedicated user of paper tissues. She never did get to know me.

Although she lived in Manhattan, I never once ate a meal at her home, nor went anywhere alone with her. I took this to be the normal state of affairs for our family relations, but used to fantasize about having a grandmother who would be more like those of my friends.

My father had bought a fruit and vegetable business which had previously gone bankrupt. He kept the founder's business name for the firm and fought an uphill battle to make it turn a profit. My mother worked with him, never taking a salary. This enabled her to keep a strict eye on the books, as well as save the company from paying out another salary. I would race home every day, hoping she would be there, but this wasn't possible and I came to accept a sad lesson about life.

We never went on family vacations together. The two trips I made with them, to Atlantic City and to Washington, D.C., were both out of season and for business purposes. When they did take a break, one of them would stay in New York to keep tabs on the business, while the other would take a train down to Florida for a solitary rest.

Throughout my childhood I was frequently ill with upper-respiratory infections. My lungs would fill and I could hardly breathe. It was like drowning. The worst part would be when I had to cough, barking like a seal, gasping for breath, leaning into a large brass urnlike steamer to try to make space for more air. If I was lucky, I could actually cough up and expel huge quantities of blackened, smoke-tasting phlegm.

Both my parents were heavy smokers. Between them they smoked more than four packs of cigarettes a day. It's only now, with the studies being done on the disastrous effects of secondhand smoke on those who live with smokers, that I have a better awareness of why I was always ill. Even today I cannot tolerate smoke and must escape from people and places that have heavy blue hazes hanging over them.

The illnesses were bad, but many times they seemed to coincide with a social engagement my parents were supposed to have attended. I was given strong insight into my position in my parents' eyes.

I remember my mother leaning over me, her face red with anger, telling me it was my fault that she and my father never got to go out and enjoy themselves. She always had to cancel and stay at home with me when I was sick. She would then toss off her final comment, to the effect that this was the price people had to pay when they had children.

Fortunately, my inner strength enabled me to be mentally healthy enough to put aside the remark with the knowledge that being sick was no plot on my part, and that if it was a problem for her, well, it just came with the territory. But still, her words hurt, because I loved her and I didn't want to make her life any more difficult than it already was. The child began to become the caretaker of the parent.

What kept me from becoming a copy of my parents was the presence of a woman who lived with us during my most important formative years.

Because my parents worked together, we needed full-time help. My saving grace was Eula Reddick, a wonderful, kind, and loving black woman who was our live-in maid six days a week for eight years. She was never a "mammy" to me, but a woman of silent strength, dignity, and awareness of how things really worked in a world larger than Brooklyn. Though many times she was a surrogate mother for me, she also became a role model.

My parents worked hard and stayed for long days, sometimes into the night. Eula did all the home-based labor at a price far below what it would have cost them to pay an accountant at the business. She provided me with my warmest images and memories of good smells that came from the kitchen, and a friend who took the time to listen.

She was my best friend, closest supporter, teacher, and most honest critic. Her pronouncements that I was the most hardheaded child she ever did know were absolutely correct. She would utter that phrase with love, anger, pride, resentment, and several other emotions, all depending upon the situation.

Through hard work on my part, I eventually turned the negative of being hardheaded around to the positive of being persistent. Still, anytime that I might come close to crossing the thin line between the two, I can faintly hear her chastising words.

Eula left us when I was twelve. By the time I was sixteen, we had moved to Brookfield, Connecticut. My mother stayed home while my father commuted the long drive into downtown New York City every day.

I was to finally get my wish. My mother and I would have time to spend together, or so I hoped. But she quickly filled her days with new friends and the discovery that she could grow things in her garden. Many times her evenings were spent playing cards with friends, while I was told how to prepare dinner for my late-arriving father.

The few times, when I was in my twenties, that we did attempt to relate to one another only served to show me how far apart we had grown, if in fact we had ever been close. She would speak knowledgeably on the topic of silverware, dish patterns, and jewelry, and I would tell her I had no idea of what she was talking about. She would then complain that she had spent a great deal of time teaching me these things years ago. There was no fighting her absolute certainty, and so I didn't try. Instead, I recognized that memory could not only be flawed, but creative as well. I was beginning to see what an amazing thing the mind was.

Still, in my life's review, I had no idea of what situations might stimulate the brain to become more active, perhaps even more in control of its functions. I needed to find other incidents which might help me to root out the mechanisms for advancing brain/mind increase. It was then that I remembered a story that was to become critical to my understanding.

In Brooklyn I lived on the first floor of a six-story apartment building. It was mandatory that anything higher than four floors have an elevator. I rarely rode in ours, usually choosing to dash up the stairs instead of waiting for the thing to finally arrive on the bottom level.

I was ten that fateful day. What happened forever changed my perception of the scheme of life.

I'd been playing with a girl who lived on the top floor of our building. She suggested that we ring for the elevator on the ground floor and then play a great game. We would wait until no other people were using it, then randomly push buttons. We'd wait to see if the elevator would stop in the proper floor sequence, or if it would open its doors in the same order as the buttons we had pushed.

We did this for some time, giggling between ourselves anytime an adult joined us. Some were more annoyed than others that the elevator seemed to stop at almost every floor. We eventually tired of our game and decided to leave at whatever floor the door opened on next.

The box stopped, jerked, and the doors opened. Instead of a long, quietly lit hallway, we were facing a menacing, dark, battleship gray wall. The pockmarks and indentations on the surface showed that it was never meant to be looked upon by elevator occupants.

We were pretty sophisticated for ten-year-olds. We weren't concerned about our fate. We knew enough to ring the emergency bell and the porter, as the assistant superintendent was titled, would come to our rescue. We pushed the button and the bell made a loud, insistent ringing noise. It reverberated up and down the shaft and through our enclosure. Nothing happened. We rang it again. The bell sounded the same, but there was a more intense feeling to it. Still no response. We punched the bell. Again, and again, and again.

Finally we heard a voice from below calling out to us.

It was a man who lived in the apartment building. He advised us to remain calm and he would search out the porter (the super). Saved at last.

He returned after an eternity with the awful news that neither man could be found. We would have to stay where we were until help could be located. We never did panic, but we began to realize where we were and what the possibilities might be.

The porter finally came and brought us down to the first-floor landing. He lectured us, but it was well past being necessary. I had received my first lesson in fear. From that moment on, I was a dedicated stair climber. I never wanted to be in an elevator again.

But other elevator incidents would help me to understand the role my emotions played in shaping my life's events. On a visit to my mother's other uncle, who lived in an apartment building in Greenwich Village, I discovered that his apartment was too high up for me to take the stairs. Unhappy and scared, I entered the elevator with my mother and the other passengers. My mind escaped my control and I began to imagine that once we reached the right floor, the door would open up and we would have just missed the mark by about a foot. I thought to myself, Wouldn't it be funny if when the door opened, I'd have to step down?

We made the stops for all the other passengers and everything operated normally. At our floor, the elevator gave a slight jerk, settled in, and the door slid open. We were a few inches off of the mark and we had to step down. I immediately recognized that this was more than curious, it was downright strange. It just couldn't have been a coincidence and I wondered if there was something more than chance happening here.

From then on, it seemed that each time I entered an elevator I would create a scenario which would stem from my fear. Each time, without control, I would think, Wouldn't it be funny if . . . Each time the exact situation would occur. By the time I was twelve, I began to suspect that the power of my raw emotion might somehow be playing a part in the events that were happening. One final emergency made me swear off thinking that special phrase of fear again.

I'd been in Connecticut with my parents and two of their friends. The three of us had to return to Brooklyn, I to school and they to their business. I left with them and they decided to make a side trip to see some other friends who lived nearby. It was a gray winter afternoon and the weather was a mixture of soft drizzle with light snow. Granules of ice would form and melt, form and melt. It was light when we entered the driveway and twilight as we left.

Our car had to cross over a small homemade bridge constructed of logs and packed dirt. A few feet beyond, toward the road, was a slight incline. In bad weather a car would need more speed to make it onto the main road. To the right side of the bridge was a short drop of about five feet into a cold, swiftly running stream. Under the span was a waterfall so that the left side dropped to more than ten feet.

My parents' friends were in the front seat, I sat in the back on the right side. We had just begun to cross the bridge when an involuntary thought jumped into my mind: Wouldn't it be funny if we didn't make it and the car almost went off the bridge?

I caught myself at the thought, squeezed my eyes shut, and tried to use my willpower to erase it. The car moved steadily over the bridge and up the incline, while I breathed a sigh of relief. We had made it without incident. My theory was wrong after all.

Suddenly we began to slow and lose ground. The wheels spun and we weren't able to move forward. The man put the gears into reverse and backed the car over the bridge. He put it into forward again, set his shoulders, grasped the steering wheel more firmly, and increased our speed.

As we approached the bridge, one of the wheels caught in a snow rut. The steering wheel wrenched from his hands and the car swerved to the left. It all happened so quickly, there was no time to think.

By pure luck the logs became dislodged in such a way

as to capture the front left and rear right tires. The car was caught on the logs and was precariously perched so that it hung swaying over the highest portion of the drop below.

I remember screaming and then becoming quiet. For a moment none of us moved. Like wands in a game of Pick Up Sticks, we were worried that the slightest motion from any of us would cause the car to move and tumble over the edge.

I was lightest, so I elected to carefully open my door and slide out. I recall being amazed at the angle of the door as I shoved it high against the fading daylight. Once free, I held on to the handle with all my might. I hoped this would give more stability to the right side and offset my exit from the car. The next day, when I ached in every fiber of my body, I realized how hard I must have been holding on.

My scream had been heard at the house, and by then the people had arrived to provide additional help. It now was easy for the two in the front to escape. The rest of the story is not at all dramatic. A tow truck was called, there was no damage to the car, and off we went to Brooklyn.

During our return home I could think of nothing but the connection between my fear, my thoughts, and my negative experience during the entire ride back. Had that fear-induced thought of "Wouldn't it be funny if . . . ?" created the possibly deadly near-accident, or had I somehow perceived it a little before it happened? I couldn't help but remember that since the incident in the elevator, all of the realized negative events in my life had been preceded by this simple statement. The only difference was how I filled in the second half.

I went round and round, becoming more confused as I thought. It was like trying to figure out which came first, the chicken or the egg.

My solution was to decide to put a permanent hold on thinking what I now called "the sentence." Perhaps by controlling my fear-filled negative thoughts I could avoid the more harrowing aspects of life.

I resolved to do just that and filed the information away for future investigation. I was ready to leave that portion of my past and move forward to search for other clues, other telling and important moments that would help me to better understand what, and how, I was learning from dolphins.

# Two

$\mathcal{A}$T SOME unknown point in my development, I realized I had become different over the years. The alterations seemed to me to be both good and bad. Every time I had managed to move forward by changing myself to fit in with those around me, I also became aware of the loss of some portion of myself. Each time I subdued my responses to people and events, I also seemed to let slip away an innocence and a joyous appreciation of the world around me.

From when I was a child, I could easily remember the feelings of wonder when I had learned something new, or the sense of excitement when something unusual might happen to me. But as I matured and looked around at others, I began to think that most people just lived from day to day, many times actively seeking to maintain an unruffled status quo to their life. My desire to experience whatever might happen, whether pleasant or unpleasant, was finally totally buried beneath the need to make those around me comfortable and happy.

It was only after I turned forty, during the years that I spent seeking to understand my present through the examination of my past, that I saw and recognized what I had done to myself. I had stripped myself of any real sense of who I was and what I wanted.

I decided to accept all that had been part of my growing up as necessary for the creation of the person I now was and would eventually become. I couldn't change what had happened, I could only see it more clearly, and so I placed the past behind me except for the most cursory review.

My teenage years were uneventful and filled with the normal stress situations. There were times of greater inner perception than others, but none stand out above the rest.

After graduating from Kentucky Wesleyan College, I

became a French teacher and was hired to teach in the F.L.E.S. (Foreign Language in the Elementary School) program at a middle school near New Haven, Connecticut. In those days the F.L.E.S. program was a new concept in teaching language. I had come up through the traditional format of learning the basics of French. F.L.E.S. required the teacher to be fluent and dramatic with the students. Only after observing the more cultural aspect of the language were they then exposed to the correct syntax.

I was allowed to be as creative as I wanted to be. I would walk into the lower grades and be outrageous in my attempts to illustrate words and sentences. In the upper grades I had the kids performing concerts in French, cooking with recipes that were written in the language, attending films without subtitles, going to restaurants, shopping at stores that sold French food, writing poetry, and creating crossword puzzles, all in French.

Although I only taught F.L.E.S. for three years, a large number of my top-level students went on to major in languages. It was a wonderful program which lost its life to budget cuts and the decision to buy jackets for the football team.

From the experience of the F.L.E.S. program, I became convinced that the only way to learn how to communicate outside of my own language and culture was to become immersed in the cultural environment of the society whose language I hoped to master. I realized that we had placed too great an emphasis upon the written and spoken word. We had evolved to the point where we relied upon and trusted language as our primary and perhaps sole means of communication.

We had neglected the other levels that create an exchange of information. Appreciation for the native people, their products, lifestyle, and culture was the true starting point of understanding.

As I taught the program, I realized that for the first time I began to love the French language I had struggled to learn since my own seventh-grade year. It suddenly took on an entirely different feeling when it was being used culturally. It was no longer a maze of verb patterns and conjugations. It was alive. French was no longer dry and without feeling. Suddenly it had beauty, humor, grace, warmth, and depth. In some ways, I learned the language along with my students. And I discovered more about myself and my heightened senses.

Over the years I had not realized how much I'd done and learned to control my high degree of sensitivity. Through daily use I had taught myself to extend and pinpoint my hearing, to pick up the sense of tension that came from those around me, and to build the filters by which I could shield out unwanted input. I was beginning to discover the role the senses were playing in interactions with other people.

Although I was generally well liked by my students, they were frequently spooked by my ability to repeat back to them whispered conversations that had taken place at the rear of the classroom. With my extended sense of hearing, it was easy for me to pick up their exchanges, and fun to catch them off guard.

That was how I first recognized my ability to hear selectively. It seemed that all I had to do to extend my range of hearing was to decide to do it, as I had with my eyes when I was training them to see together. I could filter out noises closer to me and somehow amplify those farther away.

I also learned to appreciate silence as a force stronger than loud noise. As the day would progress, students would become more restless and rowdy. In other classrooms teachers would scream and yell, trying to regain control of their students. It was sometimes embarrassing to hear their useless threats fall on deaf ears.

Rather than try to be the loudest person in my classroom, I began to practice what the kids called "the stare." I would gaze into empty space as if I had suddenly become blind to all the disorder surrounding me. Stern. Cold. Unmoving. Uncompromising, meaning absolute business. My face would turn to stone. My eyes would narrow and my jaw become set. Short as I was, I became a giant in attitude.

One by one the students would quiet down, glancing

sidelong to see if my expression had altered. My silence cut through the wall of noise and left an expanding hole in the center. Years later, returning students would always comment that they thought I was taller than five-feet-two.

I had begun to see that there were unspoken ways to communicate more loudly than using words. If I created an environment of strength based upon my use of silence, as well as the ability to act upon situations rather than try to control them, then I would have a stronger position of leadership within my own classroom.

The booming voices of my colleagues always seemed louder in the atmosphere of silence I had created around myself and my students. The teachers' lack of control and self-control became painfully obvious, even to my students.

Why had it taken me so long to learn about this technique for interacting with my students? What had I not done in my own college work to prepare me for becoming the teacher I envisioned I would be?

As I again examined my past, I saw that I had been taught to follow but not to lead, to teach but not to discover and create teachable material. I was not to ask questions, but to pursue goals that had been preset for me by others. In order to maintain control over my charges, I would always have to have the answers, but discourage them from asking the really tough questions. How had I developed such limitations?

As a student, in order to pass my tests, I had figured out how to study so I could regurgitate the correct information. Even in college there was little time or room left for learning just for the joy and sake of it. During those rare times in class that I would ask many questions, I would try to challenge what I was learning and further explore many other ramifications of the information being offered. Frequently, my fellow students would tell me to be quiet so they could learn only the material necessary to pass upcoming tests.

When I graduated, the seniors in the history division had a small party. Each of us was presented with a humorous honorary degree. Mine was "The Speaker of the Front Row." I remember the heat of my face as it turned crimson with embarrassment. It had been funny and true, but those had been the only classes where I had dared to let my inquisitive mind flow freely.

In a world rapidly turning toward the idea of competition in the marketplace for survival, the concept of education for its own sake was disappearing. All knowledge had to have a purpose, especially if it meant you could get a job by knowing something. This trained the mind in logic and retention, but also closed the pathways to creativity.

I realized that now, as a nonstudent for the first time I could remember since I was a child, I had the incredible freedom of time to begin reading what interested me. I had become so used to being told what I had to do that I had never even realized that I had finally achieved the status of full-and-free-to-choose grown adult. I no longer had to read books that would ensure that I'd be intelligent enough, in another person's opinion, to pass a course. Now I could follow my preferences and allow my mind the liberty to wander wherever I wanted it to go.

Strolling the aisles in the local library, I began to select biographies, autobiographies, and true mysteries. I also took home books that dealt with paranormal events and information.

Until it began to seep back, I never realized how diminished my sensitivity had become. I suspect I lost the intensity of my extended sensory system because I was too busy trying to graduate from high school and college, too busy trying to please others, too directed outside of myself. The world had so intruded on me that I forgot the more quiet arts. All day I was surrounded by people, sounds, time deadlines and responsibilities, and talk, talk, talk.

Each evening when I returned to my own apartment I would close the door and revel in a new feeling of freedom, a new awareness. Silence. Privacy. And the power to choose what I liked and wanted. In twenty-two years

I'd only had rare glimpses these treasures even existed. Now I possessed them all for myself.

Once I recognized and became accustomed to my altered state in life, I also had more time to concentrate on many other things. I realized that I was more interested in things paranormal than I had admitted to myself.

The study of parapsychology always seemed to carry with it a slight air of the undesirable, like the anatomy student who always smells just faintly of formaldehyde. But with my new freedom also came the increase of my sensitivity and the skills that accompanied it. In fact, they were stronger than ever and I was curious about how to control and use them.

It was difficult, in fact impossible, to find what I was searching for. I wanted to read about real people and how they handled situations in common with mine. Was I experiencing high moments of extrasensory perception, or was it something else? Were there other people like me, or was I in a tiny minority? Could I eventually learn to integrate myself into society and feel like a person on the inside of a group, or would I be doomed always to travel on the fringes of "normal" life? Was I missing something that I needed in order to fit in, or did I possess more than I needed?

I never found in books what I sought. Instead I discovered that they were divided into two categories: hard, scientific, and boring, filled with reports of endlessly repetitious experiments; or emotional, anecdotal, egotistical, juvenile, uninvestigated, and embarrassing.

My sensitivity had begun to increase because of my job demands, and it was important to me that I serve the children to the best of my ability. I wanted to find out how to use my brain, mind, and body in a more mainstream sensory application. The more I read and studied, the more I realized how stilted was the appreciation of the paranormal. Fear far outweighed joy as an emotional response. But almost all of my own personal experiences had been accompanied by a thrill of wonder and excitement as a result of the mini-miracles that had happened. I wanted to have these moments happen more often and I needed them to be applicable and useable for the improvement of my daily life.

Everything I read either coldly examined the phenomena of extrasensory perception from a far distance, or was too close and glorified it without understanding and without logic. It seemed the two camps were further divided into true believers who would accept anything, regardless of how crazy and wacky it might be, and unimpassioned rationalists who refused to accept anything as being unexplainable. Where was the third group? Where were the people who knew that there had to be a realistic cause to these events, but chose to expand their knowledge through service to others?

Neither of the first two groups appealed to me. So I began to seek out local people who were getting together to learn through experience. I had some fascinating moments with these people and I learned a lot. I also found that just because we all came together to learn, it didn't mean that we had the same goals.

Some of them were more like the story of the six blind men and the elephant. Each person was sure they knew the real truth about the paranormal. Each person derived their pleasure from their own personal application of what they learned. They created a more limited, restricted, and lesser vision of the paranormal and seemed able only to expand it as far as they themselves were expanded. Somehow they lacked the courage to move beyond their own reassuring boundaries. Most eventually sought to attract followers who would blindly echo their concepts.

Out-of-control egos were rampant. It disgusted me enough that I finally totally rejected everything I learned from working with them. This was just as bad on my part. Eventually I took a less impassioned approach and began to sift through the pieces until a clearer image of the overall puzzle began to reveal itself.

I couldn't stay away from trying to learn more about the paranormal. Uninvited events of unexplained nature continued to happen to me. Never of any major, earth-shaking importance; they were always just on the very edge of almost being normal. But not quite. The telephone call from a long-lost friend whom I had only thought of that morning, or the letter from yet other friends who hadn't written in years, but their names had popped into my mind minutes before I received my mail. The parking spot that was always in front of where I wanted to be and the vague inner warnings to slow my car down so that I averted possible accidents.

They tweaked my curiosity, twiddled my intellect, and thumbed their noses at my rational self. I had to face up to the fact that I knew there was undiscovered information waiting to be learned out there on the edges of my consciousness. I just hadn't located the proper dispenser of that data.

Because events were personal and were happening to me, I had to look to myself and was continually forced to check back into my history and find parallels to them in my past. I more than needed, I wanted, to learn as much as one lifetime could hold.

My parents and sister had no interest in any paranormal events and were unwilling to speak to me about mine. I felt separated from them because of my interest and wondered why I was so different from them. I wasn't adopted; one look in the mirror was enough to confirm that. There had to be some other sign or clue. The only two things I could come up with were my visual impairment and the exercises that followed, and my lack of socialization within the family framework of belief systems.

In other words, I had grown up free, unimpeded by their opinions and prejudices, to develop as me. I also had learned how to control my brain through my mind. My parents had never had such self-control, of their minds or their emotions.

I felt strongly that what I was doing was not extrasensory perception, but rather *extended* sensory perception. It was real. I was pushing the normal boundaries of my senses, but what I was doing was still tied to the body and the mind. There was no "extra" in there—just hard work, rational understanding, and an appreciation of the unexpected and undefined. My pushed perception had a purpose and a reason for existing, as well as a use in everyday life. For the sake of my survival I had learned to hear farther, smell more intensely, touch more aggressively, taste with greater sensitivity, and to see, but differently from others. Not until I was in my forties did I discover how important it was that I don't possess three-dimensional vision or depth perception. It would always be impossible for me to ever totally think as others do when I would never have the same type of information input as they had.

I eventually coined the term "heightened perceptual awareness" (HPA) to get away from the dread three initials of E.S.P. I didn't want to be defensive about my discoveries before I even had a chance to explain them, and needed to provide myself a little space for research and discovery.

I began to understand that my new term meant exactly what it said: perceptions, or senses, that were strengthened to meet the demand for survival. Here, at last, was where reality fit in.

I shifted my focus to the idea of "intuitive development," a gentler and less aggressive way to encompass anything that could not be categorized into the more usual events of living. As with any new and developing discipline, there were many gray areas.

In my years of intuitive development I had met people who had turned an interesting and serious subject into party games and fortune-telling. So many of them had used their strong intuitive senses to create small cults of personality which coddled and enlarged their egos. In my opinion, I felt they had used a fascinating subject purely to impress other people and increase their own self-esteem.

I saw past all of their pretensions to the realities that lay below. Heightened perceptions are available to all of us. They are not possessed by only a few fortunate individuals for the sake of self-aggrandizement. Instead, HPA is the body's way of telling the brain that it is being called upon to respond to the need for more data. If the need was true, meaning necessary for survival, then the brain's response could become strong and remarkable in its consistency.

More simply put, if we gave our intuitive senses the

same respect that we gave our logic, we would be freer to develop its strength.

Reality and need had honed and sharpened humankind's sensory perceptions, giving them a razor's edge that cut true. I discovered this through the need to survive. I began to refine it through the need to serve. The challenge would become learning how to make it possible for others to gain the same skills and techniques that would help them to develop and heighten their own sensory perceptions and awareness.

It had begun when I felt an inner certainty that what I had experienced and done was more normal than "paranormal." Mine wasn't a search for a way to identify the events, but rather how to create them at will and then find a practical use for that ability.

Perhaps the most difficult step of all was learning how to follow the threads of my inner knowledge so they could be interwoven into the very fabric of daily living. I knew that if I did attain my goals, I would also need to be able to help others do the same. I feared that I might become so engrossed in being right, in finding the solution to the problem, that I would lose sight of my original quest. Most of all, I worried about how to avoid the real dangers that were lying there, waiting for those who take themselves too seriously, who become too self-important.

Laying out my own course of education, I began to read more books about leaders who had failed, who had become mentally unstable, and those who had succeeded and still retained their real selves. I finally discovered the common thread that joined them all. It didn't matter what others thought you were, but only what you knew yourself to be.

I also found many of them had shared one other thing: They were too busy "doing" to be interested in examining their own pasts for any great length of time. They were more concerned with being the new chapters rather than rereading the old ones. Most never took themselves seriously, but they were absolutely resolute in their work.

This appealed to me, for here was a quality I could relate to—*humor*. At least I had one thing in common with them. Only time would tell if I would have the courage, vision, dedication, and understanding to explore a field that had never before existed.

# *Three*

*B*ORING, very boring, and extremely boring. The more I read about the tests, measurements, and laboratory experiments that had been used to study telepathy, clairvoyance, psychokinesis, and the rest, the more I wanted to close my eyes and sleep. In my frustration, I couldn't help but wonder where all the excitement, fun, surprise, and amazement had disappeared to.

I knew it was important to do all those tests, but the point had been badly and widely missed. Things like paranormal events rarely happen when we expect them to. They happen because of a stimulus. I had to find what that stimulus was.

In all the anecdotes I read, I discovered that in many instances there was indeed a consistent theme. Each story told of a sense of need, of danger, or of reality which surrounded involuntary occurrences of paranormal phenomena. The human spirit had to be challenged, the mind needed stimulation, the body had to be aware of a true survival imperative before the extended senses would aggressively respond.

Based on this theory, I came to believe that to correctly study the paranormal, one had to recognize the response of the physical body to the sense of human need where unexpected events were concerned. There seemed to be too little humanity in parapsychological studies, which perhaps negatively affected the subjects' overall test scores.

Those subjects involved in the experimentation and measurement of E.S.P. were faced with having to endlessly reproduce certain skills. They would have to do the same tasks over and over and over again. How could any of them maintain a high degree of enthusiasm for the boring, mind-numbing tasks set before them?

No wonder the scores would decline over a period of

time. Active minds lose their edge and their attention when called upon to do repetitive jobs that squeeze the life out of the brain. Because of my personal interest in the paranormal, I wanted not only to identify what my experiences were, but to figure out how to access them at my own will.

Although I was usually thrilled when these events happened to me, I wanted to gain more control over the situations. It wasn't so much the why of them, as the how, when, where, and what. If the events were occurring, what were the stimuli, how had they manifested themselves, where did they begin, what caused them to end, and what had I been doing just before I experienced them?

Initially, my travels through the paranormal were totally in relationship to myself. At the start, I had no idea of what my discoveries might mean to other humans and other species. My search was self-centered and I realized I'd have to put aside my dislike of looking to my own past. Once again I had to examine my own life and what part my mind might be playing in directing my brain. Perhaps, examining the drive for survival—whether physical, social, emotional, or on any other level—would be the most logical place to begin. After all, I'd already been a witness to what the mind can do in emergencies.

I knew just the experience to look at more closely. It was one which had opened the hidden corridors of my mind to me and had happened in such an innocent way. It was here I eventually found the first clue to help me solve my mystery.

In October 1971, BJ, my first husband, and I had gone on a trip to Vermont. I was newly married and for the first time ever had begun to let my inner protective barriers slip away. At last emotionally vulnerable to another human, I found I was also vulnerable to my own past.

BJ was driving south through southern Massachusetts on a major highway, returning home in midafternoon so I could finish grading tests. The sky was deep New England blue, with huge, high white clouds hanging above the horizon. I recall experiencing a deep sense of fulfillment and happiness. Everything was peaceful, perfect—a rare time in my life.

As I leaned forward to change the station on the car radio, I was suddenly overwhelmed by a deep-seated memory flooding over me. It rushed in with such speed and force that I moved upright as if someone had struck me in the solar plexus. Sitting in my place, I was immobilized, unable to see anything in front of the windshield. The present had disappeared and the past was alive again. BJ was totally unaware of my distress, having to concentrate on the heavy traffic all around us.

An awful memory had returned with such clarity and accuracy that it was as if I'd been watching a movie screen. My emotions had literally leapt up and out of me with so much intensity I was unable to place controls on them.

I remembered that at age twelve, something had happened when I was in my seventh-grade school year in Brooklyn. The event, involving my fellow classmates, was so painful, so piercing that I must have been unable to cope with the trauma of it. When it had first happened, I could see the experience had ripped through me and left a scar hidden deep inside in some secret pocket of myself.

Whatever it was, it must have been horrible, so terribly excruciating for my preteenaged self it probably would have been enough to destroy what little self-esteem I possessed at that point in my life. Now, in the present, the emotional wound was still enough to make me wince with pain.

Regaining self-control, I leaned forward to turn off the radio so I could think of how I was going to tell BJ about what had just happened. As silence enveloped us, I discovered there was nothing to think about. It was gone. I'd lost access to the memory. As quickly as it had returned, it had been snatched away and refiled, outside of my mental grasp.

I began asking myself many questions. Where could this memory have gone and why was it suddenly not available to me again? How could such a major moment have happened in my life without my ability to remember any of it?

Up until that minute, I'd prided myself on having an exceptionally accurate memory about the events of my life. What had I done to trigger the memory of something I'd forgotten had happened?

Maybe my relaxed emotions were the clue. If so, perhaps I might be able to move more freely within the mind's inner pathways by controlling the degree of emotional vulnerability present at any one time. Perhaps it could be done along the same lines as the exercises I'd practiced with my eyes when I was younger.

It was hard to believe, but I'd discovered there was an experience I'd repressed so well that, to me, it never happened—at least that I could recall. How could my mind, something I respected and trusted, have enabled me to live without this information for so many years? I felt betrayed by my own self, and concerned that there might be many more memories that I'd successfully suppressed.

I was truly stunned by the deception I'd been innocently living with. Things had happened in my life to which I'd been denied access. Maybe I was overly naive and perhaps there was more to the mind than I'd ever realized.

After several futile attempts at recall, I decided to trust my own inner sense of survival. If the memory was again buried and if I'd felt such searing pain from it, then perhaps it was right for me to "forget."

I never again tried to find it. I decided there was some special defense mechanism which must be protecting me from the deep wounds that might have incapacitated me as I grew up and might have made it difficult, perhaps impossible, for me to live a normal life. While I accepted my own inner, involuntary ability to censor my personal past, I also became curious about having discovered another level of memory that coexisted with my more accessible past.

I wondered if I had unwittingly given myself the most important key to my "psychic" experiences. I had opened an avenue, previously closed to me, and the way I had entered was through a relaxation of my line of inner defenses. Unknown to myself, I'd created a clever means for surviving the emotional pains I'd felt during childhood. Apparently it was easy enough to exit that avenue, but what about gaining entrance? What mechanism was at work here?

My unaware mind was responsible for keeping all the worst things that had happened in my past away from my conscious self. Judging by the jolt of soul-stirring pain I'd unknowingly experienced from so long ago, I decided that my conscious self had definitely come out ahead.

As I further reviewed my past, I realized I'd had several interesting experiences that were related to E.S.P. while I went to college. Almost all of them had revolved around an emotional situation. What had kept them from gaining greater importance in my life was my goal of becoming a teacher and the demands of my schoolwork which soon pushed them from my mind. My logical self had placed a barrier, or maybe just one more veil, around my intuitive half.

As I read more books about the paranormal, I realized that what I really needed was hands-on experience. All I was doing was gathering information about other people's opinions and I had to generate my own.

Occasionally I would find a group of people who were interested in looking closer at the many sides of extrasensory perception. I learned what were for me many new concepts, and did exercises which sharpened and directed my innate abilities. Most of the time I approached everything from a quasi-serious point of view. Some things I chose to accept more than others, and with good reason.

Although I'd begun my search as an inner-directed study of the paranormal, I'd lost interest and become bored with myself as the center of attention. I grew more intrigued with what the useful possibilities might be if what I'd learned was properly implemented to help others.

At first all of us in the groups appeared to be interested in the same things. But as time passed, I found that many members seemed to be looking for who they were and where they fit into life's patterns. It was now that I understood how my lack of contact with my parents in my formative years enabled me to have fewer psychological problems stemming from that time. My parental relationships had only deteriorated as my parents aged. Anything I had to handle, in relationship to my parents, was taken care of from an adult point of view.

I found I had little in common with members of the

group and with their need to confront and excise their
pasts. They had little understanding of my need to broach
the present and explore the future.

I'd always had a deep inner sense of who I was and why
I was alive in this time and space. Regardless of the many
side trips I might have taken from my path, I still knew
where my course lay. I was born to be a teacher, whether
in or out of a public school classroom. It was all I'd ever
wanted to be. As a child I would set up classrooms for my
dolls and Teddy bears. To paraphrase Descartes, I taught,
therefore I was.

So intent upon their own selves, I couldn't figure out
why these folks couldn't see the real truth that was staring
right at them. There was no need for a quest of self. It was
all so simple. We were human beings. We were born humans, would die humans. No other species but ours had
ever questioned what its role or purpose might be in life.

I wondered if we humans had too much time for intro-
spective thought without seeing or probing the greater
environment that surrounded us. Maybe we avoided
looking at ourselves in conjunction with animals, as op-
posed to being apart from them. If this was the case, then
perhaps we might be able to retrieve some of our lost
selves by learning how to access that more primal part
from an animal.

Eventually I lost interest in the last development group
and left when the members began to degenerate into identifying which one was more psychic, more powerful, or
more spiritual than another. To me, living isn't a competition, it's a challenge. Besides, I always felt it was important to learn how to work together to achieve goals, rather
than do it separately and alone. At one point I read a book
which had a huge impact on how I chose to direct my
energies in life. It was about people who had nearly died,
had similar experiences on "the other side," and had returned to life and full health, forever changed. Many of
them recounted that they'd met a spiritual being who had
asked them two questions: What had they learned, and
what had they done?

Whether or not they had really almost died was of no
interest to me. Instead, these questions seemed quite ra-

tional and of great importance. I wanted to ask them of myself and again began to look more inwardly for a short time. I saw that my answers would not have impressed me, so how could they have been satisfactory to a "being of light" on the other side? I'd learned little and done less. Book learning and earning a living didn't count as a good response.

I'd learned enough to survive, enough to teach others, and enough to socialize. I'd done run-of-the-mill, mediocre things with my life. If I chose to continue living my life in this way, I could get through it, but add little to myself and the world around me.

Unimpressed with what I found in myself, it seemed quite reasonable for me to shift my outlook on the way I wanted to live. I'd been raised to look at who I was through the image of what I owned and how that might impress others. If all of this didn't matter when I died, perhaps I'd better make a few changes.

I'd once read that some people spoke about ideas, some about things, and others about other people. As I altered my perspective, I found my conversations were slowly turning toward ideas and possibilities and became excited about the transition.

I began to consider the idea that it was important to look back at how we, as humans, had made use of our brains to survive. Perhaps in our evolution into a thinking, creative creature, we had lost some of our more primal survival, perceptive abilities. By thinking more about our actions, we slowed down our reaction time. Perhaps our "psychic" selves were more closely tied in to our need to survive than our need to think rationally and logically.

I coined the term "mental archaelogy" to refer to the idea of scraping away the layers of socialization created by parental, academic, experiential, and societal education in order to reveal a more basic brain and mind-set. It would mean pursuing the skills, techniques, and methods which would enable me to strip away all that covered my basic brain and mind. I would have to learn how to be in touch with myself in such a way that opinions, formed by others and my own life's experiences, wouldn't intrude in the operation of my brain.

I came to think of that bottom level as the survival impetus, the one that doesn't care how it looks to others, just that it protects the body from danger and harm. It sounded good, but there was a gap that had to be filled in order for my ideas to work correctly. Again, I drew upon an event from my past to uncover the necessary information.

I once had a seventh-grade student who did exceptionally well in his studies. Eric consistently made the highest grades possible. At the close of the school year I would have to write comments in my students' personal record files. When I read his, one of his former instructors had written that the boy wasn't as smart as he appeared to be.

At first I was amused at the remark. Eventually I saw something totally different than what she must have intended. I believe she meant to say that Eric was an over-achiever who had to work hard to make his good grades. Perhaps she was trying to compliment him on his efforts and achievements.

She also indicated that he wasn't intelligent enough to be doing as well as he had done, but his energy and dedication had made the difference for him.

Eric's achievement helped me to define the gap between what was available and what was possible. The missing link was the person's individual drive to move beyond his natural limitations. Through the desire to excel and achieve, the brain could be made to work beyond the intellect. It could be exercised, like any other muscle in the body, to pick up the slack where there was weakness and to increase in overall strength and ability.

I had seen this in my own work to overcome visual problems, and in others who were disabled in different ways. The only reason "normal" people couldn't use their bodies aggressively was because they didn't place the same survival demands upon it.

It seemed that strength of will and determination to succeed were the means to override problems and create a bridge between the brain and the mind. Although the difference between the two was impossible to define scientifically, my St.John's dictionary had always recognized a definite separation between them.

If this gap existed, then I would have to look for information that had already been explored about the effects of determination upon the brain so I could save myself the effort of re-creating the same data.

I spent many long hours trying to locate any work that had been done on this subject and always came away empty-handed. To me, this meant there was a place and space that needed to be explored and developed. It also meant I would have to shift my subject search and instead focus on people who might be able to teach me the basics I would need for my research.

The only role model I was able to find was the late Dr. Buckminster Fuller. His independent manner of thinking and his decision to work outside the normal framework of education gave me the courage I needed to move ahead with my concepts. He often credited his unusual clarity and creativity of mind to his inner senses and perceptions. Through his acceptance of the importance of intuition, he had designed the geodesic dome, the "correct" map of the world, the concept of "Spaceship Earth," and had become a mentor to an entire generation of "futurists." Like me, he had a visual problem and like me he had also felt this helped him to see things in a different light. If Fuller, without a college education and in the face of many failures, could rise to such prominence by using his creative mind, then perhaps there was a chance for me to achieve my goals. This change in perception and appreciation of my own capacities enabled me to evaluate everything I had done, was doing, and might do in the future from a different scale of measurement, one independent from what other people thought important.

It also enabled me to look more closely into my mind, my brain, and my behavior. If I needed to think about whether or not there was a purpose to my quest, if there was to be any reward at all, then the prize would be the means to communicate with other species, improve interaction with our own, and expand the use of our minds and brains.

I was more than intrigued by this idea, I was fascinated, hungry to follow the disarray of clues that spread before me. I felt that there were as yet unrecognized problems to be identified, but the goal was worth the effort and whatever troubles that might come as a result of my quest to learn.

It was one thing to enter into the search via paranormal studies. It was another to figure out how to use what I'd learned and developed. There had to be a way to further expand myself and my ability and then teach others to do the same. I'd set the stage for my future work, but still had so much more to discover.

All I needed now was to find the right teachers.

# Four

WHY DOLPHINS? Why not work with wolves, chimps, or other highly socialized land animals? I suppose these are the questions I've been asked most frequently. Many people assume that like them, I've had a lifelong fascination with these marine mammals. This was not so.

If love for a creature were to be enough stimulation, then I would have set about studying and trying to learn from the many collies I've owned over the years. But for me, love for a species is not a good enough reason to spend a lifetime of research with them.

A simple progression of ideas brought me to the edge of a dolphin tank.

I realized that in order to learn, I needed teachers who knew how to use the brain more fully, more aggressively. They had to be actively using these skills and techniques in their daily life. What I learned from them had to be real and not just theoretical. It had to be accurate and applicable, regardless of the religious, political, social, parental, and personal belief systems that surrounded them. I wasn't seeking concepts, but rather concrete methods for exploring and expanding the use of my mind and as well as my brain.

My teachers had to have an intellect, perhaps a sense of humor, and a defined social structure. They had to have a background of teaching their young ones how to duplicate the social responsibilities necessary for survival in a group. They had to have a developed sense of reliability, beyond meeting their own needs.

For years I had heard people question whether or not dolphins were intelligent. This idea never concerned me. As always, I was too busy pursuing my own interests elsewhere. The ocean and what lived in it were of no interest to me.

Because of my lack of respect for the artificial assign-

ment of intelligence values, I also disregarded the comments about dolphins. They just didn't seem to have any
relevance to what I was seeking.

Then, in 1979, I met a woman who had had some interesting encounters with dolphins at a location in the Florida
Keys. She claimed to have been in telepathic contact with
the animals and to have impressed the trainer with what
she had done. At that time I was not yet pursuing my
research, and so I let the subject drop for another year.
Yet in my years of study, I had still not been able to locate
the instructors I was seeking.

One night, after going through some notes from her
lecture, I recalled what she had talked about and began to
look at it from a different perspective. Perhaps I ought to
take a closer look at these animals. Maybe the word "intelligence" might lead me to discover more important information about dolphins.

I began to take out library books about the marine
mammals and then started to purchase my own books. I
spent two years reading and researching all I could about
dolphins and other marine mammals. The list of facts and
supportive anecdotes began to grow, and with it the
awareness that at last I had found the creatures I needed to
work with, to learn from.

The progression of information was like a series of
arrows pointing me toward my teachers. Dolphins are
mammals. They give birth to live calves, feed them with
milk, grow hair, and breathe air. Unlike humans, they are
voluntary breathers. This means they must think about
every breath they take from birth until they die.

I wondered how they could sleep if their breathing was
voluntary. Wouldn't they drown?

My studies showed that scientific research had proved
they do sleep, but again, not like a human. The dolphin
shuts one side of its brain down at a time, leaving the other
half on guard. There it was, staring me in the face! They
had mastered the use of their own brains, and perhaps
could select which side to use at will.

I discovered that dolphins had complex social structures
and taught their young for one and one-half to two years.
They were gregarious, but never lost sight of their need

to survive. They were also willing, under some circumstances, to interact with humans.

They were said to meet the criteria for intelligence: leisure time for recreation, humor and creativity, and in the higher orders of dolphins, sex for pleasure and not just procreation. As I looked at my prejudice against the idea of an assigned value to intelligence, whether human or dolphin, I realized that I'd be better served if I were to use a word with more far-reaching possibilities: cognition.

My American Heritage dictionary defined cognition as: (1) the mental process or faculty by which knowledge is acquired; and (2) that which comes to be known through perception, reasoning, or intuition. Cognition was the perfect word to describe the abilities of the dolphin.

Dolphins possessed a highly evolved means by which to gather information and exchange it with others in their group, called a pod. They used reasoning to do more with that data than just react to it. And as far as intuition was concerned, perhaps their bodies had also evolved in such a way as to be able to sift through their noisy and complex water environment and identify what they needed to know through the use of their highly developed senses.

Their social structure was such that the females spent at least a year and a half educating their calves. Could this mean they had an ability to teach that might be used to educate a human? I didn't know, but I grew to believe that it was time to find out.

To develop the use of my brain and to learn how to do this from dolphins was my goal, but I had absolutely no training or credentials to be able to reach it. I'd drawn a mental picture of myself trying to communicate with dolphins from the side of a tank and realized the enormous problems this would create. Being bound to dry land would never do. It would be too much of a barrier right from the start of any project I might begin. No, I would have to learn about the ocean.

I thought about returning to college to study marine biology. At no time in my four years at Kentucky Wesleyan College had I taken any classes that related to the marine world. I'd selected courses which would help me to become a history and French teacher, never thinking I would be anything else in my lifetime. Now I saw how poorly prepared I was to work with dolphins and I needed to know more, to learn more.

Over a period of months I thought about my shortcomings and saw a basic flaw in going back to study in college. Since I was seeking to learn how to communicate with dolphins, and hoped to tap into their abilities to transfer information between each other and to learn how to do the same, I realized I could never achieve my goals by being separated from the dolphins.

If I studied marine biology, I would not be actively involved with the creatures that lived in the ocean. Instead, I would be looking at them from a distance. It was this same distance I was hoping to diminish.

I came to the conclusion that if I was ever going to interact with dolphins, I had better understand the environment they lived in, as well as learn how to survive and be comfortable in it myself. So what else might provide me with a deeper understanding of the water and what lived in it? What could possibly enable me to be self-sufficient in that environment?

Scuba diving.

It was not exactly something I'd always wanted to do. But I realized I had come too far in my efforts toward researching, developing, and expanding my ideas of communication to allow my dislike of ocean sports to stop me from moving forward. How could I back down at the first thought of doing something difficult or unpleasant? If I failed myself so early in my work, then perhaps this wasn't my work after all.

After making numerous excuses not to go there, including questioning my own sanity, I finally forced myself to visit a local dive store. At first, finding the place loaded with strange-looking equipment, more fitting for athletic folks than for me, I was intimidated. I looked around expecting to see black wet suits, black masks, fins, and snorkels, and black everything. They were there, but the equipment more suited to the mystique of the Navy Seals could only be found hanging on the racks in the back of the store. I discovered enough colorful items for sale to begin to feel less intimidated. Maybe women were allowed in this macho sport after all.

I finally took the initiative and approached one of the store staff, identifying myself to a man who turned out to be the owner of the shop. I explained my hesitancy, my worries, and my reasons for being there. I wanted him to understand about my background and lack of any sports aptitude. I needed him to be aware of where I thought I might fail. We both agreed that I wasn't going to be an easy student but we would give it our best shot.

He showed me the equipment and I selected my basic mask, fins, and snorkel. Then he had me fill out the necessary forms and signed me up for the next eight-week-long class. I would begin in early October and be finished by the start of December. Great. At least I would be one step closer to my goal.

I bought the book for basic scuba and learned that the shop certified people through an organization named P.A.D.I., the Professional Association of Diving Instructors. They were perfect for my needs, taking a less physically aggressive approach to the sport, one more involved with education and making diving available to people like me.

I began my diving lessons at Canterbury School in New Milford, Connecticut, three miles from my Bridgewater home. My first night in the water went beautifully—up to a point. We were asked to swim laps around the pool as a test of our ability to be water-safe. Then we got out and began to work with our dive equipment. My heart was beating furiously with excitement and fear. I realized I cared more about passing this course than any I'd cared about any I'd ever taken in college.

Once we reentered the pool, we were told to put on all of our equipment.

There's a thing called a buoyancy compensator, a "B.C.," which is worn like a vest. Strapped to the back is a tank of compressed air, with a regulator attached to the top and hoses coming out from it. One is the primary second stage, which you use for breathing. Another is called an "octopus" and is there to provide an extra air source from which you or others can breathe. Another hose carries gauges for telling how much air remains, and extras for depth measurement, possibly a compass, and a knife. A knife?

They assured us that we would only need the knife for cutting and prying. It would be rare, rare, rare to need it to fend off the "S" word. At that time I never, ever wanted to think about the possibility of meeting a shark. Not even on my dinner plate.

I had no problem using the regulator to breathe. The mask that covered my eyes and nose made certain that I didn't try to inhale other than through my mouth. I didn't even have to think about sucking water up my nasal passages, as there was no air available to use other than through the regulator. After one dive in the pool to ten feet I decided that I loved it. I loved the feeling of floating, of being weightless, of kicking and moving almost effortlessly through the hairballs, Band-Aids, and bobby pins at the bottom of the pool. I was hooked. It was so easy, I knew the rest of the classes would be a cinch.

The instructor rapped his knife against his tank, calling us back to the shallow end of the pool.

Once we were all there, he explained the next exercise. We were to drop to our knees in the three-foot depth of the shallow end. Then we were to gently stick one finger between the mask and our face and slowly allow a small amount of water to leak in.

After we were comfortable with the fact that the water would not rise higher than the level of air that remained in our nose, we were to inhale from our regulators and exhale through our noses, tilting our heads slightly back with our hands placed on the top portion of the mask to keep it from moving. This was supposed to force the water out and clear our masks.

We were told that we would start at the shallow end and would repeat the process in the deep end. He said there were no sides of a pool in the ocean and we had to learn to manage problems at depth.

So I did just what he said. And came up gasping. I had inhaled all but three drops of water remaining in my mask. If I couldn't clear my mask, I couldn't dive.

I went down a second time, with my assigned partner looking on in distress. Peeling back the mask, I let the water in, became comfortable with it there, and then . . . inhaled it again. And again. And again. I had a major problem.

The instructor took pity on me and said I could move ahead and try it again next week. The remainder of the evening was easy, but I sure had something to look forward to during the next class.

At the next class, I still couldn't clear the mask. I could do all the other exercises but that. I was frustrated and felt like a failure. Inwardly I suspected that I had somehow created the problem on purpose.

This was all too confusing, as well as threatening—an idea for me to think about. And so I chose to try to solve the problem logically.

I called the shop the next day and asked if I could book some private pool time. They said yes and we agreed to meet the next afternoon, just before the regular session.

Arriving at the pool early, I had time to think things out. For the first time in my life, I was deeply angry at myself and disappointed in my lack of courage and my self-sabotaging behavior. I recognized what I was doing, even though it was subtle in nature. If I could build in a failure, then I could give myself an easy exit. If I couldn't dive, then I couldn't be blamed for my failure to move ahead with the dolphins.

Even though I understood the rationale, it was still pretty confusing to me. How could I want something so much, yet work so hard to deny myself access to it? I really needed to look more closely at the person I was and compare her to the person I expected myself to be.

I'd always admired courage. I don't mean the foolhardy kind that comes from placing one's life in jeopardy for foolish reasons, but the kind that is shown in quietly doing those things that are right in life.

I had always had an idea of who and what I was, believing myself to possess the quality of courage, even if I was rarely called upon to display it. Now I was allowing myself to become less of a person in my own eyes. And all because I couldn't clear my mask.

Sitting in my car, nervous and a little ashamed, I decided that this was not how I wanted to feel about myself. I also didn't want others to perceive me as a failure. I suppose I finally had come face-to-face with one self-created barrier too many. It was bad enough that over the years other walls had stood in my way. This inability to clear my dive mask was just too much, and I had finally had it with failure.

All my life I'd been too short, too fat, too this or too that. Now was the time to break that pattern and just *do* it. If clearing the mask would be the way to release me from a past filled with fear, then I would examine the problem logically, find the solution, do the assignment correctly, and advance one step closer to success in my life.

Besides, inwardly I knew that I yearned to stop being scared and start to take action. Why not now? Failure certainly never brought anything that pleased me. Perhaps this was the open door through which I could walk and locate the person that I always knew existed within me.

For the first time, I approached a problem in the same way I worked on crossword puzzles. I decided that there had to be a hidden key to the process that everyone else seemed to find so easy and took for granted. Perhaps there was a rhythm, an inner beat that I was missing. If I could find that special beat, then I might be on the right track toward success.

The instructor arrived and unlocked the doors to let us into the building. I dressed for my private session and began to mentally formulate my course of behavior. I decided that I was going to get it right no matter how long or how many tries it might take to succeed.

Once in the water, I peeled the mask, let the water in, slowly breathed through the regulator, and listened to the sound of my breath. I relaxed and become comfortable with the water sloshing around my nostrils. Then I inhaled deeply through my mouth, tilted my head backward slightly, and slowly, with force, blew air out through my nose.

Like butter. It was like hot butter melting on an ear of

corn. The water slid out through the bottom of my mask and the inside was once again filled only with air.

Incredible! A miracle had happened! I had actually cleared the mask. Could I do it again?

I repeated the movements and once again the water was expelled from my mask. Success, at last!

I didn't know it then, but it was the first time I had actually knowingly learned how to program my brain, as well as the first step toward success in my work. This experience led me to recall the earlier incident of my moveable hairline and actually initiated the aggressive search of my memory. Now I saw that I had created a program of action which had taught my brain to work against its original input. I had looked at the problem, decided upon the solution, and then just done it. This successful action became part of my inner data bank.

I also began to understand the what and why of the mask-clearing episode—and interestingly enough, it was another sport that helped me to further understand what I'd done. Whenever I had gone skiing, it was easy for me to make a right-hand downhill turn, but when I went to turn left, my left side would stiffen, almost becoming paralyzed. I needed to know why that was happening.

It was so simple once I figured it all out. The basic understanding seemed to come to me in a quantum leap of awareness, though processing the information took me longer.

Because I lacked three-dimensional vision and depth perception, I was not able to use my brain the same way most "normal" people do. In my daily life I had always tried to keep up with others and either couldn't or found myself passing them by and winding up in front. I was either a woeful underachiever, or a supersuccessful person. There had never been any in between.

I began to understand that there were times when information was missing that I needed to complete a task, missing because my eyes couldn't gather it. Once I recognized the existence of a hole, or a missing piece of the puzzle, I began to figure out ways to fill in the gaps.

I'd have to think about the situation and assess where

the problem actually started. I'd question myself about whether or not I really wanted to succeed in that area. If I did, then I'd go to the second step.

I would observe others to see what I might be doing incorrectly and what they were doing to succeed. I'd try to identify the missing link, or what I eventually came to call the midpoint. I'd then create a simple mental training program so I could place the missing data into my brain in order to have all the pieces to the puzzle stored in one place.

The final step would be to test and see if the newly gained information was enough to allow me to be successful at the desired task. If it was, then I moved ahead; if not then I would try to find another path by which to learn. I would only stop when I'd achieved my goal.

Once I understood why I couldn't make left-hand downhill turns, I began to take charge of my life and develop the means to glide down the slopes with a smoother style. There were no more humorous excuses for why I couldn't do anything anymore, especially ski well.

I'd start out the season on the baby slopes. Every time I went to make a left turn, I would stop, take a breath, and literally have a conversation with my brain. I'd tell it I was now going to perform a physical action which was designed to place information into it. This was to show that my body was safe (as safe as it could be on a ski slope), and to use that input to free my left side to move more naturally, the way my right side did. Then I would gently and firmly force myself to place my weight on my left ski edge. In this manner I trained my brain to appraise situations in such a way that my body could respond correctly. The more often I did it, the more confident I would become. Within a short period of time I would then be able to graduate to more difficult slopes.

I finally understood that I was doing the same thing I had done when I had taught my eyes to work together when I was eight. Nothing done and learned in life is ever without value. It worked for me then, and it still works for me now.

In the cold Canterbury pool, I saw that this same principle had to be applied to mask clearing, and ultimately to any problem which I was to face in the future. For me, clearing was and will always be a skill that would have to be refreshed every time I went diving after a long absence in the water.

So, in the fall of 1982, I cleared my mask, and I cleared my way toward working with dolphins. I learned how to dive, eventually becoming a professionally certified Divemaster. And I tasted success in a different way. I had discovered how to repeat my triumphs, how to admire myself, how to cultivate courage. I had begun diving to work with dolphins, but before I ever met one I had already been forever changed.

It was because I was a diver that I was given my first opportunity to interact with dolphins.

## Five

*E*VEN BEFORE I'd begun diving lessons, I had made the vow to do whatever I would have to do in order to do whatever it was that I had to do. I knew at the start that this might mean my life would change, that things could get tough, and sacrifices would have to be made. I adopted the attitude that change was life and status quo was death. Change might mean a lack of security, but it also could bring immeasurable growth. I might have to learn to live with and accept a precarious existence.

In those earlier days, I never realized how true this would be, but from the beginning I was tested and faced with the worst problem of all—money, or the lack of it.

There are no textbooks on how to do innovative research, there are only other people who might serve as role models. Having read about individuals who had achieved their goals in the face of overwhelming difficulties, I set about laying a plan of action to achieve my objectives.

This placed such stress on my first marriage that it broke apart several years later.

I wrote to every major and minor dolphinarium in the United States outlining my project and asking them for time with their animals. Some turned me down right away, some took a little longer. Others had not yet responded and never would.

It was traditional for our dive class to attack food after each session. I had poured out all my impassioned hopes and desires to them over pizza. Looking back, it seems like a simple start to such a convoluted course of action.

In early January, after having completed all my certification dives, I received a phone call from my friend Jack Kinney. He'd just attended a small diving conference in mid-Connecticut and had met a man who worked with dolphins in Cape Cod. He'd gotten his name and phone number and wanted to know if I was interested. I just about leapt through the phone wires trying to get the information.

I finally got through after many tries. I started slowly, knowing from all the rejections I'd received that this was a potentially dangerous time for me. If I sounded too eager, too unprofessional, then I would lose my first and best chance to come face-to-face with dolphins.

The man's name was Bob Peck and he was a sports instructor at Springfield College in Massachusetts. He also taught science at a nearby private school.

I began the conversation by explaining that I was a former schoolteacher and went on to explain how and why I'd become a scuba diver, and finally revealed what I wanted to do with the dolphins. He listened carefully and then told me that before he would consider me as a candidate we would have to meet each other. Could I come up to the college next week?

We set a day and time and ended our conversation. I've always been amazed at what a strange sense of humor God must have. The future of my project lay in the hands of a man dedicated to sports, and here I was, the least sporty woman I knew.

The next week passed rapidly and I drove up to the college. I walked into the school and easily found Bob. I quickly introduced myself and he looked me over, eyeing my rather full, five-foot-two figure, short curly hair (so dark brown that it's been called black), and enormous owl-eyed glasses. I didn't look too difficult to deal with, but I wasn't a candidate for the Olympics, and even to this day I don't know whether that worked for or against me.

We spoke at length and then moved into the cafeteria, where we were met by Tim, Bob's sports assistant who also worked with the dolphins. Bob explained that the location I would be working at was in Brewster, Massachusetts, in the crook of the elbow of the arm that forms Cape Cod. I found it hard to follow some of his words because my mind had begun to react to what he was really saying. He was going to allow me to have access to dolphins! With difficulty, I forced myself to refocus my attention back to him and listened as he continued his briefing.

Sealand of Cape Cod was a small, private operation owned by George King and his wife. Bob explained that he had worked there during the summers since he was a young boy. Recently he'd put together a small nonprofit organization called Underwater Education Program, or U.E.P., and had hopes of running programs for all age levels. These courses would cover marine education and would use the animals and resources of not only the dolphinarium, but the local natural area as well. The program was in its infancy and for fifty dollars per hour, he would allow me to get in the water with Scotty and Spray, the two Atlantic Bottlenose dolphins in residence.

I made arrangements with Bob for me to do three weekend sessions. BJ and I would come every other weekend beginning in March and ending in early April. If things went well, then we would continue from there. It would only cost me six hundred dollars.

I didn't have enough money to pay the telephone bill or the mortgage on the house, but I told him it was a deal and drove back to Connecticut trying to figure out how to get the necessary funds to finally get in a dolphin tank.

When I returned from my visit to Springfield, I spoke with Tom Scott about what had happened. To my great surprise, he volunteered the necessary funds to make my first weekend of encounters with dolphins a reality.

I had met Tom because of our mutual interest in paranormal events. We had forged a firmer friendship over several months. One evening he had asked me what my personal goals were and I had told him about the "dolphin project." His answer was that he could make it happen for me.

Having heard the same thing from many other people who had never followed through, I just smiled and quietly said thank you. Tom must have recognized my slight air of skepticism, because he immediately asked me what I would need to move ahead. In the end, he actually followed through, covering all the expenses of my learning to dive. Still, nothing ever seems to happen that easily.

He told me to expect a check to arrive a few days before we were to go to Cape Cod and explained he would have to wait that long for the arrival of some stock dividends, then hung up.

February flew by, March came, and the moment I'd looked forward to for so long seemed to arrive almost overnight. That last week I went to the post office early every day. I didn't even wait for the mail to be delivered. I needed to have the check deposited in the bank so I could be certain the funds would be there for the weekend. By Thursday it still hadn't arrived.

That Friday afternoon BJ and I packed our clothes and gear for our trip to the Cape. We took turns trying to reach Tom Scott. He had called two days before, in response to the increasingly worried phone messages I'd left on his machine. He spoke in reassuring tones and once again pledged to send the two hundred dollars necessary for our first encounter. That was the last we heard from him.

BJ suggested that in light of our negative bank balance, perhaps we ought to give Bob Peck a call and reschedule the date. I refused with the insistence of a person who knows on some inner, intuitive level that there are some opportunities which only come once. I had a feeling that if I allowed the lack of money to stop me now, I would never have another chance to do this.

I told BJ that we would drive the five hours to Brewster, Massachusetts. Once there we would explain our problem to Peck and hope he would take pity on us and not tell us to turn around and go home. If it didn't work out that way, well at least we would have given it our best shot.

We arrived late in the evening and met with Bob in the parking lot of Sealand. He was not thrilled with what we told him, and he looked at me, then moved off for a moment to think. When he turned around I could see in his face that he had decided to allow us to be with the dolphins.

He invited us to stay at his summer cottage, in the next town toward the tip of the Cape. BJ and I followed his car in silence, our emotions bouncing back and forth between relief and anticipation.

Once there, Bob asked me to tell him again why we didn't have the two hundred dollars with us. Gracious as he was, I could tell he was unhappy about the money situation.

We got up early the next day. Bob explained that he would introduce me to the dolphins and show me the entire operation of Sealand. Then we would have a chance to get in the water with the animals for three sessions—that evening, the next morning, and late in the afternoon.

I was never to feel the excitement of this first opportunity to start my work because I was too angry and under too much stress, thanks to Tom's having stranded me. I had lost a tremendous amount of credibility in Bob's eyes and I knew I would have to work hard to regain his trust.

The Sealand I saw in 1983 was in pretty bad shape. It was just as Bob Peck had originally described it to me. This was definitely no Sea World. I came to understand the meaning of a "mom-and-pop operation."

The Kings had also owned a small business in Maine. It, too, involved the display of animals, although not marine mammals. After the second place closed, they'd sold all of the animals except one. This was how Humphrey the humpback camel came to be a resident at an aquarium.

There was a small gift shop which was also the entrance, exit, and restaurant. To the left were two small tanks which held sea turtles and local saltwater fish. Down the same corridor was a door which opened to the main displays.

On the right was a building which housed the aquarium which had a small display of local and tropical fish. In the center were two bathrooms which also were used as changing rooms for divers. Behind that, in the second half of the building, was where the trainers prepared the fish for the dolphins, seals, and sea lions, as well as transient rescued small whales and dolphins that might be in the pool at any given time.

The marine biologist kept a saltwater tank on a countertop. It was brimming with mussels, which he told me he was raising for his lunch.

There was a grassy knoll to the left of the entrance door. On the farthest side was a small one-room building which housed the Underwater Education Program. In it were various samples taken from local saltwater marshes, bottles containing dolphin fetuses, dolphin brains, shark embryos, and other miscellaneous items that made the place look like the laboratory of a mad scientist.

Next to the office was a small penned-in area where Humphrey would amble, occasionally staring back at visitors with a look that seemed to say it all. If you've seen a camel at an aquarium, what's left to see in the world?

Behind the aquarium/operations building was a double pool which housed stranded seals, sea lions, and Dennis, a Horsehead seal that would blow bubbles on command. He'd also been rescued, from an area nearby, and was to live out the rest of his life in the pool.

Beyond that was a small building that looked like it housed a carousel. At any one time there would be rescued cetaceans swimming in there, trying to decide whether to live or die. Over the years there would be Atlantic White-sided dolphins, Harbor Porpoises, and in the end, a large black Pilot Whale.

The long building facing the entrance door, farthest to the back was where the Atlantic Bottlenose dolphins lived. It was here that my work would begin.

I don't know quite what I had expected to see—perhaps a miniature Sea World at worst. Instead, I was looking at a small operation which was limping by, living off the receipts of the fleeting summer season of visitors. The long, narrow enclosure was not my idea of a place to house dolphins.

I had never attended a dolphin show before—in fact, had never had the slightest interest in seeing one—but I could see that this place had never been sparkling clean and was considerably less than that now.

The building ran long, like a freight car. The flank was a series of glass doors which could be left open in the summer to catch any errant breeze that might be lurking about. In the winter they were kept shut against the cold and a heater was constantly run in a losing battle against the wind.

The other side of the flank was a series of concrete seats, in bleacher form. They were closed off by wooden boards during the winter. This not only diminished the amount of natural sunlight entering the building, but also made any exit from that side impossible. At the time, this fact held no importance for me. Later on it would become a critical problem.

The tank itself ran almost the full length of the building. Toward the left was a small area which could be used to separate animals from each other. At that time there was a small Harbor Porpoise named Holly in the pool. She had been rescued the winter before. There was also a pipe that flushed water into the tank, which operated on a natural algae basis. I suspect that the algae sometimes lost the fight and the feces won.

The main body of the tank ran to a depth of sixteen feet. At the deep end were two platforms which were cornered on either side. A thin wooden plank connected the two areas. The wall behind this place was painted in what once must have been bright yellows, oranges, and reds, alternating with thin stripes of white.

The place had a distinct odor—slightly pungent, not quite pleasant, but tolerable. I later came to identify it as salt water mixed with dolphin feces. They say that odors are the strongest stimulators of memory. Regardless of what dolphinarium I may be at, every time I get a whiff of that particular "perfume" my mind speeds back to Sealand.

Bob wanted me to be dry for my first encounter with Scotty and Spray. He felt I should know more about his animals before I went into the tank with them, and I agreed, although I was a little disappointed at the delay. He climbed over the railing and stood on the platform. A few sharp raps and the animals appeared from the black depths.

He explained that dolphins can be quite jealous for affection and attention, then proceeded to give me a graphic demonstration. I should have paid more attention, because this conduct would cause my first major understanding of basic animal behavior once I was finally in the tank with them.

Bob showed me the signals he used. I strained to try to remember them so I wouldn't inadvertently do them later. I wanted all of my interactions to be natural and unforced.

I'd long ago decided never to offer any food reward as a means of attracting the dolphins to me, and I didn't want to give them signals which might lead them to expect payment.

If they were to be with me, it had to be because I had behaved correctly. They had to feel that the contact was reward enough. And perhaps they might be curious about a human who listened and tried to understand, rather than attempted to impose their will upon them.

BJ had come equipped with the camera he had borrowed for the occasion. He was to document all of the interactions so we could have a record of the work from the very first day.

Bob looked at me and decided it was time for me to mount the platform. I knew I ought to be excited, but with all of the problems getting there, I suddenly found myself devoid of any feelings. A cloud of calm settled over my mind and I realized I was suddenly taking in my immediate situation and surroundings without judging them at the same time. It was as if I was living in a space devoid of time, sound, motion, and life. I was actually part of the moment, rather than outside it.

It was strange to not feel anything. I've since realized that when I need to concentrate on a situation as it unfolds, I seem to lose all emotional feeling. Being in this state coalesces and intensifies my energies and directs my attention to the conditions at hand. It was the first of many times yet to come that I experienced such a void.

I climbed over the rail and kneeled on the platform. Bob had suggested that I wear something comfortable and old. He had warned me that a dolphin's favorite joke was to see how wet it could get a human. He was definitely right.

Scotty and Spray came up to me on Bob's unspoken command. I looked hard at their markings, trying to learn who was who. It was easy to see the difference between the scars and scrapes, especially around the top of the area, just behind the long beaklike rostrum, called the melon. Bob explained that the series of stripes which ran from the center of this area were caused by years of water flowing to the sides of the bulbous hump. The marks were called laminar flow lines and they followed the paths of least

resistance when the inner oil sacs would shift to cut down
on drag.

It was also easy to see which dolphin was darker. I
looked at them with the same practiced eye that could
identify which of my five collies I was seeing in the distance. People would always ask me how I could tell the
difference. It was simple for me to pick out the specific
markings. Finding who is who has always been the first
step in my work with dolphins.

Scotty was obviously the dominant animal. I had read
that dominance was not gender-related, but here it was
definitely the male who was in charge.

With some indiscernible signal from the dolphin, at least
to me, Scotty made certain that Spray kept her distance
from me. As I kneeled, I tried to get closer to him. Each
time I felt I was too separated, too distant.

By now my knees were sopping wet. Scotty, at Bob's
cue, had been rising from the water to plant a "kiss" on
my head. Each time he had returned fully to the water he
had hit it with a stronger belly flop. This would spew
water in my direction. It became quite obvious that this
dolphin had a sense of humor. And I was his straight man.

I decided that I had to get closer. I lay down full-length
on the platform. What the heck, I thought, I can always
get dry later.

I extended my right hand toward Scotty. He opened his
mouth and I suddenly realized that he owned a beautiful,
and quite complete, set of *teeth*.

I had never given much thought to those teeth. I knew
dolphins used them to grasp and flip fish down their gul-
let. They didn't chew their food, just allowed their three
stomachs to do the work.

But they did use teeth to grasp, and their jaw strength
was such that they could take an inflated beach ball in their
mouth and dive it deep down beneath the water. Fun for
them was releasing the ball so it would rocket straight up
to the twenty-foot ceiling, making deep indentations from
the force and speed of the rising missile.

Now Scotty's mouth had total possession of my arm.
Immediately the image of a Doberman pinscher came to
mind. Scotty definitely had more teeth and better control

than a dog. He also seemed to have claimed my arm for himself.

I drew in a deep breath and decided that this was his first act of dominance. It was a watery Mexican stand-off, with my arm as the prize. I verbally asked him to let go. Nothing. I then explained that he was scaring me. Nothing. I told him he was the boss, and I meant it. Nothing.

By now my arm was wet, very cold, and quite soft. The angle and the pressure were becoming too hard for me to continue negotiations. I pulled my arm toward me, gently prying it out of his mouth.

He allowed me to do this, but not without a penalty. As I looked down at my arm, I could see a series of red welts rapidly rising. In the middle of each was a small, red dot of blood.

Bob's reaction was concern for the health of the dolphin, which I totally understood and agreed with. He was worried that Scotty might become ill from any germs my blood might be carrying. But I also recognized that I needed a little consideration as well. I could see right away that if I sustained any injury at all, I had better keep the information to myself.

I waited for Scotty to finish circling and return to the side of the deck. He came up with his perpetual smile and looked me in the eye. It was impossible to detect what he was trying to tell me, but my human self thought I saw a hint of a dare in his glance.

*Are you brave enough to stick your hand back in my mouth?* I looked back and decided that, yes, I was dumb enough to do that.

I tentatively extended my right hand. Scotty moved forward and took it in his mouth. My action flew in the face of all my life's training. Never stick your hand in the mouth of a Doberman. So what about a dolphin?

He again held my hand in his jaws with the same intensive pressure. I began to fantasize about being pulled into the 52-degree water, with nothing but a pair of old blue jeans and a blue shirt to keep me from freezing to death.

Scotty never changed pressure, but my mind began to race with creative endings to my life.

Once more I begged him to let go. He again stared at

me with his impassive smile. So, once again, I made the
move to rescue my fingers.

This time I watched as a thin trail of blood escaped from
my cuticles. Bob caught a quick glimpse of the ribbon and
a worried look crossed his face.

"This is not good for the dolphin," he said.

This ain't so good for the human, I thought.

Once again Scotty cruised up to me. I took a big breath
to try to hide my growing fears and attempted to bury
them someplace deep in my mind. He opened his mouth
and I returned my hand into the opening.

Looking him in the eye, I firmly explained to him that
he was really scaring me. He looked back, then gently
released my right hand into the water.

He slowly made a wide circle and returned to the side
of the deck. Picking up my hand, he was ever so gentle.
The touch was that of a small feather. He shifted his body,
which seemed to adopt a purposeful attitude, caught my
eye, then dropped my hand.

He circled, returned, and reclaimed the hand. This time
the pressure was slightly firmer. Then he released the
hand.

He did this no less than ten times, each time increasing
the strength of his grasp just a little more. Finally he took
my hand in his mouth and held it with the same strong
pressure as he had the first time. Now I was totally relaxed
and allowed him to hold on to my fingers with trust and
confidence, expecting that he wouldn't pull me into the
pool.

As I met his stare, I was suddenly aware of an amazing,
incredible understanding. Scotty had used behavior modification training on me. He had gained my trust by showing me he was in control of the amount of pressure he
chose to use to hold my hand. He had revealed the mind
that lay beneath, had shown me he was capable of making
choices in regard to me, my well-being, and my safety.
The only way that I could conceive of his figuring out this
form of training was that he had been intelligent enough
to have replicated what his trainers had done when they
were teaching him show skills.

I had had my first lesson in cognition and communication from a dolphin. He had shown me, through his be-havior, that he understood my fears and was able to moderate and regulate the degree and intensity of his actions in relation to my needs. At that time, I had no idea how I might have transmitted information to him, but somehow he had achieved an accurate awareness of both my feelings and my thoughts.

As astonishing as this was, the best was to come a few short hours later.

## Six

*T*HE THREE of us were asked to leave the tank area while training was going on. Such requests for me to leave the pool so shows and training can go on always seem to come at a critical moment of discovery, and have been a perennial source of frustration in my work.

Still, in my opinion it's more important to work with and give in to the needs of my host than to grumble about my demands. This keeps the doors of communication and interaction open for future work. Compromise is a very vital part of my work and my life.

We left Sealand and went out for breakfast. Having found, in the past that I would rapidly become seasick when I did breath-hold dives with any frequency, I gobbled down two seasick-prevention pills. I suppose I may be the only person in the world who can get green from being in a tank with dolphins. But better to take the pill than to suffer.

Bob explained what the procedure would be once we went back for my first in-water session. He wanted me to enter at the shallow end of the pool. He advised me not to reach out and try to touch the dolphins, but to wait for them to approach me and show their interest. If one of them presented the dorsal fin and pushed it into my hand, it would be a signal for me to grasp the fin lightly and allow the dolphin to tow me around for a ride.

I was to avoid positioning myself over the top so that the dolphin would be able to pull me more easily. If I felt a shake of the fin, I should release my hold and let the animal go. I asked Bob to give me a bucket of warm water. I'd been told that if I flushed my wetsuit with warm water I wouldn't have to work so hard to adjust my body temperature to the shock of 52 degrees. It would give me a running, or floating, chance.

A wetsuit is not designed to keep you dry. That's what

a drysuit does. The drysuit wearer can control the amount of warmth by the type of clothing worn and the amount of air inside the suit.

Wetsuits come in various thicknesses. The thinner the suit, the less warmth is provided. The idea is to trap water between the suit and the body, which then reduces the amount of liquid passing over the surface of the skin, thereby reducing the loss of body heat.

My suit was three-sixteenths inch thick, which was a middle-range width. This meant that it would reduce heat loss, but eventually my body would lose the battle and begin to relinquish core heat. Thus there would be a threat of hypothermia, a real danger to the life support system.

My plea for warm water was not an idle request. The warmer water would mean I could extend my time in the pool and reduce body stress.

We returned to the dolphinarium in the afternoon. Light was quickly fading, even though the days were getting longer—March is still a time of early darkness in New England.

I set up all of my equipment at the shallow end. Mask, fins, weight belt to keep me from being too buoyant and floating at the surface like a cork, wetsuit and gloves, which would protect my hands from the cold water and keep my sharp nails from slicing through the skin of the dolphins.

I walked to the platform at the deep end of the tank and again climbed the rail. I lay prone in my clothes, this time with my bathing suit underneath. Scotty and Spray both approached me and each took one of my hands in their mouth. They then slowly moved back and looked at me expectantly. I supposed it was now or never.

As I moved off the deck, Bob walked up to me and began quizzing me again about why I didn't have the money I had agreed to pay. Great. At the very moment I most needed to be concentrating on the task at hand, he was needling me about money and Tom Scott.

I again gave him my solemn word that the postdated check I'd handed him earlier was good. I told him Tom was my problem, not his, and turned to begin to suit up.

My wetsuit came in two parts, with extras. A long "farmer john" went over the full body, including the legs. The yoke at the top slipped over my head and zipped closed at the chest. Over that was a jacket which zipped up the front and up from the wrists to the elbow. Booties of the same material went on the feet, providing warmth and giving the heel strap fins a place to hold on to. Last to go on would be the gloves.

I looked around for the bucket of water and couldn't find it. I made a quiet inquiry about it but quickly caught on that the bucket was not going to make an appearance. It was the first test of my determination. Real divers don't need to prewarm their wetsuits. Bob wanted to see if I was good enough to pass the test.

OK. So I'm a real diver. And a real dummy as well. But I was too close to back out now.

Bob decided to put in his assistant, Tim, first. This would be for my protection. Seeing that I wasn't quite dressed, he directed BJ to enter the pool.

I watched as BJ slowly allowed himself to slip into the water. As the coldness crept up and into his suit, the sounds he made were less than reassuring. He whispered to me that it was a good thing that we had already had a son—at the moment he thought he would never be able to reproduce again.

By the time my turn came, I was overheated inside the suit, stressed about the money, and anxious about the dolphins. This was not the way I had pictured my work starting. I climbed over the side of the pool and inched along the top until I could reach my fins and put them on. I felt and looked like a gray stuffed sausage with fins. With Bob Peck looking at me bemusedly I began my long, controlled slide into the water.

*Cold.* I mean really cold. How did I ever get myself into this predicament? For the first but not the last time, I asked myself why I was here. I could be baking pies. I could be doing laundry. I could be doing anything else except freezing in this pool.

As the water invaded the suit, I settled into a vertical position. I quickly placed my masked face in the water and looked for dolphins. Nothing. All I could see was tiny debris, called particulate matter, floating past my eyes. I didn't even want to consider what part of that matter was coming from the bottom end of the dolphins.

As I slowly adjusted to a lowered body temperature, I began to think about Bob's questioning me about money again. The more I considered the situation, the angrier I became. Before I realized it, I had wasted ten minutes of my precious time thinking stressful thoughts which had no bearing on my present position in the water.

At that moment BJ yelled out, "Hey, look at me!" Glancing toward the deeper end of the pool, I saw that he was being swiftly towed through the water by Scotty. They both seemed to be having a wonderful time.

My first and most socialized thought was that this was great. How nice for BJ that the dolphin liked him and he was having this great experience.

Then, almost as if it had a life of its own, an emotion I didn't even know I could have slipped out from the very depths of my being. I'd spent a lifetime creating filters that worked, holding back unpleasant, even threatening feelings. If my life wasn't perfect, well, I could live with it. I was glad to have what was mine, and never window-shopped for something I couldn't afford to buy or would never own. Jealousy was not something I had ever experienced. I had been successful in holding my emotions in check, including the one I was to experience next.

As if I had no control over it, my mind formulated a series of thoughts. Wait a minute. This is *my* project. I should be the one being taken for a ride, not *him!* I could hardly believe what I was feeling. I was *jealous!* For the first time in my entire life. And it filled me with a sensation I'd never had before. It was raw and totally uninhibited.

No more than three seconds later, Spray came up to me and shoved her top, or dorsal, fin into my hand. I gracefully reached out and forward, as if I had done this every day of my life. She moved into my cupped palm, and off we went for a heart-stopping ride.

When she was done, she lightly shook her body, dipped

down below me, and off she went. There I was, floating
in the center of the tank in a state of amazement.

What could have been the reason for this incredible contact? As I bobbed in the small waves of the pool, I tried to
review the events leading up to that moment of contact.

I had done nothing to bring Spray to me. In fact, with
all of my worries, perhaps I had kept her away. But I had
suddenly experienced a rare moment of unrestrained, un-
filtered emotion. I had been deeply jealous, and she had
appeared from nowhere. Had my full feeling of emotion
been the key? Nothing else seemed to fit.

Right then and there, I decided to totally alter my approach to my work. Instead of trying to control my
thoughts, I would allow them and my feelings to run free
and unfettered. After all, that morning I had witnessed
Scotty and Spray exhibit natural and rampant jealousy for
Bob's attention. Perhaps this behavioral model would be
closer to a dolphin's.

I calmed myself, closed my eyes, and waited. The sound
of a quick exhalation started me enough that I opened my
eyes to find Spray once again in front of my hand. I
reached forward. Again she slid her fin into my palm and
treated me to a ride.

After she let go of me, I floated at the surface. I watched
two dorsal fins as they circled and moved toward me, then
I reached out. Both dolphins came in and took me away.

I had become infected with "dolphin fever." This is a
term I now use to describe the behavior of people who
meet dolphins in the water for the first time. They lose all
sense of the real purpose for their being with the animals.
Suddenly they are caught up in the sheer exhilaration and
beauty of the experience. They lose all perspective of how
they ought to behave. All they want is more—more of
everything, as long as it includes a dolphin and the real
world doesn't intrude.

Here I was, enraptured in my first interaction, totally
overcome with being in the water with dolphins. This in
itself was a miracle. The cautious, controlled life I'd led
was beginning to slip away in the wake of a dolphin's tail.
I had lived my entire life as a conservative person, protec-

tive of who and what I gave myself and my energies to. I had never gone steady in high school, never joined a fan club, never marched for any cause. Now, here I was at the age of thirty-seven, steamrollered by emotions created by being in the water with two dolphins. Reeling, I felt I needed to get a hold of myself and regain contact with reality. Scotty was more than willing to help put things into their proper perspective.

In retrospect, I have often wondered what outcome my dedication to my work would have had if the sequence of the next two events had been reversed. While they were happening, there seemed to be a sense of unreality about all the interactions. Afterward, when I reviewed the session under my mental microscope, I saw a larger, broader picture.

Scotty offered me his fin once again. He towed me around the pool, then dropped me off in the far corner at the eight-foot-deep shallow end. This was where the bleachers had been boarded up, so there was no way that anyone could come to my assistance if that became necessary.

He moved back, looked me over, uttered a string of high-pitched sounds, quickly slid forward, and began to batter me. His actions totally surprised me. He pushed, shoved, and bumped me hard. If my pulse had been taken at that time, it would have been over the top. I was more than scared. He had caught me completely off guard and unawares. I'd thought that we had built this sense of tender trust; now he was dissolving it in an instant. At one point, hoping to distract him, I had dropped below the surface and seen his erect penis. It was then I realized he was being sexual with me. Dolphins can sometimes be quite humanlike.

I was rapidly stripped of my innocence, as well as my ignorance. Once again, nothing I had read had prepared me for this situation.

Here I had spent my entire life working hard at being safe. Now I was sure I was about to die in a dolphin pool, at the mercy of an enamored animal. Whatever happened to Flipper, the Lassie of the sea? Why hadn't I read anywhere that dolphins could be aggressive toward humans, not just toward other dolphins and sharks? And why had I been too stupid even to figure it out for myself? It was too late for that now.

Suddenly, I had an incredible realization: I could die. I don't mean that I could die there. I mean, I could die. I had been immediately forced to come face-to-face with my own mortality.

I once read that the body has no means to recall pain. It's great with pleasure, but pain doesn't stay in the memory cells. Thank God the full awareness of one's mortality passes away swiftly as well. No one could live a full life, always aware they could die at any moment.

Each time Scotty hit me, my heart raced and my emotions peaked. He was being sexual, but he was also getting great pleasure out of my discomfort.

Bob heard my *oofff* sounds and looked at me to see if I was panicking. He yelled across, in a controlled but quavery voice, "Uh. Do you want to come over here and get out of the water?"

I immediately turned my attention to his invitation, for a brief moment actually forgetting Scotty and his assault. My mind raced with the proper response. I was sure that if I got out, he would probably never let me back in.

Even as Scotty continued his pummeling, all in the name of sex, I yelled back to Bob in a not too strong tone of voice, "No. I'll stay in, but I'll swim over to you."

With my eyes focused on my goal, I began to move slowly through the water to the opposite corner where Bob, BJ, and Tim stood. I had been so busy with the dolphins I had never even realized the other two had already exited the water some time before.

As I turned my back to the corner, I discovered I had achieved some sense of self-protection. Now if Scotty came at me, at least I could see him. Before, with my back to the center of the pool, I felt too vulnerable. This change in position helped.

Suddenly I realized that Scotty had stopped his advances. What was the reason? It had coincided with the instant I had stopped paying attention to him. I hadn't reinforced his attacks through my emotional responses. Perhaps I had again found something important and was on the right track.

I saw that Scotty had pushed me into a game of stimulus, response, stimulus, stimulus. When he shoved me, that was stimulus. When I reacted, that was response. My response then became a stimulus for him, which meant he would again stimulate me with a hit. Great fun for him. Petrifying for me.

I had interrupted this chain of behavior when I shifted my attention to Bob and to swimming purposefully to the other corner. By removing my attention from my emotions and redirecting it toward another goal, one that had enabled me to control my inner feelings, I had stopped making myself an object of interest to the dolphin. I later came to understand that if I behaved as I had when I had done lunch and bus duty as a schoolteacher, I was in better control of my attitudes. I would have to modify, or set conditions on, my decision to allow both my thoughts and feelings free rein.

I'd accidentally hit upon a way of conducting myself which I still use in all of my interactions with dolphins today. I had discovered that my thoughts and emotions were totally tied in to my physical being. Everything I thought and felt could be transmitted through the water to the dolphin by my pulse rate and whatever other signals he was retrieving by using his sonar. If I were to limit my responses, then I could limit his reception, which would ultimately limit his responses to me.

Once I realized I wasn't going to die at that moment, I relaxed and began to play with Scotty and Spray. I was amazed by their creativity and their ability to use their bodies and behavior to indicate the rules of the game. Nothing I had read had prepared me for the vibrancy, the humor, and the joie de vivre they exuded.

At one point during our play they had given me a double dorsal fin ride and dropped me at the center of the pool. The water was pitch black and it was impossible to see beyond a few feet. I decided I was going to keep a watch for them through my face mask. Hanging in a vertical position, but with my face fully in the water, I was ready. I was concentrating. I was sure I'd be able to spot them coming in to me, even from the sides and bottom.

Two taps under my armpits, from behind, made me almost jump out of the water. Surprised? I was stunned. How had they managed to sneak up behind me? Actually, how had they even known I was waiting to spot them?

I'd never seen them at all. Somehow they had eluded my vigilance and come up directly behind me. In twin movements, they had poked me in my most vulnerable spot, one guaranteed to get my immediate attention. How had they known to tease me in this way? All these years later I have no answer. I just assume they had a great sense of humor.

Well, at least the three of us had something in common.

I took off after them, laughing through my snorkel, eager to play. They rolled around me and joined in the fun. I'd never felt so free and uninhibited. At last I didn't have to excuse my unrestrained sense of humor. All I had to do was appreciate the joke and join in. What a feeling of ultimate freedom!

Suddenly Scotty disappeared and Spray approached me slowly, purposefully. She moved back with her left eye just below the water's surface. I became prone and placed my head down so I could see her better.

Her eye opened wide, focused, and looked directly into mine. She moved forward, closer to my mask, as if she was seeking a clearer and stronger visual connection.

As she pursued the eye contact, I became aware of a startling feeling. Where once Spray had been looking at me, now she seemed to be looking *in* me. She had created a stronger, more mindful eye lock than I had ever experienced with any person.

At the same time, I realized that in some way she was actually bonding with me. It was as if she was scanning me, not only through my body, but beyond, into my personality, my sense of self, my innermost being. She was reading me, inside and out. With my heightened perceptions tingling, I could feel the billions of bubbles of sound moving into every part of me, places I hadn't even known existed.

Somehow, and for some unknown reason, Spray had chosen to reveal her intelligence, her cognition, her "dolphinness" to me. Yet, at the same time, I also felt she was revealing my "humanness" to me. I was stunned. This couldn't be happening. But even as it was happening, I was trying to figure out what "this" was.

Why was this eye contact with Spray so important? I have mentally replayed that moment more times than I know, and each time I experience the same rush of astonishment. It becomes a sudden pulling of the edges of my consciousness. It was for me a first, true and equal exchange between species—not the first for humankind, but the first for me.

I look at one of the few underwater slides of Spray, eyes wide, staring into the camera with an indefinable gaze. Huge, interested, knowledgeable, and knowing. Perhaps "this" was a contact with an alien. But who was the alien?

Well, I was in her environment, so I suppose that made me the outsider. If I'm honest with myself, I don't suppose; I knew this was so, which only increased my gratitude for the sense of acceptance she was extending toward me.

It wasn't her intelligence that caught my soul. It was her cognition. Here, within Spray, was that awareness, the sense of soul and spirit, the ability to do more than gather data and store it for later use. I sensed that there was so much more than intelligence in this animal. There was the desire and initiative to use information to create a style of living, not just a drive to exist and survive.

With Scotty, I could see how much of his behavior was directed toward being dominant and sexual. With Spray, there should never have been an underlying reason for her to bother with me other than to play. But she had chosen to allow me to see further into her than I'd thought possible, and she made the effort to try to educate me over the next year.

That first session was a brief moment in my life, but it altered me forever. I was no longer interested in pursuing my own personal theories. I wanted to spend the rest of my life trying to understand more about the essence that was housed in the creature called dolphin. More than that,

I wanted to test my ability to learn from what promised to be a phenomenal species of teacher. I had somehow shifted my priorities from searching for methods to expand the use of the brain to trying to learn how to communicate beyond words.

# *Seven*

**M**ONTHS had passed since my first dolphin interactions in March and April. Now it was August 1983, and I was again prone on the platform, waiting for the dolphins to approach me. I looked out at the water and waited to spot the dorsal fins rising to the surface. The pool was so calm that it was hard to believe living creatures of power and grace were swimming below.

Suddenly, with loud exhalations, the dolphins broke the water's calm and rose together in front of me. Heart in my throat, I realized that they had once again caught me off guard and were pleased with my genuine surprise.

Shaking their heads, they swam away, then back toward me. As usual, Spray hung back a little, waiting for the dominant Scotty to check me out.

Remembering what had happened during our original meetings, I extended my right hand and allowed it to loll in the water, an obvious invitation to him. He approached it, opened his mouth wide, but only rubbed his teeth against my fingers. I'd expected him to mouth my hand, but he didn't bother.

Spray glided in, rolled to one side, and looked me directly in the eye. I had the distinct impression that both of them recognized and remembered me. Their behavior was more a reaffirmation than a reintroduction, as if they were refreshing their memories of our past meetings. They bellied up so I could stroke their stomachs and flanks, allowing me to massage whatever body part they presented. After a while the dolphins finned backward and hung in the water facing me. I waited for them to come to the deck's edge. And waited. By not returning, they seemed to indicate that now was a good time for me to join them in the water.

Climbing off the platform, I moved down to the shallower end of the pool. By now, our eighth session, I'd

become smart enough to have changed into my wetsuit
before entering the tank area. Donning my mask, fins,
snorkel, gloves, and weight belt, I chose to leave my hood
off. When I'd worn it in the spring, it had blocked my ears
to the point that I hadn't been able to hear the sounds the
dolphins had made. I didn't want to be deprived of the
experience now.

I climbed over the rail, then inched my body across the
top of the tank edge, my feet dangling in the water. It felt
warmer than it had been in March, but not by much.
Scotty came over and began to nuzzle my fins, and I knew
it was the right time to enter the pool.

Sliding in cautiously, so as not to kick him inadvertently
with my fins, I waited for the wet coldness to envelop my
skin. It was better this time; I'd probably be able to stay
in longer than during the spring interactions.

As soon as I'd acclimated myself, Spray again came
over, pushed against my hand, and off we went for a brisk
tow around the pool. Scotty soon joined her.

I didn't want to be passive and force them to carry my
full weight, so I began to gently fin, hoping to reduce the
strain of towing me around. As if they sensed the change
in drag, the dolphins slowed their pace, allowing me to
try to keep up with them while still grasping their fins.

It was wonderful, exhilarating, but I hadn't come for
rides or play. I'd come prepared to try to learn from them.

I'd spent many hours reviewing my notes and my memory, trying to find the logic in what had happened in
March and April. All of my original theories, now unim-
portant, seemed pitiful and inadequate once I'd had direct
contact with the animals. I'd originally wondered if dolphins might communicate telepathically. Perhaps they
were using only sound, which might translate into a language of some kind. Could it also be that I wouldn't find
this true and instead come to see that humans had given
dolphins more credit for comprehension than they deserved?

None of these ideas seemed to fit my experiences. It was
easy to see that I'd be better off if I started from total zero,
from nothing, seeking nothing, and found a way to allow

the dolphins to teach me. Questioning where I'd made my mistakes, I was always drawn back to examine the emotional, nonrational moments which had been so important.

Perhaps I might do better if I redesigned my methods. Instead of trying to identify only what I was seeing, I might consider adding what I was feeling and what I'd intuited. There might even be more I was missing.

It was possible the dolphins' behavior could be understood not as individual events, but as a sequence of interrelated occurrences with a syntax like the nouns, verbs, adjectives, etc., of human sentences. Like sign language, it might be that their basic language, the one enhanced and accompanied by sounds they made, was constructed of specific actions performed in concert with each other.

I'd reviewed whatever resources I had that would enable me to succeed. I recognized that my background as a foreign language teacher would help me enormously. When in the water with the dolphins, I would behave like a visitor to a foreign country. I would allow my body movements and my mental attitude to indicate to Scotty and Spray my willingness and eagerness to learn from them. I'd even allow them to select the subjects they believed were important for me to understand, rather than make those decisions for them myself. After all, who else would know better what they needed to survive?

As I dropped off Spray's dorsal, I tried to figure out how I was going to make them aware of what I wanted to do. Ignoring them for a moment, I began to review the pieces of our present interactions.

I'd noticed that in our first earlier encounters, they'd always returned me to the shallower end of the pool each time the ride was done. As the interactions progressed and they became more comfortable with me, they would drop me further toward the center. I wondered if there was any significance for this. I began to look more closely at how they behaved in relationship to me, to each other, to the pool, and to their overall environment. If I accepted that the tank was their territory and I was just a transient visitor, then there might be more to the fact that I was in the water. Perhaps there was a protocol I was supposed to be observing, something like knocking on the door of someone's home before entering.

If this was true, then maybe this socially correct way of behaving would accelerate my ability to interact with them. But if there was such a set of rules, what were they, and where did I begin with them?

I thought back to the times when I'd been lying on the deck. Bob had noticed that I seemed to be able to interact with the dolphins more quickly than most other visitors. Had I stumbled onto something important? Had I created a midpoint, a safe space, half water, half air, for all of us?

As I was thinking about protocols, Scotty came up and took my right hand in his mouth. I allowed him to munch on it without fear. The neoprene glove kept my hand warm. And safe. I'd already accepted his dominance. Could putting my hand in his mouth be the correct physical way of showing him I understood what was happening and accepted the situation?

Scotty pulled my attention back to him, pushing against me in a gentle way that also demanded my notice. He then moved in front and slightly to my left and began to shake his head. Acting more on instinct than on thought, I extended my left hand to him and he engulfed it gently in his mouth. I allowed my right one to drift lazily on the water's surface.

Next, he placidly moved his head back and forth, sending little sonar sounds rippling to and through my left fingertips. With my head in the water, I actually was able to hear them for the first time. It had been right not to wear the hood.

I wondered if he was trying to indicate something to me and so placed my right hand over my left. Immediately Scotty stopped sonaring and moved forward, taking my overlapped hands in his mouth. The entire time, he had been looking directly at me with widely opened eyes.

At some unknown signal, he stopped this behavior and moved back, still keeping his eyes on mine. It was as if he was moving his body in such a way as to say, *Now did you get that? Did you understand what we just did?*

What I figured out was that if I held my hands in front

of me, one over the other, and moved them up and down in a flowing motion, he would then glide forward and take them into his mouth. Time after time, he would do the same thing in the same way. The behavior was consistent enough that I began to think he might be training me —for what, I had no idea.

As the first session progressed, it appeared that all Scotty and Spray wanted to do was reinforce my understanding of the importance of my hand movement. It was the same movement that I'd done while on the platform, and it brought an identical and immediate response from them each time I did it.

I also noticed that they emitted the same sequence of sounds whenever the movements were performed. Perhaps this string of sounds, in concert with their body motions, might also have some importance in the scheme of things.

I left the pool because my body temperature had decreased enough over the ninety-minute interaction to make me uncomfortable. Hypothermia was a real threat and I'd have to be cautious on my own behalf. The cold drew water away from my extremities in order to protect the warmth of the body core. I would always have to be aware of the immediate needs of my body and not allow the loss of inner heat to incapacitate me in any way.

The next morning I again lay prone on the platform. Scotty and Spray quickly came to me. I extended my hands, folded into the now familiar "prayer" position. Scotty moved to my hands and took them in his mouth, applied a gentle pressure, and then released them.

To my surprise, Spray now came in and did the same thing. She vocalized sounds loudly enough to be heard above the water; they were the same ones she'd made the day before. The dolphins moved back and waited expectantly for me to ready myself to get in the water and join them.

This time they dispensed with the dorsal ride and, on either side, immediately began to push my arms. They moved in front of me and I again performed the protocol movements. After this was completed, Spray slid backward and again allowed Scotty to be in charge.

Once more, he moved toward me, then to my left. Opening his mouth, Scotty engulfed my entire upper arm and held it steady. Then, with a series of soft sounds, he moved the arm in an up-and-down manner.

His lower jaw gently lifted my arm. As soon as it broke the surface, he used his upper mouth to apply a slight downstroke pressure. I had no sensation that he was controlling my arm, just that he was guiding it in some thoughtful direction. It was also clear that he had a reason for doing this.

When he'd finished, he then moved back in front of me and took my hands in his mouth, and followed with another string of connected sounds. Letting go of my hands, he finned backward, stopped, and just stared at me.

OK. Now what?

Well, I obviously didn't get it the first time, so he repeated the entire chain of behaviors, ending with an expectant stare.

OK. Now what?

Once again, I hadn't caught what he was attempting to communicate. So he did it again.

By now, Scotty's insistent movements on my arm had attracted Bob Peck's attention. He came to the poolside and called my name, firmly asking me not to do that with Scotty. He explained that it wasn't a behavior Scotty had ever done with anyone else, and he didn't want the dolphin to be reinforced in the actions. He was worried that the animal might do the same with other unsuspecting people, and that they might be injured.

I turned to him and tried to explain that Scotty was not acting in his usual gruff and aggressive way—he was barely holding on to my arm with the lightest, gentlest touch.

The dolphin wasn't forcing me to move my arm; I was allowing him to do it. This was so unusual for Scotty that I knew something important was going on. I just couldn't figure out what it was.

Bob was unimpressed, and insisted I stop.

I swam away from Scotty, trying to do as Bob asked. I felt it was necessary to obey his requests, especially in view of all the hospitalities he'd extended to me. I was able to distract the animals for a short time, but ultimately all they wanted to do was return to holding on to my arm.

I looked around and saw that Bob had left.

If I was ever going to learn anything from a dolphin, it would have to be on their terms, not on mine. I made a decision to ignore Bob's request. If the animals wanted me to do this, then that's what I was going to do. Whatever "this" was.

Scotty resumed the sequence. He did the same movements, made the same sounds, ended it all in the same way.

What *was* he trying to show me? I could see the frustration all over his body. Each time I didn't follow with the mysterious correct response, he would move back and begin to shiver, then to shake. The water silently conducted the message and sensation of a dynamo, humming at top pitch, full to bursting with pent-up energy.

I could hear his sounds increase in loudness and intensity. He was making this enormous effort to teach me something and at best, I was a fool.

As if to spell him awhile, and take some of the energy away from his inability to teach me, Spray took over. Now it was even worse for me. She did the exact same thing as Scotty had, including running the same scale of sounds.

How could I be so dense? What were they trying to show me?

I began to use my rational mind to attempt to figure it out. Every time I thought of a new idea, it wouldn't fit. Did they want me to initiate a movement through the water, like surface diving toward the bottom or swimming away from them? Was I to mimic the sounds they made, or ought I react to them in some manner? Was I missing something too obvious or even too subtle to recognize? It grew to be as frustrating for me as it seemed to be for the dolphins.

Scotty returned and once again assumed the role of teacher. This time, he did it all very slowly, as if he was working with a very dull pupil. Which he was.

In a serious and almost regal manner, he once more grasped and moved my left arm in an up-and-down mo-

tion. I concentrated on his actions, desperately hoping to
hit on the answer. I was so engrossed in the interaction I
didn't realize Bob had quietly reentered the building. Suddenly his loud, agitated voice brought me to attention.
Frowning, he told me once again not to allow Scotty to
pursue his strange behavior, then threatened to end the
session right then if I didn't stop.

I turned to him, tried to explain what was happening,
but he would hear none of what I said. The ultimatum
had been issued.

Spray was to my right, and I turned to face her. In a
very sullen, childish tone, I muttered, "He won't let me
continue with this." I was really angry and unhappy at
Bob's demands and intrusions.

Spray moved back, and then with a slow and deliberate
manner, moved forward. She opened her mouth in response to my properly positioned hands. As if she were
saying, *Now listen carefully to me, you slow, stupid, human
woman,* she moved my hands in the now familiar up-and-
down motion. I'd never experienced anything like it in
my life, but I instantly recognized what had happened.

I'd suddenly had a quantum leap in understanding. I
*knew.* I understood what was happening. I had no reason
to know, but I knew!

It was the rhythm of the movement that held the answer.

Spray had taken my hands and moved them up quickly,
then down slowly. Up quickly, down slowly. Like
Scotty, she hadn't been grasping my hands in her mouth,
but rather had manipulated them to move upward
quickly, downward slowly.

I looked at her, presented my hands, allowed her to pull
them into her mouth, and then moved them up quickly,
down slowly, without her assistance. Her eyes literally
flew open. She began to chatter excitedly and again captured my hands in her mouth.

Up fast, down slow.

She seemed to swell with joy, her fixed smile appeared
more radiant, even though I knew this was not physically
possible. How had she done that?

Next, she moved from a horizontal position to a vertical

one. With her entire body length visible to me through my mask, I watched her undulate toward me in a shimmying fashion.

Her front pectoral fins approached me, slid under my armpits, then pressed close to me. I was stunned to realize she was pulling me into a true embrace. As our bodies touched, she squeezed harder, almost forcing me to place my arms around her girth. Without thinking, I clasped my arms around her and returned her embrace.

I'd never done this before, never even attempted to. Bob had warned me that dolphins didn't like to be held in this manner. But here she was, initiating the hold all by herself. At that thought, I turned to check and see if Bob was still there. Luckily, he must have slipped out at some point before all the excitement occurred.

Returning my attention to Spray, I clung to her and she slowly drifted into a horizontal position. Still hugging me to her, still looking me in the eye, still allowing me to encircle her with my arms, she softly, almost lovingly, repeated the series of now familiar sounds.

She seemed to be saying I'd been a good and perhaps a promising student. Perhaps there was hope for this human female after all. Now she was giving me a proper behavior reward for my success. I felt proud of myself, thrilled and exalted that I could learn. For the first time in my life, I understood how a mentally challenged person must feel grasping a concept that is simple to others, yet difficult to them.

In some ways, it was like being a child again. My world had expanded to include other realms, other species and unknown information. There was a freshness, a newness to what I was learning and an excitement within me as I realized I was able to be simply taught.

Once I'd calmed down, I realized yet another amazing fact. Spray's actions were more than delight at what we had achieved together. They were well thought-out, directly appropriate to the situation. It was then that I recognized the procedure: As she had been trained through behavior modification, so she was now training me.

Repeat the desired behavior until it is understood. Once grasped, reward it with positive reinforcement, such as affection. After several repeats of the behavior to ensure that it has really been understood and accepted, move on to the next step.

Whatever it was I'd just experienced and discovered, it was light-years ahead of what I'd initially looked for so long ago. I would forever leave behind thoughts of telepathy or language as I knew it to exist for humankind. Now I would have to attempt to identify the very basic nature of what had transpired.

I'd recognized the first hand movement, mouthing sequence as a protocol. The second seemed to be the specific up-and-down motions. The third was the emission of the exact string of sounds. That completed the chain of behavior from start to end. I had begun to understand the rudiments of their language.

I had no idea what it all meant, or why it was important to Scotty and Spray. I only knew how much joy it had brought all three of us when I'd passed my first test in dolphin communication.

# *Eight*

*I* HAD a serious problem. By the last of my original set of three weekend sessions at Sealand I was thrilled with what I was learning, but confused about what to do with the information. I had discovered a world filled with heightened sensory perception, a watery realm whose most evolved inhabitants had expanded the use of their senses to survive. Instead of finding sparse bits of clues to follow the path of a mystery, I had been overwhelmed with a profusion of information far beyond any expectation I might have had.

People had always been my primary interest, not dolphins. I had originally been concerned with finding out important information relating to the increased use of the brain. Instead, I realized I had been exploring virgin territory, perhaps even places no human had knowingly visited before. I came to see that I had created a problem along with my discoveries. What should, what could I do with what I was learning? I began to worry about how to use my new understandings, and realized that what I truly wanted to do was to help humans.

The problem intensified as the weeks went by. It gnawed at me like a guilty conscience. I knew I had to do more with my budding work than just collect information. I understood that I needed to have a goal, a place to apply my findings, both present and future. Accepting this as a fact helped to lessen my discomfort, but not by much.

I never expected that a simple course of action on my part would lead to finding just the right people.

Once I'd completed my final April sessions, I called a local newspaper. I hoped that an article on my research might attract an interested person who would donate funds to help me continue my work.

When the article came out the following Thursday, I

found it to be a mixture of fluff and serious information. I was embarrassed about the pose they'd photographed me in: kneeling on the grass, dressed in a wetsuit, holding a stuffed dolphin toy in my arms. That about summed up the way they handled the piece. It wasn't bad for a first article on my budding efforts, but it wasn't good enough to bring in what I'd wanted. Or so I thought. Still, it did have its readers.

The next week I was contacted by a journalism teacher from a nearby high school who had read the article. He had a small class of students who needed to practice interviewing on someone. Would I volunteer?

I've always loved doing anything related to students, so I agreed and we set a date in early May.

The class of fifteen students was made up from different grade levels, all less than eager to throw questions at me. As far as most schoolbound kids are concerned, May only stands in the way of June, which means vacation. These teens were already vacating.

I did my best not only to give in-depth responses to their lethargic inquiries, but to capture their attention and create some sort of kinetic energy between us. Most of their questions were standard, with a few giving me pause to really think.

They made me ask myself the hows, wheres, and whys I'd never looked at before. For the first time I was called upon to give rational explanations of events I'd experienced subjectively. Now I had to enable others to understand my experience from a less personal, more logical approach.

The time went by quickly, at least for me, and the bell signaling the end of the class startled me more than it did them. I'd enjoyed talking with the group about my experiences and hoped they had gotten as much from the session as I had.

After the majority of the flock had flown off to other places, a serious young girl approached me. She had hoped to catch a few minutes alone with me. I was free to spend the time and pleased at her interest, so we went back inside the classroom.

Settling into the standard school chairs, we began to

discuss the behavior of the animals and how the dolphins would relate to me as an individual. Seemingly satisfied with what I'd said, she revealed that she had a brother who was autistic. "What's an autistic?" I asked her. He was a boy who had severe problems in communicating with people, even his parents. She was the only person he had any real interaction with. She felt that the difference between herself and others was in how she behaved with him, which she said was very close to how I'd behaved in my interactions with Scotty and Spray. She was never demanding, never judgmental. She just wanted to spend any time with him that he wanted to spend with her.

At that time I had no idea what autism was, and wasn't very interested. What caught my attention was her relationship with her brother, and nothing other than that. We exchanged telephone numbers and I told her I'd call her soon.

Casual and easy as that was, it was a momentous encounter just the same.

I went home and began to think about what she'd told me. I still had no idea what autism was, but I was interested in her story because of its behavioral aspect. Obviously, she thought there was a connection, and it did involve humans in need. Perhaps I'd better give her idea a closer look.

I decided to work a little differently this time. Rather than read all I could on the subject of autism, as I'd done on the topic of dolphins, I chose to try to locate a family with an autistic child. I would attempt to arrange for a meeting so I could interact with the child.

I hoped a firsthand setting would enable me to do what I'd done with the dolphins. Perhaps I might be able to learn from an autistic person how they felt about and dealt with the disability, as well as how I ought to behave when I was with them. It was my only plan at the time.

I thought about the type of parents I wanted to speak with. I needed people who were open-minded and willing to try something that might be a little off the beaten path.

I lacked any connections or training in interacting with disabled populations. I didn't know any psychologists, had no connections to the medical world, and no back-

ground in autism. I would need to contact an organization
or a group which was made up of people who were willing to examine possibilities.

My background in paranormal work had made me
aware of several organizations. One of them had been in
existence since the 1950s and had a solid reputation as
serious folks doing serious examination of a serious subject. There were two chapters of Spiritual Frontiers Fellowship, or S.F.F., in Connecticut. My home was
equidistant from both, but I chose the one in the southern
part of the state. I called the office one afternoon in late
May of 1983 and outlined what I hoped to do. I explained
that I would like to meet with an autistic child and his or
her parents. All I wanted to do was have a short interaction with them and then take it from there. If something
interesting or important were to come as a result of the
session, then there might be more interaction in the future.

The woman with whom I spoke was gracious and understanding but unable to be of help. She knew of no such
parents, but took my name and phone number in case she
met someone who might want to call me. As I placed the
receiver back on the telephone hook, I thought this was
perhaps the end of the matter and pushed the idea to the
storage shelf in my mind. It never dawned on me to call
elsewhere.

I was surprised when the very next week I received a
telephone call from a woman with a cultured, soft voice
that carried a hint of a foreign accent. She said she was
calling from the southern portion of the state and wasn't
certain if I was the person she was looking for. Was I the
woman who was working with dolphins, but wanted to
meet an autistic child?

I assured her I was the one and asked her to identify
herself and how she'd heard of my work.

Her name was Beatrice—Bea for short—and she had a
twelve-year-old autistic daughter named Beth. A friend of
hers had suggested that she call Spiritual Frontiers Fellowship to see if anyone was doing any unusual research in
helping autistic children to communicate. She'd just gotten off the phone with them, having been given my number.

I gave Bea a brief explanation of my background and my not-too-clear goals. At that time I had no idea of what to expect, but she seemed willing to work with my open attitude and so I made a date to get together with her and Beth.

She filled me in about her and her daughter and explained that she had been divorced for many years. She lived near her mother's home and, together, they provided the primary care for Beth.

Once off the phone, I fished out the paper with the student's name and phone number from my pocketbook and called her. I spoke with her mother and invited her and her daughter to my home to meet Bea. Unfortunately, they weren't able to come and I never heard from them again.

The woman who knocked on my door looked like her voice. Slim, neat, attractive, and a bit taller than my five feet two inches, she seemed somewhat nervous. Of course, having been overwhelmed by my four barking, cavorting collies probably didn't help.

Beth was next to her, holding Bea's hand in a tight grip. I barely looked at her, wanting to bring them into the house as quickly as possible.

I forced a pathway through the assembled and eager animals, all the while mumbling apologies. Bea took it all in stride, saying she was accustomed to long-haired dogs. I whisked them in through the kitchen and into the living room, showing them to the couch.

It was a bright afternoon in late spring and the sun was splashing rainbows through the crystals that hung in the windows. The walls were glittering with colors, some shaking, some still, others moving in a rhythmic pattern caused by the traffic that passed in front of the house and produced tremors in the glass panes.

I'd always loved the display of colors, but today I seemed to be more acutely aware of them and how confusing they made the world around me. Interesting. I'd never viewed them in this way. I shook the thoughts from my mind and asked Bea if they would like something to eat or drink. She said no and so I sat down with them on the long couch.

Now I was able to look at Beth for the first time.

Bea had warned me that her daughter had never uttered an intelligible word in her entire life, so I was unsurprised by the guttural grunts and squawks coming from her.

She was beautiful, in a porcelain way. Her skin seemed to be made of translucent china, almost as if it held an inner pastel light of its own. Her full, attractive lips, without artificial color, were of a cherry, cranberry hue. Her shining brown hair was cut in a bob. Her eyes, of the same color, were unusual. As I watched, they began to roll, independently of each other. The left eye seemed to have no relationship to the right, but both moved off into separate realms. Even during my worst times with a lack of eye muscle control, I could never have done that.

When she had walked through the house, I'd noticed her uneven gait, like the rolling movement of a person with cerebral palsy. She moved smoothly, yet with difficulty. It was as if she'd figured out alternate ways to use her leg muscles in order to propel herself through the world.

Beth was slim, like her mother, with long legs, a lanky torso, and slender fingers. Upon closer inspection, I saw that the knuckle on her left index finger was enlarged. Seeing my steady gaze, Bea explained that Beth spent a good amount of her time with the knuckle in her mouth. Although she used it like a pacifier to calm herself when anxious, there were some serious by-products of the action. The disfigurement had come as a result of her constant chewing and gnawing on the finger.

As I gazed around the room, trying to follow Beth's line of vision as best as I could, I suddenly became aware of the incredibly large number of items, forms, colors, smells, sounds, and stimulation present in just this one room. I watched as she reacted to the overwhelming sensory input which surrounded her, slowly becoming aware of how she was perceiving this environment. Clearly she was having to deal with too much. I saw her discomfort, which showed in her eyes and body positioning.

I sensed her need to be reassured and rose and began to

slowly explain some of what was in the room and why it had meaning for me. Her distress seemed to lessen perceptibly and I felt I'd made my first decision with some accuracy. It was Beth's response, and Bea's agreement with this assessment, that told me I was on the right track.

I also realized I'd made an innocent mistake even before I'd begun. I ought to have traveled to Beth's home, where she was comfortable and safe in her own environment. In my home, she had to deal with an overload of new stimuli. How could I ever get to know her when instead of having the leeway to relax and be herself, she was fighting to assimilate all the strangeness that surrounded her? I could see her trying to decide how best to survive in this strange situation.

I had to figure out a way of showing her how well I understood her problem and my willingness to help her surmount it. Perhaps if I was below her it might help in some way. I slowly and gently slid down and off the couch, curling my legs under me as I settled onto the carpet. Intuitively, I'd chosen a physical posture which conveyed an important message to her: You are above me. I'm below you. You are in charge. You have nothing to fear from me.

I'd recalled how the dolphins had been willing to interact with me as long as I knew, respected, and accepted who was supposed to be in charge. That meant them, not me. As we had first settled our ranking while I was on the platform, I now tried to make the same information available to Beth. I wanted her to understand and accept my willingness to allow her to take the lead, to be in control of how I would relate to her.

A subtle but unmistakable change came over her. Somehow she had immediately picked up my nonverbal message. She'd done it with the same effortless examination of her environment, and those in it, as had Scotty and Spray. Surely she was exhibiting an enhanced sensitivity to her surroundings and those who moved through them.

I listened to Bea as she told me how she'd discovered that Beth was autistic. It was not so different from the stories I was to hear from many parents over the next few years. The ending was always the same. What might they have done differently that would have saved their child from being unable or unwilling to communicate?

"Communicate." This was a word I was hearing more and more frequently, from myself in relationship to my work with dolphins, and now with autistic children. Could it be that instead of searching to find out how to increase the use of the brain, I was really on a quest to enlarge and expand a human's ability to communicate? If this was so, then I would have to look at my work from a totally different perspective.

Up until then, I'd merely been fulfilling a personal need to understand how my body and my brain worked. Now I realized that my interactions with the dolphins had taught me many new skills and techniques about communication, almost by-products of my original goals. I'd made many important discoveries about protocol, attitude, and behavior which could definitely help humans. What I'd already done had greater substance than anything I could have ever imagined or projected.

I pushed those thoughts aside, letting them wait for further and closer examination, and returned to the interaction at hand.

Still seated on the carpet, I found my attention being split. Part of me was still listening and making the proper responses to Bea, who was sitting on the far end of the sofa, while the other half had subtly shifted my attention to Beth. To my amazement, Beth seemed to have become instantly aware of this change. Her nervousness all but disappeared as she tentatively reached her hand out for mine. I leaned closer to her and with her strong hands, she drew my face toward hers.

Beth firmly placed her lips on mine. I kept my eyes open and watched as her eyes began a slow roll toward the back of her head. Bea immediately told Beth to stop what she was doing and move back.

The meld couldn't have lasted more than a moment, but in that instant of touch I became intuitively aware of Beth's emotional state. The transference of information was quick, simple, and totally reminiscent of my exchanges with the dolphins.

It was like the quantum leap in understanding I would have with Spray in August later that year. I had no way of knowing what I suddenly knew, unless the information had come from Beth. She'd used her lips to seek me out and explore who and what I was in relationship to her, then made her sensory experiences available to me as well. It was as if I was seeing myself though her own perceptions of me.

I turned to Bea, groping for the right words to share the experience with her. She listened carefully, but with a look of deep concern. She explained that Beth did this all the time, with everyone. It startled some people and put others off. It was unsocialized behavior and she was trying to teach Beth the correct way to act. She added that her daughter would soon be growing into puberty and she was afraid the girl's simple actions could be misunderstood, creating a sexual situation with the wrong people.

This was something I hadn't thought about. I had a young son and understood the need to protect children in an increasingly hostile world. She was right to be concerned, but I couldn't escape the need to further examine what I'd just experienced.

We compromised and agreed to give Beth the freedom to touch her mouth to mine as a means to communicate, but mine alone. If she were to attempt the same behavior with others, Bea would let her know that her action was inappropriate.

Even as the pact was made, Beth again moved forward to mash her lips against mine. I tried to empty all of my socialized thoughts from my head. This wasn't a girl or woman with a sexual agenda, who was pressing me so closely. Instead, this was another human who was attempting to tell me something in a primitive way, through touch. It was my job to learn how to decipher what she was saying.

As our lips met, I mentally reviewed what I was perceiving. Her eyes again rolled backward and held no hint, no clue as to what she was thinking. As her saliva ran out of her mouth and down the side of mine, I had a sense of nothingness. I'd never felt such an utter lack of intent from anyone else's mouth. It was a stunning development in its own right. Her touch held no emotion. It was flat, without caring or passionate content.

Her lips reminded me of a siphon which was picking up on the "me-ness" of me and transferring that data to Beth for examination and review. I tried to quantify, to classify what was happening. It was as if, in her inability to communicate in a "normal" way, without speech or writing, she'd developed a means by which to test those around her and gather information by which to judge them.

The thought struck me that the dolphins, with their sonar, did the exact same thing, but at a greater distance. Beth, being young and without tutors, had to get right on top of her subject and actually touch the person in order to acquire what she sought.

If this was true, then I was naked to her inquisition. It would almost be as if she had a pipeline to my brain. I could not store my private and truer evaluations of people and situations in some hidden place. I'd have to be honest with myself, ergo with Beth, about the choices, likes and dislikes, which constructed how I formed my opinions and how I emotionally responded to them once created.

I decided right then that I'd better behave with her exactly as I had with the dolphins. I would not try to cover any part of myself but would allow her free access to everything, good and bad. I would not place socialized categorization on anything that I thought or felt. It would all just be a part of me, take it or leave it. And none of it would reflect back upon how I expected Beth to behave in response to my being with her.

Here I was once again, back to basics. My attitude, or the decision to be positive in my thoughts, would control my behavior. My mind-set, or the decision to filter out all that was happening around me, would control my attitude. My mental self, that sense of control over my thoughts, would then create a means by which my brain would transmit information through my body.

As I sat next to her, Beth drew me even closer, but disconnected her lips from mine and turned her head toward the center of the room. Her left hand slowly dropped down to my leg, almost as a blind person seeks a page of

Braille to read. Her hand traced a path along the seam of my worn blue jeans and then came to rest on my thigh. Slowly she began to gently rub the fabric, down, then up. Down, then up. Down, then up.

Again I sensed that her fingers were explorers, seeking out sensory input to be gathered in her brain. I had no feeling that she understood the warmth and existence, the life's essence of the human body that lay below the surface of the fabric.

Each time she touched me I felt no difference in the pressure of her movements. It was the denim she was feeling, not the thigh. The fabric was soft and pliable, the product of many washings with bleach and softener. Yet it was also rough in places where I'd indelibly spotted the jeans as I was gardening and wiping my hands on whatever was available.

As she ran her hand up and down in the same place with the same pattern, it was as if she was discovering the same information fresh and anew with each touch. Where had the data gone? Why wasn't she storing it?

The questions stirred an old memory, and suddenly I understood and appreciated what she was doing. I was seven and my mother had come home with a new coat. It was a blond sheared beaver with a rich brown mink collar. She'd put it on and paraded around for all of us to admire. Then she'd sat down in a chair and allowed me to stroke the collar, which smelled like a lifeless animal but felt soft. I rubbed my hand on it for a moment and felt it tickle my palms. It had an interesting texture but not much else to attract me.

As I moved my child's hand further down to explore the broad expanse of the coat's back, I was amazed to see the trail of altered color left behind. I ran my hand up the pelt and watched the fur shift to a darker hue, then down and saw it lighten again. It wasn't just the color change I could perceive. With each swipe I felt the difference in the texture of the hairs of the fur as it was moved up, then down. I had discovered what grain meant, and it fascinated me.

I was intrigued by my discovery, caught up in the flood

of sensory exploration and input it provided. I couldn't stop stroking the coat and began to rub it up, down, up and down, over and over again. My brain told me that I was touching the fur, my eyes saw the changes, my fingers held the feeling for the tiny instants that they roamed the surface. Together, the entire action and perception of that action ought to have produced identifiable results. But it hadn't, and seemingly couldn't. I was unable to retain the data my hands were gathering. It all seemed to literally slip through my fingers and my mind at the same time.

I could have and would have gone on forever, except for one little problem: My mother was wearing the coat as I had been rubbing against it. We'd never had a cat because she despised having animals rub against her legs with their bodies. She felt the same about my unceasing stroking of the coat and commanded me to stop immediately.

The coat now hung in my closet. I would have to find it later, and reacquaint my fingers and eyes with the sensory experience.

Bea's command to Beth to stop rubbing my leg returned me to the present. I'd learned yet another behavior in a growing list common to autistics. They loved to perseverate, or totally focus their behavior on objects, and would spend hours stroking them if left alone without supervision. I was learning so much, so quickly.

I wondered if autism might not be a learning disability, like dyslexia, an inability to process information in the same way as other humans did. If this was true, then the success of one's approach to communicating with these children might well depend upon one's ability to recognize what was going on and how one interacted with the child.

I wondered if Beth's movement had revealed yet another facet of her autism to me. I suspected this was so and was amazed that somehow this young girl had been able to transmit so much of her world to me. Through a shared intuitive awareness I had been guided to an appreciation of what Beth felt was important, of how things were tactilely evaluated, of why she had to repeat her actions over and over again. I had begun to understand her universe through what was of value to her, even as Scotty and Spray had done with me.

In years to come, the one comment I would hear most often about autistic children was that they try to block out the world around them and they don't, or won't, communicate. From the first moment of really getting to know Beth, and from working with so many other autistics, I found this statement to be totally, absolutely incorrect. Instead, I saw that autistics, like dolphins, were constantly bombarded with sensory input, constantly attempting to communicate with others, and more attuned to their environment, and the people in it, than most other humans. Their approach to living, again like the dolphins, was more basic, more survival-oriented. The information they were constantly receiving was telling them how to act or react in situations, without any social restrictions accepted by them at the same time.

I wondered if rather than hope for them to interact with me on my terms, perhaps it would be more rewarding to seek out and identify the methods the children used for communication, then learn how to interact with them. Exactly as I was learning to do with the dolphins.

I recognized that I'd learned as much from Beth as I had from the dolphins. Although I hadn't performed standard psychological tests in order to come to this conclusion, through our interactions I'd sensed a sharp intellect below her nonverbal behavior. I'd quickly come to care for her and her mother and suggested we continue to interact with each other as often as feasible.

Bea agreed, with the proviso that it was also acceptable to her daughter. Happily, Beth, through her positive session with me, also seemed to want our relationship to continue and grow. We set another date for our next meeting and they left for home.

Once alone, I began to closely examine all I'd learned from Beth's visit, all I'd shared with her and her mother, and all the possibilities that were present. Only one course of action seemed possible. I wanted to, had to interact with autistic children as much as I wanted and had to work with dolphins. Doubtless, I had much to learn from both populations and I felt they really wanted to share with me as well.

My life's work was now beginning to take form, to develop function, purpose, and identifiable goals. I found myself in an odd situation of totally understanding something I didn't understand at all. It was nebulous, like the wispy moments of intuition at the ends of my consciousness, but I "knew" that if I pursued it all the way, I might be able to open new frontiers of understanding, of communication, and of interaction.

Three months had passed since that first session with Scotty and Spray in the icy waters of Cape Cod. I had started on this path because of my curiosity about a childhood disability and how it had shaped my life, my personality, my world. Nothing I'd experienced before had ever gripped me in the same way. I'd somehow stumbled onto some great and important secrets which had been waiting for the right moment to reveal themselves.

There was an entire world of awareness which humankind had somehow evolved past or perhaps chosen to overlook and devalue. This world is where the most basic forms of communication exist. In our sophistication we had overshot our goals and lost the ability to interpret the simpler forms of exchange. I would have to go back to the beginning of the roots of communication in order to improve the skills I possessed. I knew it would not be an easy choice to make, that it would force me to live my life on their totally different and demanding levels. I would have to be able to switch instantly and easily between the other humans with whom I interacted and dolphins and people with autism.

Fortunately for me, I wanted not only to learn more about all of them, but also to share what I'd learned. Not only had I found and identified my teachers—dolphins and autistic children—but in the process I'd also found the human population which could most benefit from what I was discovering. There was no mistaking what was unfolding. I was absolutely certain that given enough time, enough experience, I could show the world exactly what dolphins and autistic children had in common. Beyond their sensitivity, their heightened perceptions, their behavioral responses, beyond the many lines of similarity, the common ground began to reveal itself.

It was communication.

# Nine

*1* HAD BEGUN my quest in such an innocent fashion. Originally, I didn't even have to worry about failing. After all, if my theories were wrong, if nothing came from my efforts, or even if I decided not to move forward, who would be hurt other than me?

Now I found I was responsible not just to myself, but to marine mammals and to autistic children. I was uncovering new concepts and applications everywhere I looked. There were moments when I felt I was forgetting more than I was remembering, and I worried how that might affect my future work. Often, when the money was low or nonexistent, I thought of not going ahead, not continuing my explorations. I certainly seemed to have more going against me than for me. But I also had what I came to think of as a "fail-safe scenario." It was what forced me to slog on ahead and do "it" anyway.

I would envision myself twenty years later. In my fantasy, I'd be sitting in my home, by then quite wealthy, having sold my pie-baking business to a large gobbling corporation for an astronomical price. I'd fed the world great pies. Sure, other people could do it, but I'd done it better.

I would turn on the television and there would be a news feature about a person who had finally been able to figure out how to communicate with dolphins, and with autistic children. I would feel a surge of jealousy. Jealousy? What an absurd and horrifying feeling! I'd remember having felt the same way that time years ago with Scotty and Spray. Jealousy was a terrible, enervating emotion, one I'd never wanted to experience again in my life.

As I turned away from the news show, I would be thinking, I could have done that, but I gave it all up for money and a baking business that specialized in pies. Then I would know I'd be jealous of that other person for the rest of my life. I'd have to live with jealousy forever, an unwanted emotion I had newly rediscovered. All because I'd been too afraid of being poor, of being unqualified, of not being good enough.

Next I would imagine how I'd feel if I continued my work, regardless of success or failure. I knew I wouldn't be jealous of a person who had become rich at baking pies, only a tiny bit regretful.

It was the fear of having to live with jealousy, of knowing I could have made a difference for humankind many years earlier and had allowed myself to give up because things were tough for a while, that kept me going during those rough first years. It was also the worry that I would have lied to myself about the person I really was. Did I or did I not have the courage to pursue the research?

So I kept working with Beth and with Scotty and Spray. Eventually, however, I began to feel as if I was developing ideas, not realities. I was overwhelmed by concepts, frustrated by not knowing how and where to apply them. Every time I wondered whether or not there was more to learn, I'd uncover yet another amazing discovery about the children or the dolphins, but no way to use it to help others. I began to feel overwhelmed and disorganized. I seriously needed help to sort out the growing amount of work.

A friend pointed out where the problem really was. I had started out with a personal idea which had grown beyond my expectations. I was results-oriented; I needed to have something larger than myself in which to house all I'd discovered and done, and to share it with others. I needed an organization.

After thinking it over, I finally agreed that my friend was accurate in his appraisal, and so in 1984, MID★POINT: A Research Foundation For Creative Communications, Inc., was born. From the moment of its conception, I knew it had to be a nonprofit organization which would find a means to donate services to those who truly needed them.

The name wasn't difficult to choose. It came from the midpoint of interaction which had been established when I was on a platform creating a bond with dolphins, as well as the place of respect created between myself and an autistic child. It stood for the middle ground where both sides are safe and feel free to pursue further communications with one another. I liked the name. It felt good, sounded solid, and held the promise of being able to include any of the expanding facets of my research.

It was also easy for me to create the logo of a nongendered human reclining on the word MID★POINT, extending a hand to almost touch the flipper of a dolphin rising from below. The word was split to allow the top half to be uncolored, symbolizing the air, and the bottom section was blue, signifying water. In between is a space, to indicate neither water or air, but a place for humans and cetaceans to meet. At first I had been concerned that no one would know what MID★POINT was or what it did. Another friend had suggested I add a clarification to the title. He said I could put anything I wanted to in the main title, and so I did.

A woman who had read an article about my work donated the money necessary for us to become incorporated and then to seek a 501(c)(3), or nonprofit, status from the government. If there ever was an organization that earned the right to be called nonprofit, it was and still is MID★POINT.

The mission statement was simple. This was a foundation which would research and expand the frontiers of communication, then would apply its findings, as well as educate others about them.

Research, application, and education. This was a more perfect combination than a Reese's Peanut Butter Cup.

Now I was free to move in whatever direction was

necessary for me to pursue my research. I could work with any human population that needed my help. Now I could make the information available to any organization or individual that needed to learn about it.

There was only one problem. There was basically only one person doing the work—me. Other people were supportive, but physically uninvolved. Once again I'd moved ahead and opened a new direction, only to find there were unexpected problems. For every solution, there seemed to be three new problems to be solved.

By that time, I'd had several successful interactions with Scotty and Spray. I'd also had many more sessions with Beth and Bea, all in their home, and had found I loved being with them and learning from Beth. I had also been able to test my work with other dolphins than the two from the Cape.

A friend of mine had donated the funds for me to fly to Bermuda and work with the dolphins at the Blue Grotto Dolphin Show. I'd remembered about the show from a previous visit to the island some years before. I'd written to the head trainer and asked if I could do some research with his animals. He'd written back and agreed to allow me to work with them. The idea was to test what I'd learned from Scotty and Spray and see if it applied only to them, or if the protocols and information were more universal in nature.

Nolly Robinson was the head trainer at the show. He had been properly cautious about me and my credentials. He made certain not only to interview me once I'd come to the show, but to have the marine mammal veterinarian look me over as well.

Once they agreed I was all right, they gave me total freedom to interact with their three dolphins. Nolly's generosity over the next years made it possible for me to rapidly expand my knowledge and test my findings. He would hand me the keys to the dolphinarium and ask me to lock it up in the evening, and to be certain to be there in the morning so he could get in. What more could anyone ask?

The setting was so unlike that of the one in Cape Cod. The large pool was natural, having been carved out of a limestone system which honeycombs through a section of the island. Everything was open to the elements. Kiskadee birds flew to the treetops, singing the songs from which they took their names. Wild cats could be seen walking on the ledges covered with trees and undergrowth. The air was fresh, the breezes warm and cozy. Silence would sometimes settle all around, magnifying the gentle *plooosh* sound of the dolphins' exhalations as they swam in circles in the pool below.

There were two smaller enclosures in the back and a larger show pool in the front. A tiered section of boards provided seating for the thousands of guests who visited each year. A large tentlike tarp protected them from the occasional driving rainstorms that could fall from the sky without a moment's notice.

In the water were fish, crabs, starfish, and a million other life forms which came and went as the daily tides turned. To the left side were hundreds of young mangrove trees, roots snarled around one another in an endless tangle. Occasional mangrove pods, long and slim, would float at the water's surface to be used as playthings by the dolphins and myself. On the right was a tall, sheer cliff where a platform was extended so Nolly could hold fish between his teeth and hands, enticing the dolphins to leap high enough to snatch them away as a reward.

I climbed down the six steps to the deck. As I sat on the platform, Nolly introduced me to his charges. He explained that Spike was the dominant male, Rebel was aggressive, to say the least, and Patrick O'Grady was passive. They'd worked together for many years and Nolly had been the only real trainer they'd ever known. He had not often entered the water with them, and I found the animals' behavior to be very fundamental and not overly humanized. This was ideal for my purposes, as Scotty and Spray were quite sophisticated in the ways of handling humans.

As I watched the animals and how they related to each other, I had no doubt of Spike's leadership. When I sat on the deck, with my feet dangling in the water, he would come to me, mouth my hands and bootie-covered toes, and block the other two from having contact with me.

Spike, like Scotty and Spray, seemed to have a great interest in my feet and the calves of my legs.

I was fascinated to watch as he behaved in the same manner as Scotty had. The only difference was in how he moved my hands at the end of the sequence of motions I would make with them. I wondered if perhaps the lead, dominant dolphins used part of the movement in the same consistent manner and then made slight adjustments to indicate a difference in personality.

After seeing him slide backward and stop interacting, I hoped I was making the correct decision to enter the water. Putting on my gloves, mask, snorkel, and fins, I turned my body around and lowered myself into the pool. It was a much easier process here than at Sealand.

Once I was in, Spike rapidly approached me, shoving his dorsal fin into my hand. I curled my fingers around it and off we went for what now seemed to be the requisite dorsal tow. We circled the area twice and then he headed back to the platform.

Once there, he shrugged down and away and waited for me to exit the water. When I didn't, he repeated the actions again, ending in the same way. He was obviously confused. He'd given me what most humans want and yet I was still in the water. Slowly I paddled out to the center of the pool and just allowed myself to bob like a cork, making no moves toward him at all.

To occupy my thoughts, I looked around at the environment. It was beautiful, peaceful, almost dreamlike. I realized that I truly loved being where I was at that space and place in time.

Suddenly Spike appeared in front of me. He was different now, I could see by his movements. It was as if he realized what I'd been thinking, how I'd been feeling. His response was to treat me differently as well. Now he allowed me to swim next to him, almost as an equal. We made several circles of the pool, then returned to the center area, rather than the deck.

He began to exhibit his dominance by keeping the other dolphins away from me as much as possible, and seemed to prefer that I remain in one specific section of the natural pool. As I watched, I also compared what I'd seen in the

Cape Cod tank. I was witnessing a large number of behaviors which absolutely corresponded with those of Scotty and Spray. I was amazed to have spotted these behaviors so easily, but curious to see if there were also differences.

The absence of a resident female appeared to be one factor in some of the dissimilarities. Without sexual partners, the animals had considerable pent-up energy to deal with. I could see that not only was I an object of interest, but I had been identified by them as a female. They played differently with me than they would have with a human male. They were less physical, less macho in their interactions. With these dolphins, there was never any sexual play with me, at least not in the same way as I later came to see with Scotty and many other dolphins. But there was a real sense of who had priority over my time—and clearly that was Spike.

Once he'd decided to allow the other two to have some interactions, I was surprised to see that Rebel no longer wanted to have anything to do with me. He behaved petulantly, staying in his area. He would take water in his mouth, then flip it up into the air, not once or twice, but over and over and over again. It was the first time I was to witness perseverating behavior in a dolphin, which closely matched that of autistic children—and it wasn't the last.

After a while, I realized that not much was happening. There I was, floating in the center of the pool, surrounded by dolphins and none of them was coming near me. I looked to the rear of the area and for the first time noticed Patrick's dorsal fin. It was aimed in my direction, which meant the rest of his body was facing away from me. I was later to understand that this position gave him a speedy means to get away from me, if necessary.

I fixed my eyes on his fin and watched as it drifted imperceptibly toward me. Because of the distance, the only way I could measure the forward movement was by judging it against the links in the chain fence that separated the pools.

Patrick didn't just drift toward me. Just when it looked like he would move even closer, he would right himself, circle me at a good distance, make clicking noises, and then return to the safety of his corner. This was definitely one shy fella.

I remained unmoving for over an hour as he repeated his motions. Finally, as if he had made some great decision, he began to slide closer to me until he was within touching distance.

He stayed that way, with his back toward me, for a few minutes, then turned so our eyes could meet. Once we had made eye contact, he again rolled onto his side and glided a bit closer to me.

I tried to figure out what he wanted me to do, never thinking that doing nothing was the right something to be doing.

I decided he wanted me to reach out for him, so I gently slipped my right hand through the water in his direction. I barely brushed the tip of his fins when he turned on me and began to chatter wildly. *Yah-dah-dah-dah-yah-dah!* And away he swam.

I was cold and had obviously done something wrong, so now was a great time for a lunch break.

The tide had gone down and the stationary deck had not. There was a gap between the water and the platform that looked like the Grand Canyon. I looked for a way to exit the pool and realized I would have to select a likely-looking mangrove branch and haul myself up, out, and over the mud which held hundreds of skittering crabs.

I wondered what in God's name this woman from Brooklyn was doing in this situation. The thought became a private joke which has sustained me over the years. And I still don't have the proper response.

After lunch and a long, hot bath, I came back later in the afternoon and again went through the platform protocol with Spike. After I was in the water for a short time, Spike and Rebel again disappeared to the far left-hand end of the pool. I had a feeling that this was so I could continue my interactions with Patrick. I finned in a circle, keeping myself in the center of the pool, and saw Pat's dorsal fin rise to the surface, poised in the now familiar backward tilted position.

Hanging motionless in the water, I was grateful to my buoyant wetsuit for making it possible for me to keep afloat at the surface without even moving my hands. Without eighteen pounds of lead weight in a belt attached around my waist, I wouldn't be able to move below the surface even if my life depended upon it, so I didn't have to waste my precious energy in that direction.

Once more I waited patiently for Patrick to approach. The situation seemed to be so much a matter of my creating trust by my behavior and my ability to identify his needs.

Eventually, after what seemed a lifetime, Patrick was again in front of me. This time I kept my hands floating loosely at the surface on either side of me. Pat drew closer and closer until he again turned to look at me. I held my breath, hoping to control my shivers and any other movement on my part that might scare him off again. My body had long ago exhausted its stockpile of warmth and was now working on sheer willpower. Although 78 degrees is warmer than 52 degrees, it's still considerably lower than 98.6.

Pat floated to the surface in a horizontal position. He then maneuvered his entire flank along the palm of my hands and slowly worked himself in an up-and-down motion. He was using my hands to pet him, but was totally in control of the interaction. If this is what he wanted, and my stillness made it possible for me to be with him, then so be it. I accepted that I'd once more learned a valuable lesson from a dolphin.

It might not have held the cryptic data and high energy of what I'd learned from Scotty and Spray, but at least Pat had been willing to share with me how he needed me to behave with him, what he wanted, what his terms were for interaction. I was thankful I was able to learn this, and fascinated to discover that all dolphins were not alike. They were as different in personality and desires as humans were. I also saw that with the three animals from Bermuda, there would always be unexplored areas of mystery which would take months, even years, for me to unravel.

As I had more in-water sessions with dolphins, I realized I needed to know more about the ocean and my ability to survive in it. Although I'd been certified as an

Advanced Open Water diver in 1982, it was obvious that I had to learn additional information. I began to take specialty diving courses, culminating in my final goal of becoming a Divemaster. I had no desire to be an instructor, knowing I'd never been able to stay in one area for the seven consecutive weeks necessary to certify students.

During the three years it took for me to gain my credentials, I would not only take classes, but assist instructors with their students. It was a required part of the Divemaster training course. Although I had several instructors to choose from, and did work with many of them, I found I definitely preferred helping out my friend Jack Kinney. I saw that he was thorough, eager to work with students, didn't seem to need to show them how superior he was, and really enjoyed what he was doing and making available to his students.

I can't recall the exact class that I first met his wife, Hedy Kinney. I'd worked with many other Divemaster candidates, but she and I were the only two women who had chosen to achieve this rating. It was natural that we would draw closer to each other.

Although the classes always ended at eleven in the evening, as when I was first learning how to dive, large hordes of pizza-hungry divers would descend upon a local restaurant. Frequently, Jack, Hedy, and I were the only people there who had any diving experiences, so we would hold the others' attention by telling our best scuba stories. Eventually I would tell a short tale about my dolphin work, always secretly hoping to solicit funds for interest for my research.

One night Hedy turned to me and said that she had once spent time in the water with captive dolphins. I was interested and listened to her story of the encounter. She casually mentioned that she would be willing to go with me on my next trip, wherever that might be.

I'd had many offers of help in the past. People always want to help me with the dolphins, but not with much else. Hedy's proposal was different. She included an offer to take slides for photo identification of the interactions.

This was something I really needed to have. Since my first sessions, I'd had only fifteen slides taken of the encounters, by a friend who had offered to take land-based shots. I knew it was important to have good documentation, but couldn't take pictures at the same time I was having interactions. Besides, a camera always separates the photographer from the subject of the shot.

I had been making plans to return to Bermuda in February of 1985 for my third trip to the dolphinarium. I extended a casual invitation to Hedy to join me, not really expecting her to take me up on it.

She said yes and changed my life forever.

I was glad to have her. I felt I wanted to have someone else there in the pool if something dangerous happened. On a previous stay I'd recruited help from people who lived in Bermuda, including Judy, a Navy officer who was stationed on the island, and Jim, her ex-Marine husband who taught scuba for one of the local businesses. All of these people would be off the island when I returned for my next visit, so I really needed an assistant.

I hadn't taken a good look at Hedy until that time, only seeing her from an external point of view. I guess I'd always thought of her as Jack's wife. Even women can be guilty of male chauvinistic ideas.

It had taken me years to find another person who wanted to work with me, as hard as I did. Once again, thanks to diving, I'd finally found someone who was as eager and as curious as I was to follow the course wherever it might take us, regardless of the danger involved in our quest.

## Ten

*B*ERMUDA in February is not like Bermuda in April. While its winter bears no resemblance to New England's, it can still be cold at that time. I had chosen February as the date for my next research visit for many practical reasons. The best was that the dolphins would be on a five-week furlough of no shows and no training. This would give me a large amount of uninterrupted time with them. Hedy and I landed on the island expecting full sun and warm breezes, a mini-respite from the frozen New England we'd just left behind. Once we passed through customs with our load of suitcases and equipment, we headed out to flag a taxi. The opening door allowed the first blast of chilly air to hit our skin and created masses of enormous goose bumps all over our bodies.

It was *cold*. Not as cold as Connecticut at that time of the year, but it sure wasn't like southern Florida. I knew immediately that cold weather meant cold water again for our interactions. I decided I must have a secret death wish.

We checked into the hotel and unpacked our suitcases, and after eating lunch at the hotel, trudged up the hill to rent mopeds. These were absolutely necessary on the island. Tourists aren't allowed to rent cars, so it was travel by bus, taxi, or moped. We had packed our street clothing in a small bag, along with our masks, gloves, hoods, booties, flippers, snorkels, cameras, and purses. We wore our street shoes over the wetsuits, which were warmer to wear on our backs than to carry in our baskets. Over the gray and blue coverings, which made us look like refugees from a Cousteau film, we wore thin windbreakers. On our heads we wore hard helmets (now required), to prevent brain injuries from possible moped accidents. In our case, with the heavy equipment we were toting, this was a high probability.

We arrived at the Blue Grotto an hour and a half later

and returned to a place just a mile short of the airport, visible across the water. We rode down to the small shed that housed Nolly's belongings and parked the bikes in front of the cave where he had his office. I called down to him and he yelled back that he'd meet us down by the dolphins. Hedy and I unloaded the bikes and brought the gear to the dolphin area.

When he appeared, I introduced Nolly to Hedy as my assistant researcher and photographer. As I looked around, I saw there were some changes being made. The floating dock had been removed from the far side of the pool and was now perched high above the lower platform. It had undergone repairs and was almost ready to be placed back in the water. There was also a long extension ladder hanging over the area.

Looking down in the water, I easily spotted Rebel and Patrick. They both swam as if they had a lot of pent-up energy to get rid of. But I couldn't find Spike.

When I asked Nolly where Spike was, he sadly told me the dolphin had died the month before. Nolly had gone away to the States for his first vacation in years. When he'd returned, Spike had already passed away. The necropsy had revealed that some years before he'd swallowed a fish bone which had eventually lodged itself in such a position that over the years an abscess had been created. It was just coincidence that the wound had burst at the same time Nolly was gone.

This was bad news, but I had no idea how bad it would turn out to be for Hedy and me.

We climbed down the steps to the platform and Nolly handed us our equipment. The peace of previous visits was long gone, supplanted by the sound of saws, drills, workmen calling to each other, and the telephone's insistent ringing. So much for paradise.

As we finished our preparations, the sky clouded over, turning day into dusk. At first a cold but gentle rain fell, but the winds picked up, and even in our soaking wet suits we could feel it begin to cut to the bone.

Shrugging aside my feelings of coldness, I explained to Hedy what I was going to do, then lay prone on the deck, not knowing what to expect now that Spike was gone.

I was surprised to see both Rebel and Patrick O'Grady now appear in front of me. Pat seemed less shy, Rebel more in command of himself. They both came to me and each took one hand in their mouths. Gentle crunchings commenced, then they backed off.

I wanted to introduce them to Hedy, to let them know we were a team, even as the dolphins were. I turned around and sat up, placing my bootied feet in the water to dangle.

Now only Rebel came to me. He nudged my feet and then began to play with them. Eventually he would come from below and lift them up and out of the water. This was a new behavior, and I had no idea what it meant.

Hedy suggested that he might not want me to have my feet in the water, so I pulled them out. As soon as I put them in again, he repeated the same behavior as before.

I wondered if he didn't want my feet in the water, or if he didn't want them in where they were. Telling Hedy in advance what I intended to do and why, I slid down the edge of the platform, to my left, by about two feet. We watched as Rebel approached, then swam to the spot where I had previously been sitting. He didn't seem to have a problem with where my feet were now, but his repeated presence where I'd been before seemed to indicate a definite territoriality which I was bound to respect.

Well, things had certainly changed since my last visit, and he wanted me to know that Spike was no longer the head dolphin in charge. Even though this was Hedy's first encounter with him, she too could see his intent.

We'd come this far, braved bad weather and menacing mopeds, so we finally decided there was no better time than that moment to get in the water. I slid in as usual and waited for my body to acclimate to the cold, cold water. As I did, I caught glimpses of circling dorsal fins in the water around me. For one short moment my imagination got the best of me and I had a visceral, knee-jerk reaction to what I was seeing. It looked like two sharks circling for a closer investigation.

This accelerated my heartbeat as well as my adrenaline, which in turn brought the dolphins even closer.

I dropped my head below the surface so I could see their

full bodies and calm and control my fear. Then I again turned my attention to admiring the view and the environment. Hedy called out that Rebel was directly behind me, so I slowly finned around to face him.

Moving forward toward me, he glided into position as I reached out my hand for a dorsal ride. He moved slowly at first, then picked up speed. I was trying to move my legs with enough momentum to relieve some of my weight from his body.

He took me twice around the pool, then dropped me at the deck. With a slight shove to my upper right arm, he indicated exactly where the edge of the platform was. The tide was high and so I easily lifted myself out of the water for a second, then relowered myself.

He came to me again, but this time he pushed me toward the deck again. No more dorsal rides, he seemed to be saying.

That was fine with me. I looked him in the eye, turned on my back so I could continue to keep him in sight, and back-paddled to the center of the pool. All this time, Pat was happily and safely situated in the rear right portion of the area, which was obviously his territory.

Rebel again came to me, placed his fin in my hand, and towed me back to the deck. It was curious that each time he had done this he'd positioned me where previously he hadn't wanted my feet to be.

The days are as short in Bermuda in February as they are in Connecticut. I noticed the brightness beginning to fade from the sky and decided it was time to get Hedy in with the dolphins.

Part of me was insecure as to whether or not my desire to have her join me was premature, another part worried that she would feel I was hogging time with them. I needn't have had either concern.

I instructed her to gear up, bobbing in the water near the deck as I waited. She sat on the platform with her feet in the water, but neither dolphin came near us. I asked her to join me in the water, then moved back a bit to allow her entry.

She made little squeaking noises as the water seeped

1. Spray, an Atlantic Bottlenose dolphin at Sealand on Cape Cod, introduced me to the world of dolphin communication.

2. My meetings with captive dolphins always begin at a platform, where I introduce myself to them and determine if further interaction will occur.

WILLIAM KURZ/MID★POINT

3. Scotty's grip reminds me who is really in charge.

4. Shy, passive Patrick at the Blue Grotto Dolphin Show in Bermuda. Contact with him was always special because he did not befriend people easily.

TWO PHOTOS: HEDY KINNEY/MID★POINT

5. I film Patrick with an underwater video camera. It took one hour of my floating motionless for him to feel safe enough to come this close to me. He died the next year.

6. The dolphins at Hershey Park, Pennsylvania, dramatically increased my knowledge of dolphin communication. It was a very active pod made up of a teaching dominant, an aggressive, and a passive dolphin working together. Here I make eye contact with Buddy, the teaching dominant dolphin.

7–10. The dolphins use me to help them learn about Frederica Cadmus, a member of the Mid★Point team. Buddy, Cooter, and Tessie have placed my hands so that I hold Freddie's legs still while they use their sonar to explore her leg muscles. Then they move my hands to a new location, articulate, or bend, the leg, and repeat the behavior.

HEDY KINNEY/MID★POINT

11. Buddy and Tessie pose for Hedy Kinney.

12. In the water at Hershey Park, making friends with Buddy and Cooter.

LARRY ARNOLD/MID★POINT

Christopher, an autistic child, went from total lack of involvement to deep interaction in fifteen minutes when I communicated with him using the skills and techniques I learned from dolphins.

13. Christopher is looking away from me, and I am not forcing eye contact.

14. Christopher chooses to make eye contact.

15. Christopher allows me to touch him while he holds a glass of lemonade in his hand.

16. I have nonverbally asked Christopher for a drink of lemonade, and he reaches out and hands me the glass.

17. Christopher decides to take my hand and hold it.

18. I tell Christopher a joke. He looks at me for a moment, a smile moves across his face, and he begins to laugh—music to his parents' ears.

19. Buddy, the leader of the dolphin pod. He taught me how to behave correctly with the other dolphins in relation to their status in the group.

THREE PHOTOS: HEDY KINNEY/MID★POINT

20. My real goal was to help people. I found a link between the behavior of dolphins and the behavior of people with autism when I set out to communicate with autistic children as I had with dolphins. What we all had in common was the desire to learn from one another, which created a middle ground of understanding. Here I am with Beth, an autistic child, at the YMCA. Even though Beth did not like swimming, she was willing to go into the water with me because she trusted me as her friend.

21. Beth and I learn to trust each other.

through her suit and around her body. Playfully, I welcomed her to the exciting world of dolphin research and she let me know, in dry, witty, sarcastic, and concise terms, exactly how she felt about that. This was starting to work out as a good team.

A few more minutes passed, and then slowly Rebel came to her. After a moment of sonaring, he allowed her to reach forward and take a dorsal ride. The only difference between our rides was that he dropped her at the center of the pool, not at the deck. I wondered if there was any significance to this. I'd always been the object of the dolphins' attention, never having a chance to observe encounters, interactions, and behaviors between them and other humans. Watching Hedy with Rebel was as interesting and educational for me as being the target myself. I decided to take a backseat and observe how the dolphins related to her.

At first there was some flurry of attention by both the dolphins; then, curiously enough, Rebel swam away to the left rear of the pool. He settled into what was clearly his area and began to flip water into the air with his mouth. There was that autistic behavior again.

Now I watched as Patrick began imperceptibly to back toward Hedy, as he had once done with me. I yelled across the water to her, advising her to remain where she was, and not to move. From then on I gave her a running commentary on his actions and movements.

After several minutes had passed, she wanted to know whether or not she could move. Hypothermia was beginning to set in because of her lack of activity, and she was beginning to turn as blue as her wet suit.

As if he understood the need to intensify the action, Pat glided closer to her, stopped, sonared, then turned to face her. It was almost nose-to-rostrum and the world seemed to quiet down into a vacuum. No birds, no workmen, no sounds at all, not even water being flipped from Rebel's mouth—he'd stopped this behavior as soon as Pat had faced Hedy. It was as if he was also curious to see what would transpire.

If ignorance is no excuse for breaking the law, I can

truly testify that innocence is no excuse either. We both found out the hard way.

I'd always been responsible for myself in interactions with dolphins and with autistic children. That all changed when Hedy, in a cold and shivery voice called out to me, "What do I do now? What do you think he wants me to do?"

I thought for a moment, remembering the time before when he'd presented his body for stroking, totally forgetting his initial and more violent basic reaction. Perhaps, I thought, he wants her to touch him.

I told her to gently reach out, present her hand, and then if he didn't move away, touch him. So she did.

Patrick recoiled like a gun had gone off. He looked at her and began to chatter madly. His *yah-dah-dah* of our past encounter was nothing compared to what he was saying to Hedy now. A good start at translation might have gone along the lines of, "Hey, you stupid lady!" and gone downhill from there.

When he was done yelling at her, he began to swim around her, quickly at first, then with increasing speed. I could sense that she was in danger. His erratic movements made me frightened for her. She was in the center of the pool, and I was a million miles away in the water at deckside. I couldn't tell whether or not I ought to move toward her or if that would further aggravate the situation.

I knew I couldn't leave her there, so I began to paddle gently toward her. Instantaneously Rebel moved from his spot and approached me. He snapped, jaw-popped (a warning sound made by angry dolphins), and blew water toward me, pointing all the time in the direction of the platform. Well, there was no way I couldn't understand his directions, so I retreated.

Yelling across to her, I let Hedy know what had happened, hoping she'd regain some confidence in me because I'd made an effort to help. There was no reply. She was in the middle of an even more dangerous situation now.

After Patrick had chattered and then swirled about her, he'd disappeared. Hedy was later to say the silence was worse than the movement and noise. At least then she'd known where the dolphin was. Now all was quiet and calm and she had absolutely no idea of what to expect, nor did I.

Suddenly the water exploded. Patrick O'Grady was vertical and directly in front of Hedy's face. He paused for a second, then reared back and forcefully bonked Hedy's face mask.

She closed her eyes at that point, and I guess it was a good thing she did. Patrick sank down, gathered speed, and leapt straight up out of the water and over her.

All I could think was that if he were to flatten his body out at the apex of the leap and come down in a belly flop, I would be minus a partner very quickly. I also wondered how I would explain the loss of his wife to Jack Kinney. After all, weren't dolphins the friendliest things on earth? Didn't they just love humans?

But Patrick did not flatten out. He completed his jump in a perfect arc, cut the water with hardly a splash, then swam away to the safety of his right-hand pool area.

Now Hedy was able to speak in a strong voice. She'd never been the type to curse, but her words were full-bodied in intent. "Get me out of here. NOW!"

During this time I'd come to recognize that Rebel's movements towards me had constituted a designation of where my area was, as his was to the rear left and Pat's to the rear right. Calling back, I said she ought not to swim through my area as long as I was still in the water. She strongly suggested that I exit the water as rapidly as possible. I turned to do this and realized I now had a large problem. During the time we'd been freezing ourselves in the name of research, the tides of nature had turned. The water had lowered and the deck was way beyond my reach.

I yelled this out to her, and, still in control of her fears, she suggested I find an alternative route out. *"Now!* Do you hear me? *Now!"*

Caught between concern for her and dislike for mangrove roots and crabs, I swam to the side of the deck, located a likely root, grabbed hold, and hauled myself out of the water. Hedy then swam, without interruption from either dolphin, to the same root and I helped her lift out of the water.

It had certainly been a learning experience for both of us.

We gathered our things, afraid to discuss the events in case Nolly was nearby to overhear our comments. He might have denied us access if he thought there had been a problem, and this we did not want to happen. Shaking from the edges of hypothermia, as well as the downside of fear, we squished our way up the hill to the bathroom so we could change into our warm street clothes. We packed our gear, shoving the wetsuits into garbage bags, waved to Nolly, and let him know we'd see him the next day. Then we drove off on our bikes into the fading daylight, for our hour-and-a-half ride back to the hotel.

We were both too tired and chilled to care about our recalcitrant mopeds, and neither of us gave a thought to the problems we'd had with our shifting gear on the trip to the dolphinarium earlier that day. All we wanted was warmth, dinner, and peace.

Once back in the room, we washed our gear and then ourselves. Each of us took turns having a long soak in a hot tub. Water could be our friend as well as our enemy.

We dressed and went to the hotel restaurant for dinner, quietly amused that we now looked like any other tourists in the room. Somehow we never got around to discussing what had happened. Perhaps we were too tired, or too close to the events to think about them, but we ate dinner, spoke about shopping, about children, about diving, but not one word about dolphins.

The next morning, after breakfast, we took a little time off for ourselves and explored the natural beauties of the island. Then we returned to the hotel to gather our things for the return trip to the dolphinarium. During the entire time, we still did not discuss what had happened the day before.

By some silent agreement, we decided it was time to return to the Blue Grotto Dolphin Show. Once again we rode across the island looking like two creatures from the Black Lagoon. By now Nolly was accustomed to our strange appearance and never even cracked a smile.

We took our time unloading the gear, checking it all out more thoroughly than was necessary. When there was absolutely nothing left to do, we finished dressing and moved everything to the platform.

Hedy and I sat on the edge of the deck with our feet extended into the water. Once again we tested the placement of our feet and Rebel's response. Again he seemed not to mind when they dangled to the left of the right edge of the platform. He was specific in his response when we did have them in the wrong area. I could see that more than with Scotty and Spray, these animals were quite precise about their territories.

From now on I would respect not only the individual personalities of the animals, but the possibility of assigned territories when I was in the water with captive dolphins. Over the years that followed, I was to see similar behaviors in slightly different forms, which enabled me to respect unseen boundaries and eliminated a lot of possible problems.

The encounters with Rebel and Patrick that day, as well as on the days that followed, were thankfully less dramatic and considerably more peaceful. Hedy was able to take photographs both on the deck and in the water. All went well from then on, as long as we respected the dolphins' well-defined areas, understood their differing personalities, abided by who was in charge, and no longer made such gigantic errors in etiquette.

From that trip I gained a realization of how little I knew about working with others in a group situation. I had a great amount to learn about what it took to be responsible for the safety of both humans and dolphins, as well as for myself.

I was fortunate to have found such a gap at a time when it was only crucial to two people. In later years, when I would be in charge of twenty-seven people, all swimming with wild Spotted dolphins in the Bahamas, through seven-foot waves, I would take a moment to silently thank Rebel, Patrick O'Grady, and Hedy Kinney for what they'd taught me.

Best of all, I gained a special friend, one whose courage, stamina, dedication, and support were indisputable. I was in awe of the fact that even though Hedy had faced real danger and had performed well, she had apparently never thought of not returning to the pool the next day. Many people think Hedy is soft, genteel, weak, shy. She can be tough but they are never aware of this.

Eventually, years later, I asked her why she hadn't backed out as any sane and normal person would have done. She answered without hesitation. "How could I have not returned? I was curious to find out what had happened, why it had happened, and what would happen next. I had to return." This was something that I could understand.

Danger be damned. It was a partnership formed in heaven, confirmed in danger, and promising for the future. And I had come back home from one of my trips with great slides to tell the story.

# Eleven

*E*XSPURT: *ex,* meaning out of. *Spurt:* meaning a drip under pressure. *Exspurt:* information out of a drip under pressure. Perhaps "exspurt" would be a more accurate way of spelling "expert."

As time passed and my research progressed, I found little understanding among experts regarding the nature of what I was doing. I also discovered that few would bother to take the time to discuss what I was discovering and developing.

At first the experts seemed to need to classify me, as if, by judging me, they could make pronouncements and placements regarding my research.

"Patricia St.John was a therapist." Wrong. My work was light-years away from therapy. Therapy was a designed form of manipulation for the improvement of an individual. To the contrary, I was allowing the dolphins and the kids to manipulate me so I could better understand how they perceived the world around them and how they chose to communicate.

"Patricia St.John was a quack, New-Ager, one of the weirdos who wanted to do telepathy with dolphins." Wrong. I'd spent years studying what had been written about the animals and as much time having in-water interactions with them. My research was developing along lines of behavior, interactive experiences, and sensory perception. I'd done my work from the center of the pool, not comfortably from the sidelines.

"Patricia St.John was one of 'them.' " "Them" meant someone not belonging to a closed clique of insiders who had degrees, titles, and high places in a pecking order. I hadn't progressed through proper channels, which showed my lack of respect for my betters. This was only partially true.

I'd become a GDI, or Gosh Darned Independent, but I

respected the input, knowledge, and experience others might be able to offer me. I was never affiliated with a university, a dolphinarium, or any other organization which would provide me with a seemingly respectable and stable base of operations. MID★POINT would grow on its own to be the sole provider of support for my efforts. As the years passed I joined professional organizations involved with marine mammals and wrote and delivered papers. Several papers were published in journals, sponsored by many organizations ranging from autism to dolphins and whales, as well as in paranormal research. What I wrote about charted my discoveries, my physical interactions with dolphins as well as autistics, the most interesting events that seemed to hold promise for future examination, as well as some theories I had begun to develop as to what was happening and why. The information began to be used in colleges and university classes and was included in some major libraries.

In spite of all that, many hard-liners in each field—meaning those who were dead set against learning more about my efforts—still chose to keep the doors closed.

Fortunately, there were also professionals whose interest was piqued by what I was doing. These were the people who allowed me access to their dolphins, or invited me to do Grand Rounds at their psychiatric hospitals, or the folks at institutions who wanted to hear what I'd done and helped me further my work with their clients.

Most of all, there were the parents who welcomed me to work with and learn from their children, eventually enabling me to move ahead and be able to help others freely.

Bea and I came a long way together over the next two years. We learned much from each other, always keeping our attention on Beth's needs.

I discovered how large a part guilt played in the life of parents of autistic children. Right from the start the blame was placed on them, especially the mothers, for not having bonded with their child at an early age. How could parents refute the ideas of the very man who, in the mid-1940s, had identified the disability, Dr. Bruno Bettelheim?

In an October 8, 1990, letter to the editors of *Newsweek* magazine, Dr. Bernard Rimland, director of the Autism Research Institute in San Diego, California, wrote, "Bruno Bettelheim was cruel—viciously cruel—not only to the children under his care, . . . but also to parents. His writings, considered gospel by many at the time, likened the mothers of autistic children to guards in Nazi concentration camps and blamed them for causing autism in their children. Bettelheim aggravated the guilt he instilled in these parents by criticizing them and limiting their contact with the children in his school. It is now well known that autism is a biological disorder, totally unrelated to supposed maternal rejection of the child."

Other parents, fed up with being assigned the role of bad people, had educated me in ways not found in books. Each time pronouncements from "experts" were made as to the "real" causes of autism, they would show me where the hidden prejudices lay.

My first real understanding of the impact of assigned blame came when I was approached by a woman who had provided direct service care for teenaged male autistic twins. She desperately wanted me to speak with the boys' father and offer my help to him.

Money wouldn't have been a problem. Even at the start I'd decided that regardless of the financial situation of parents of autistic children, MID★POINT would not charge them for our services. We would, and still do, accept consultation fees from institutions, schools, hospitals, and any facility or organization which uses MID★POINT as a resource.

Offering help freely to parents was good for two reasons. The first was that we wanted to be altruistic and give back freely some of what we'd learned freely. We also hoped to mirror a dolphin pod's intrinsic behavior in some fashion.

The second was more practical. If we accepted money for our services, then there would be a silent contract which would say we were also responsible for getting results from what we taught. Not taking recompense placed the accountability back on the parent. Besides, we might see their son or daughter once or twice, but they lived with the child and spent the most time with them.

Not knowing this, the direct service worker begged me to call the twins' father and told me not to worry about naming a price. He was well-off and would want to do anything to help his sons.

I resisted making the call. I'd always felt that the delicate nature of our work demanded that we not try to market a concept. Parents had to be willing to make the effort, not be sold, convinced, or coerced into doing it. So naturally, I'd also made the decision not to pursue people, whether they were connected with dolphins or with autistic children. We didn't want to have to convince them of our abilities; we wanted them to invite us to work. This way we all understood and accepted the research aspect of what we were doing.

Breaking my own rule, I gave in and told the woman I'd call the man. But I also reminded her that even though the man might be able to well afford our services, there would still be no charge for them.

That night I telephoned him. He answered with a deep, warm, and cultured voice. The woman had told him to expect me and it wasn't difficult to begin our conversation.

He listened politely and then responded.

"Look," he said, "you sound like a nice woman who seems to know what she's doing. You also sound sincere, so I'll be honest with you. I took my sons to Yale New Haven Hospital for observation. After lots of time and even more money, the doctor called me in to his office. He made no bones about it. He said it was all my fault that the boys were autistic and it was because I was a shit."

I couldn't believe what I was hearing, and even before I could come back with a shocked comment, the man continued.

"I've worked hard to help my boys out. I realize they aren't living in the best place in the world for them, but it's the best there is at this time. I think you really care, but I don't want to go through this again. I'm not willing to have anyone else call me a shit."

Well, I certainly couldn't argue with that, although I made a feeble attempt to explain that what I did was an assessment of the ways autistic children communicate on an individual level. Again he reassured me that his remarks weren't directed toward me in any way, and then he hung up.

Moments like this made me doubly appreciate my sessions with Bea and Beth.

After their first session at my home, I'd gone to their house to see them. Small and neat, it was also airy and comfortable. On its best days, my home had never looked as neat and clean. Of course, living in a constantly increasing amount of fur, as I do, does take the edge off neatness.

On my first visit to them I was amazed to find that Beth remembered me. Although I kept my distance from her once I'd come through her doorway, allowing her the opportunity to escape from me if she wanted, she walked right up to me. With her eyes wide open, she placed her unemotional lips directly on mine, then pulled away.

I'd already decided that if she did just that, I would steel myself and pull all emotion from my mind, all feeling from my body. Again she touched me with her lips, and as they stayed together, I could feel her body becoming less rigid, less stressed. She pulled away, took a firm hold of my chin in her hands, and again pulled my face close to hers for lip contact.

Once she was totally satisfied, she moved away to a small couch and sat down on it. I followed and sat next to her. Beth allowed me to put my left arm around her, crossing over her neck, with my hand resting on her left arm. Suddenly I felt her left hand spasm uncontrollably.

It happened again, then twice more. Each time the arm moved I could see a look of fear enter her eyes, as if she was nervous about not being able to control her body movements. Thinking there must be something I could do to help her, I reached around with my right hand and whispered into her ear, "I am in control. Tell your hand, 'I am in control.' "

I didn't have to explain that I was telling her to say to her hand that she was in control, not that I was. Somehow she'd understood the implied meaning and began working with it.

Her left hand slowed and then stopped. It lay unmoving and quiet for a minute, then began to jerk once more. Again I whispered, "I am in control," and again the tremor lessened and faded away.

It was a spur-of-the-moment decision on my part to try to show her how to control her body by controlling her mind. It was easy for me—after all, I'd been doing it with my eye muscles since I was eight years old. I was just passing along knowledge to my friend, which she quickly grasped and used.

During the rest of the visit, each time the involuntary movement would begin, Beth would get a look of deep concentration, then stop the muscle from jumping.

Although my visits were infrequent, they were always rewarding. I discovered so much about the nature of autism and what both the child and the parent had to deal with.

Every new concept goes through its own Dark Ages. This was also true of autism. In the beginning, in the late 1940s and through the 1950s, autism was really considered to be caused by parental coldness; the child was responding to insufficient caring and emotional response by limiting his or her own in return. My interactions with Beth had shown me that instead of blocking out her environment and being unaware of what was happening in her surroundings, she was hypersensitive. She would react, either subtly or in a grand manner, to so much going on around her.

Having had to learn to control and filter an overload of sensory information myself when I was a child, I could easily observe many of her attempts to control the degree and nature of the input constantly flooding her senses. They made perfect sense to me.

Scientifically speaking, my observations were flawed because I was interacting with my subject. But I was dealing with a human being as a person, not as an object of scientific inquiry, so I operated on a one-to-one level.

I watched as this supposedly tuned-out young girl reacted in subtle, almost indiscernible ways to stimuli. It wasn't only things around her that she would respond to, but conversations as well.

One memorable time Beth and I were cuddled together on the couch. Bea was sitting across from us and I began to talk with her about the need for Beth to begin to take some responsibility for her own actions. I said Beth was bright, quick, and could learn when and if she chose to. Adding the clincher, I said it was even more important because someday Bea would not be alive to provide care for Beth.

Immediately the girl began to move, as if uncomfortable. She placed her hands over her ears and I watched as a faraway look started to come over her eyes.

Bea quickly sat up and in a loud tone of voice yelled, "Beth, come back. Don't go away. Come back."

I watched in amazement as changing expressions passed over the girl's face, as if she was making decisions about whether or not she would mentally leave, and if so, then how far she would go, or if she was going to stay.

Beth chose to stay. Never having seen such a thing, I decided not to allow myself to react, either emotionally or externally, in any way. I hoped my nonresponse, having changed Scotty's behavior so long ago, would also work positively for me with Beth. And it did.

It was fascinating to see how she had manipulated the course of our conversation with her behavior. But, as always, I gave in to my stubborn streak and picked up our discussion where it had been interrupted.

This time Beth didn't go away. Now she lay calmly in my arms, occasionally sending sidelong glances to Bea, then back to me. It was a small victory for all of us. She'd chosen to stay and listen, even though the topic was not pleasing to her.

Bea worked hard to help her daughter. She knew Beth possessed more ability than her teachers said was present. They had repeatedly kept Beth in a first-grade environment, saying the best that could be expected of her was that she would be able to make her bed. Bea fought a constant battle with the school authorities, desperately trying to get them to do more for her child. It was usually a lost cause.

Conflicting professional opinions had indicated that Beth might either be mentally retarded, normal, or highly intelligent. The most common comment was that she was normal, although autistic.

Bea had also been working with a doctor who was based in southern Connecticut. The woman had commented that there was nothing mentally wrong with Beth, and the remark stuck in Bea's mind. One day, her temper shortened, and worn down by trying to make life better for the girl, Bea turned to her daughter and yelled, "They tell me there's nothing wrong with you. Write! Show me you know your name!"

Bea picked up a piece of paper and pushed it on the table in front of Beth. Then she picked up a pen, placed it in the girl's hand, put her own underneath to provide support and to steady Beth's, and waited.

Slowly, painfully, instead of the endless circles and scribbles which she'd always drawn, the letters B E T H appeared. Her mother was stunned. Beth could write! She could write her own name.

From that point on, Beth would begin to communicate, not through speaking, but through writing. Her wording, spelling, and punctuation indicated she was far beyond being a first-grade student.

Eventually Bea asked her daughter how she was able to write. In a halting, palsied print, Beth wrote that she'd been sneaking out of her room at night and taking books down from the bookshelf. She would memorize their position, then return them to it exactly. This way her excursions would remain her secret.

She went on to explain to her mother, in writing, that her favorite author was Dostoyevsky, whom she preferred because "I am very interested in dostoyevsky [sic] and don't want to degrade him by not reading him despite it being sad and I would like to read him. I don't easily

despair about depressing things so I want to read Dostoyevsky . . . a dove flew over a wood and cooed to other
doves decorating devoted nests. we love our children so
we want all good things adoring delights and the dove
missed whenever he overshot the evening star . . . dostoyevsky [sic] does words write which speak to me. I
read him at school despite whoever said I didn't. Some
people don't deduct I can read and I despise their doubt-
ing me."

Although she had actually never read Dostoyevsky in
school, there was no mistaking her frustration with her
teachers and their lack of faith in her abilities. She wrote
often of her anger towards them.

Beth later wrote a poem about the author, titled *"Dostoyevsky, a poem."*

> *I am deciding to only sow seeds of soulful sorrow*
> *and will harvest them all tomorrow*
> *I despair despite what devouring oafs say*
> *of the every day world we inhabit today*
> *I don't pretend we can cancel out crime*
> *I won't pretend I am sane all the time*
> *We go on our way one day at a time*
> *We won't care over sin to sigh*
> *Or sorrowful slow justice to cry*
> *I describe our plight as our world might*
> *As woe and sorrow would some fight*
> *but I believe God soon will give*
> *us each another chance to live.*

How it was that she'd begun to write, and why at that
exact moment, we were never able to figure out. But Beth
had chosen on her own to make her inner self known to
the world. No one deserved more credit for this than her
mother, who had worked so hard to enable her daughter
to communicate.

As months passed, her writing ability improved dramatically, her subject matter even more so. Her poetry
and prose were musical and remarkable, but she was no
idiot savant. She also made her everyday frustrations, an-
gers, desires, and demands known, but only through

writing and with the support of her mother's hand, placed below her own. Beth still refused to speak.

The more my research progressed, the more I began to recognize why others had failed in their quest to understand dolphins and autistic children and how they were communicating. I saw that well-meaning adults had placed their own value systems upon the children and the dolphins. There was only one "proper" path to correct communication and that was through the accepted use of language, either oral or written. This left little or no room for reciprocation, for expressing themselves in their own way, in their own "language." Any communication would have to be standardized to fit mainstream needs, not theirs. If they didn't, wouldn't, couldn't do it "our way" or the "right way" then there was obviously no real, important, intelligent communication occurring from their end.

In order to make true exchange possible between dolphins and autistics and "normal" humans, it would be necessary to alter our approach.

In my initial findings, I thought the reasons seemed simple enough. As the number of my encounters with both populations increased and grew in complexity, I saw that I could never make my findings, and how they were gathered, fit into normal scientific research paradigms. Although I'd hoped to be able to develop data that was absolutely reproducible, instead I was constantly bumping into inconstants. The sprightliness of the inner spirit, the individual's demand for diversity, nonidentical personalities, and differing degrees of intelligence immediately negated my hopes. Still, if these inconstants, occurrences which indicated progress or change but weren't always repeatable, were present in each case, and if there might be enough other events that were constants, then perhaps I might be able to allow my research to follow its own pathways.

I began to gather anecdotes and store them in my memory and my notes. I became my own best resource. As I came to rely more heavily upon my own body of work, I found myself to be the only person, at least to my knowledge, who was exploring and examining communication through interactions with dolphins and with autistic children.

As an "authority" of one, I realized I was on the way to becoming an ex-spurt.

## Twelve

_I_'D MET the director of the Developmental Center for Autistic Children, a day school on the outskirts of Philadelphia, in 1985, at a luncheon given in my honor. When he invited me to visit his school I eagerly accepted. He asked me to observe and interact with the school's young students and to address the staff and help them in any way I could. As it turned out, my time there would provide my most crucial experiences yet for the formulation and understanding of my research.

On my first visit I was introduced to a boy about nine years old. I was told that John was the school's most difficult client, one who made the staff ache inside. He'd originally been identified as autistic-like rather than fully autistic. Now, seemingly in response to some family crises over the years, he was exhibiting full-blown dysfunctional behavior.

Thanks to the movie _Rainman,_ public awareness of the existence of autistic populations has increased. Very few people actually understand what that term means. They think that to be disabled in this manner is also to be like Dustin Hoffman's character, Raymond, who was an "idiot savant." Many, but not all, autistic children or adults behave in this fashion. A movie showing head banging, feces smearing, body rending, and other totally unsocialized behavior wouldn't sell many tickets at the box office.

It's hard to do fund-raising for autism. Photos show normal-looking children, many of them beautiful in a fey, fairylike way. Unlike kids in wheelchairs or in braces, all you see is a child who looks like any other child.

This is also one of the reasons autism is so hard to detect and identify at any early age. There are no real tests for the disability. It can only be identified over long-term observations. We are all autistic in some form, but what

separates us from the truly impaired is the degree of per-
severation—the uncontrollable repetition of words,
phrases, or gestures—which accompanies the behaviors.

There are fourteen identifiable behaviors in the rating of
infantile autism. Accurate diagnosis may be difficult because so many of the characteristics can resemble other
problems, such as mental retardation, deafness, or severe
reactive disturbances. If a child exhibits one to six of the
behaviors, he or she is sometimes labeled autistic-like. If
the child exhibits seven or more of these traits, in any
combination, and the behavior is constant and inappropriate to the age, then he or she is labeled autistic.

This information, as well as that which follows, can be
found in a Pennsylvania Society for Autistic Children
(PennSAC) brochure. A high percentage of what I eventually learned about autism came from many of the members of this hardworking and aggressive organization. In
fact, until I began working in Pennsylvania, I knew none
of this information, having learned all I knew from Beth
and Bea.

Autism is a severely incapacitating, lifelong developmental disability which appears during the first three years
of life. It occurs in approximately five out of every 10,000
births and is four times more common in boys than girls.
It has been found throughout the world in families of all
racial, ethnic, and social backgrounds. No known factors
in the psychological environment of a child have been
shown to cause autism.

My developing research indicated that in certain cases it
was possible for an autistic individual to make a decision
to work around the disability and to significantly improve
communications with others. I had witnessed many such
moments.

The symptoms of autism are caused by a physical disorder of the brain and include:

Disturbances in the rate of appearance of physical,
social, and language skills.

Abnormal responses to sensations. Any one or a
combination of sight, hearing, touch, pain, balance,
smell, taste, and body carriage are affected.

Absence or delay of speech and language, though specific thinking capabilities may be present. Immature speech rhythms, limited understanding of ideas, and the use of words without attaching the usual meaning to them is common.

Abnormal ways of relating to people and things. Autistics do not respond appropriately to adults and other children. Objects and toys are not used as normally intended.

The brochure continues to explain that autism occurs by itself or in association with other disorders which affect the function of the brain such as viral infections, metabolic disturbances, mental retardation, and epilepsy.

On IQ testing, approximately 60 percent of autistics have scores below 50, 20 percent between 50 and 70, and only 20 percent greater than 79. Most show wide variations of performances on different tests. (To my understanding, most autistics don't test, or don't test well, so I've always considered this a meaningless piece of information.)

I'm frequently asked what happens to autistic children and whether or not they outgrow their disability. The truth is that they live a normal life span. Sometimes their symptoms change, and some may disappear with age, so periodic reevaluations are necessary to respond to their changing needs. But most remain autistic throughout their life.

Much of my emphasis in working with parents is to get them to see what will happen to their child in the future. It's important to do as much as possible for their kids when they are young and most educable. But few, if any, parents like to think about what happens to these children when they become adults.

What usually occurs is that they are placed in a different category of diagnosis so they can be included with other programs that have funding streams. Almost nothing exists in the way of specialized programs for adult autistics. That's why they seem to disappear as they pass age twenty-one.

The diagnostic checklist of the fourteen behaviors which are used to determine the presence of autism are:

Difficulty in mixing with other children.
Acts as if deaf.
Resists learning.
No fear of real dangers.
Resists change in routine.
Indicates needs by gesture.
Inappropriate laughing and giggling.
Not cuddly or affectionate.
Marked physical overactivity.
No eye contact.
Inappropriate attachment to objects.
Spins objects.
Sustained odd play.
Acts in a standoffish manner.

The common denominator in all of my sessions with autistics was a lack of eye contact. I was told that each of the children would not look a person directly in the eye. But I found that by using the skills I'd developed from my interactions with dolphins, I could have a remarkably high rate of eye contact with all the kids I'd met.

I'd had enough encounters with autistics to know not to expect any one child to be like another. I also knew that their own home provided the best environment for a non-stressful interaction. But the invitation to visit the Developmental Center for Autistic Children and be with the students was too tempting to turn down.

At the school, John was definitely no longer "autistic-like." Physically he was beautiful, with the now familiar porcelain transparent look to his face. With his dark brown hair and liquid brown eyes, he was a good-looking child whose face sometimes shifted suddenly to appear crafty and old.

Unlike most of the other kids I'd met, who were non-verbal save for the occasional scream or grunt, this boy never stopped talking. What made this even more eerie was that his words and intonations seemed to be those of an ancient woman from the back woods of Kentucky or West Virginia. The voice was deep, scratchy, ridden with twangs, and edged in anger and age. No one in his family came from the South, and no one could figure out where this boy's familiarity with the regional jargon came from.

Over the years I've come across many a story told by parents, siblings, and direct service staff that pointed to the presence of a high degree of paranormal ability in autistic children. This was the first time I'd ever heard professional staff wonder out loud whether or not a client was possessed. After hearing him speak, I could understand why they thought this was a possibility.

It wasn't an area I was willing to look into, regardless of my background and training. I felt that to pursue it would be to totally muddy the waters of my research. Besides, I suspected there might be a simpler, more normal reason for his strange way of speaking. I never found out what it was, but what did happen was even more interesting.

Before meeting John, I'd been shown around the facility. There were a string of classrooms, back-to-back, through which ran a darkened hallway. This was a place for visitors to stand and view the activities going on in the rooms, without being seen by the children. Loudspeakers could be turned on and off so sounds could also be heard.

In the room where I was to meet the children, there was a long, rectangular two-way mirror on the far side of the wall. There were no decorations on the wall and only a thin blue fitness mat on the floor. Lodged on the wall high above, in the right-hand corner of the room, was a fixed camera, so there was no way to follow the action if I were to move out of range of the television's eye.

I met John in an office just outside of the room. We joined hands and walked down the three steps that led to the door. I opened it and we went in together. I sat on the floor and allowed him to move around me, hoping that, like Beth and the dolphins, he would have a sense of dominance and control because he was higher than me. I tilted my head down and a bit to the side so I could still watch him as he moved. I'd positioned my body in such a way that the camera would be able to record our session for later review. He circled me cautiously, all the while speaking nonstop. I kept my attention on his movements, but gradually realized there was more important information coming from his speech.

"If you touch that, I'm gonna smack you. You put those shoes back. Don't you dare do that." And so on, building a list of behavioral restrictions, all spoken in a true twang of the hills. I began to understand that he wasn't so much telling me what he couldn't do as how he was being trained to respect boundaries.

I answered by explaining that I thought I understood what it was he was saying and that I would also try to respect any boundaries he might create for me.

He immediately slowed down his speaking, relaxed the tightness of the accent, and gave me a long, silent, appraising stare. Shaking his shoulders, he then launched back into his rapid-fire words.

The subject and content of his sentences had changed. His comments were filled with other topics and only an occasional reference to limits. By now he seemed to have accepted me and settled down somewhat. He slid closer, then sat next to me.

I'd removed my shoes, but he was still wearing his sneakers. He began to play with the laces, twirling them, then sticking the ends into the eyelets. I picked up the laces on his other shoe and did the same. If John was receiving positive stimulation from his play, as Beth had when she'd stroked my blue jeans, then I wanted to experience the same thing too.

We played like that for a few moments and I listened as his voice wound down. Now he was speaking with less energy and in a less stressful manner. Listening intently, hearing intently, I began to discern one word spoken more loudly than any other.

*Drum.*

I know from my later review of the tapes that John never really said "drum" more loudly than any other word. I also know that I "heard" it more audibly and that he had uttered it more frequently than other words he'd spoken.

I stopped and looked directly at him, then told him in a low voice that I understood. With my fingers, I slowly began to tap his foot like a drum.

He stopped talking and placed his hand on mine, allowing me to tap, bump, and make noises. Then he took his hand away and did the same thing to my leg. Together we made a variety of noises, laughing and giggling like old friends.

The moment was warm, filled with camaraderie, trust, and appreciation.

But I had another boy to meet with, and so I bent my head to sneak a look at my watch. I saw that our session would soon have to end and remember silently thinking how much I hated to have to close it down.

No sooner had I thought this than John lifted his head and stared directly and piercingly into my eyes. The director of the school, who had been watching the entire session from behind the mirror, later questioned me about the moment. He remarked that John seemed to be totally normal for that instant and he was curious about what had transpired. How could I tell him that I suspected John had somehow read my mind?

John's eyes held mine for an eternity, but the contact was over in an instant. His face clouded over and, dropping his head, he lifted his hands and placed them tightly over his ears like earmuffs. As a child, I'd done this when I'd wanted to shut out external noises. I was struck by this parallel and wondered whether or not John was doing it for the same reason. Perhaps the noises he was hearing and hoping to silence were being perceived from inside his head rather than externally. He immediately resumed his rapid-fire stream of Southern-accented words, once more laying out the boundaries. It was almost as if the last half hour had never happened.

That had been in September. My next visit to the school was in November, the week of Thanksgiving, and John was not on my schedule of students to see. It was my second day back and the boy with whom I was scheduled to meet had to leave early due to illness. At the last minute, John was put in the time slot. I wasn't told until just before the session. I sat in the office, wondering what his reaction would be when he saw me again. I heard footsteps advancing down the corridor and raised my head to see who was coming. The teacher, holding the boy's hand in his, entered the door. John, seeing me, smiled widely and with total recognition. He broke away from the teacher, drew close, hugged me, and planted a kiss on my cheek.

I got up and took his hand in mine, telling him we were going to spend time together again. He understood and took the lead, pulling me down the stairs and past the door to the room. It was like being tugged by Scotty and Spray, on our way to a new adventure.

The director called to me that we'd passed the door, but I told him we'd be back in a minute. John obviously wanted to take me somewhere and I wanted him to know I'd accepted his leadership.

He tugged me past two more doors and then stopped in front of one on the left. Reaching out, he opened the door and pulled me past a large piano and to the rear of the room. Then, with exaggerated movements, he took my hands and placed them firmly on the set of drums in front of us. He looked up at me wordlessly, a flush of expectancy in his face as he waited for my response.

I was astounded. He'd found a way to show me he hadn't forgotten our last visit, or what had transpired in it.

I was so moved. I felt a lump rising in my throat and my head pulsed with surprise as I searched for a proper response. Then came a quiet, but insistent *tap, tap* on the mirrored window. The moment was broken by the director, who wanted to remind me which room I was really supposed to be in.

I can't remember what happened during the rest of our visit. I know it went well, but nothing else was as important as the fact that John had figured out a way to let me know what he was thinking, that he'd found a way to communicate. Once again I'd seen that learning and communication were, by definition, a two-way street.

It nagged at me that the director had felt it was so important for me to follow his schedule, rather than pursue the interaction with John. It was like having Bob Peck interrupt my breakthrough session with Spray. I felt as frustrated as I had been then. The question bothered me enough that I began to give my next sessions with the other two boys broader attention. I would have to split my awareness between what the boys were seeing and feeling, how I was perceiving and reacting to it, and how the administration was judging the encounters.

I'd met with several children in September, but John was the only repeat in November. Bobby was the second boy. He was the total opposite of John. Slender, blond, and silent, he was also nervous and extremely hyperactive. About John's age, he was more cautious and guarded with me. At first he refused to take my hand or meet my eyes, but he did sneak occasional sidelong glances at me from under his long, pale eyelashes.

We entered the room and removed our shoes. I sat in my now familiar spot in the middle of the floor, within camera range. I could see that Bobby was concerned about my presence. No one had told him what to expect, and he couldn't fit me into any mold. I watched as he began to circle me where I sat so quietly. Suddenly, he emitted a string of clicking noises. The sounds moved up and down a scale and seemed to repeat every few bars. Adding to this, he would approach and thrust out his arms, hands formed into tight fists. I would move backward each time, being sure to show him proper respect, allowing him to be in control.

Circling, ever circling, the rate and pitch of his clicking noises increased. The more he moved, the less emotional I became. The more he acted, the less I reacted.

Suddenly he stopped. No movements, no clicks, no thrusts. Then, without any warning, Bobby backed into me, stood for a second as if making up his mind, and collapsed into my lap.

This behavior was so familiar. I knew I'd seen it before, but where?

As his body tension lessened, I began to gently stroke his back in a downward massage. Then his legs, his hands, his neck, and once more his back. Now he was totally relaxed and willing to stay quietly where we were together.

I picked up his right hand and gently opened the fingers, unfurling the small fist. Lightly pulling on the pinkie, I

said, "One." Then grabbing the next finger I followed
with, "Two," and so on.

I watched as his face grew soft with interest and attention. This was the same boy who, moments before, had
been whirling around me, ready to strike out and run at
the first sign of a problem I might cause. We played with
his fingers over and over again until he finally lost interest.
Rising, he danced about a bit and then pulled me up to
join him.

By the end of the session, we were close friends, so I
was again amazed at what happened once we were done.

I helped him put his shoes back on, donned mine,
opened the door, and walked calmly up the stairs. At that
moment, a woman opened the office door. Bobby jerked
his hand from mine, let out a howl, bolted into the office,
jumped up on the desk, and with broad swipes, one-two-
three, cleared the desk of everything.

Two women inside the office acted quickly. One took
his arms and pinned them to his sides, the other spoke
soothingly to him but also reprimanded him for his negative behavior. While I walked next to Bobby, they
brought him, most unwillingly, back to his classroom.

It was almost as if he'd suddenly remembered he was
supposed to behave in a negative manner and had awak-
ened from a trance or a dream where he'd acted positively
with me. Now he had to make up for lost time.

That night I couldn't forget what had happened with
Bobby. I kept trying to place the circling and clicking
behavior and where I might have seen it with other autistic
children I'd visited.

Putting the problem aside, I picked up my new Stephen
King book, melted into his world of horror, and let my
mind rest. It was then the light bulb lit and the eureka sign
popped up. Patrick O'Grady. I'd witnessed the exact same
actions when I'd been with Patrick O'Grady in Bermuda.

Pat had circled me, then backed in, but had been ready
to slide away if things got bad. Even as he'd gone around
me, I could hear the clicking and whistling sounds he was
making.

This very day I'd seen and heard the same thing with

Bobby. In the end, by behaving in the same way with both, I'd had successful and peaceful interactions with them. I could hardly sleep that night, eagerly looking forward to the next day's session with Bobby and what I'd learn next.

Fortunately I'd already discovered that a good day or a good session doesn't necessarily mean a repeat at the next meeting. Bobby was in no mood to do anything except what he wanted to do. It was just luck that the director had informed me that he would be unable to observe my interactions with Bobby; he would be occupied with parents of another student. This meant I could bend to Bobby's desires, rather than having to accede to those of the director.

Karen, Bobby's social worker, brought him to me, but I could immediately see he wasn't going to cooperate. She explained that when he was like this, nothing worked. I suggested we allow him to go about his normal routine and see his response to my presence. She agreed, so we walked a little farther and went into a room that resembled a home economics center.

To the left was a small kitchen. In front stood a long bank of pine cabinets, with an equally long counter below and more cabinets underneath. Immediately in front of the door was a low, large, long table with several kid-sized chairs pushed in around it. Bobby immediately walked to the chair at the head of the table and sat with an air of finality. He seemed to be saying, "Well, here I am. This is about all you'll get from me."

Ignoring him, I walked to Karen's side. I wanted Bobby to understand that I was not going to be any sort of a threat to him. I told her of our meeting the day before and how he'd allowed me to stroke him, even placing his hands in mine. She remarked that she'd been working with him for the past six months and he'd never voluntarily offered her his hand. How had that happened?

I explained the technique and how crucial my inner attitude was to the entire encounter. It didn't matter whether or not something happened between us. I didn't have to always be in control. I could share dominance with him. Then I picked up her arm and taught her how to move her hands and what pressure to use when stroking.

Bobby began to make noises, so I turned to give him a little more of my attention. He looked up, directly into my eyes. There was not much to interpret, but even if there had been, I would have tried to stay away from that possible pitfall. It was always better not to assume, and instead to allow the child to express himself.

Strewn in front of him were a number of children's books. Karen volunteered that he loved books, especially those from the school library. He wasn't very interested in what was in them, but felt really possessive about having them in front of him. He almost never allowed anyone near him when he had books.

I moved away from the counter, deciding to duplicate some of his behavior from the day before. Keeping a suitable distance, I walked past him to his right side and stopped. Then I walked back to his left side and stopped. Neither time did I make any movement in his direction.

I did this several times, stopping after completing the two laps. He eventually lessened his defensive body posture and seemed not to mind my presence. Finally I slipped into a chair on his right, but kitty-corner to where he sat. He momentarily raised his guard again, then looked directly at me and relaxed.

I softly asked him about the books, watching his face for any sign of a stress reaction. Each time I saw him relax further, I would extend my hand, slowly but inexorably closer to the book nearest my hand. Eventually I rested my index finger next to the book. Then I let it creep over the top and stop.

He brought his hand forward and snatched the book away.

We did this many times, until Bobby finally allowed me to touch the book without interference. Then I turned the tables on him and slowly pushed the book back toward him.

I wanted through my actions to show him how willing I was to allow him dominance over me and the book. I needed him to see that I could be three times more than reasonable—I could agree with his desires.

He changed his expression, considered me carefully, then selected a specific book and pushed it toward me. I opened it and began to slowly read to him. Bobby listened for a minute, then pulled it back to him, only to replace it with another.

We were playing a game within a game. He was allowing me to have the book, but was testing me every second.

Letting out a deep sigh that emanated from the soles of his shoes and the soul of his being, he turned his back to me and became a boy made of Jell-O. Keeping his bottom on his chair, he lay languidly across my lap and slipped into my arms. Karen let out a gasp as I started to stroke his neck, shoulders, arms, and hands. With a jerk, he rose and went into the kitchen. Under Karen's supervision, he prepared himself some crackers and pieces of cheese.

Bobby returned to the table and ate, casting furtive glances in my direction. When he saw that I made no claims on his food, as he'd done with the books, he slid me a small broken piece of cracker.

I waited, making certain he wouldn't want it back again. When it looked as if it was to be mine, I picked it up and daintily nibbled at the cracker, being sure to allow pleasure to cross my face.

The remainder of the session continued in the same way. Bobby would push a book to me and I would read him some short passages. He'd grab it back and shove another one to me. At no special signal, he'd collapse in my arms for a massage, then sit up and eat more crackers.

When the session ended, I stood up and thanked him for being so cooperative, so special. Turning to Karen, I began to thank her as well. From the corner of my eye, I saw a streak of movement.

It was Bobby. As he'd done the day before, he ran toward the back of the room, jumped on a table, and began to clear it of everything. Karen singlehandedly restrained him as I watched.

Twice now he'd behaved this way at the end of our interaction. Could he be showing me that he didn't want to see me go or the session to end? Or was it possible that, as I'd wondered the day before, he was only able to control himself for a short period before all his energy burst loose in some outward direction? I never found out, but the questions his behavior raised were tantalizing, as was pondering the answers.

That afternoon I sat at another long table. I'd been given some after-school time to speak with staff who chose to stay after work to talk with me. The conversation was half comments, half questions, all of them stimulating. These were dedicated, bright, eager, and concerned professionals. Toward the end of the meeting, Karen began to speak in a halting voice.

"I have a story to tell you and I'm not quite certain what to say about it, so I'll just relate it and see what your opinion is."

Tilting my head to show my puzzlement, I remained silent, eager to listen.

"Bobby and I went out to the back area where the swings are after you left the room. I asked him if he wanted to be pushed on them, but he shook his head to say no. I leaned back against the wall of the building and he followed suit. We shared that companionable silence you'd told me about and I decided just to enjoy being with him, instead of trying to help him do something.

"He pushed my arm and I turned to look at him. Quietly he said, 'Arm hurts.' He'd never said that before and I tried to figure out what it really meant. I took a chance and decided he wanted me to stroke and massage his arm as you had done. So I picked up his left arm and began to move my fingers over it lightly. When my hands grew too tired to continue, I looked down at him, smiled, and then allowed his arm to fall by his side.

My attention was caught by another child and as I was looking away, I felt a hand being slowly and stealthily placed in mine. Holding my breath, almost afraid to look, I glanced down and saw that Bobby had given me his hand for the first time since I've worked with him. It was as if he was rewarding me for my good behavior, like I do with him when he's good.

"I can only believe that from what I've seen when you were with him, from what we spoke about, and from what happened to me, you are on the right track. I know you are doing something important and valuable."

I had no answering remark for her. I was as impressed and thrilled as she was. I was also thankful for her honesty and her praise. It was the first time in the two years I'd worked with autistics that I had heard such comments from a professional staff person.

I'd always felt it was great that I was able to interact with children and dolphins, but my goal was that others would be able to do the same. Here at last was my first anecdote indicating I was on the right track.

These encounters with John and Bobby were of major importance to me, both professionally and personally. Through John I was to see that my behavior had so impressed him that even over the space of three months, after a single short encounter, he was determined enough to have found a means to make his recollection known to me. He hadn't responded to the personal "me," but rather to the correct "me." As with Scotty, a lack of emotion on my part was able to stimulate the first bonds of a successful and mutually respectful relationship.

As for Bobby and Karen, for the first time I saw that my efforts could be taught successfully to others and be received with equal acceptance by an autistic child. Also for the first time, I clearly saw how the behavior of some autistic individuals actually and truly could be compared to the actions of some dolphins.

Exciting as all this was for me, it was the shortest and the least physical of the three encounters during that week that really changed the nature of my work as well as my understanding of it.

# *Thirteen*

THE LAST student I was to see that day was also the youngest. Small, pale, and tired-looking, Lindsey was brought to me in the late afternoon. It had been an unseasonably warm day and he looked like any child who badly needed a nap and a cool, damp face cloth to wipe the dried sweat from his brow.

I was tired too. Seeing many children in one day was too heavy a schedule. I'd only had short intervals to clear my head, reset my inner awareness to Empty, and write my hurried notes on scraps of yellow paper.

The child who approached me emitted no sounds like John had made, but displayed none of Bobby's hyperkinetic energy. I could see the boy was almost too tired for the interview.

Lindsey was listless, almost too quiet. My imagination created a scenario where the camera, and those observing us from behind the mirror, would watch as he and I curled around each other for a short snooze. Not a bad idea at that.

We walked into the room. I let out a small sigh of relief, knowing I would soon be able to have my staff meeting and then drive the four hours back to Connecticut. My thoughts had already begun to turn to how long I would have to leave the turkey in the oven for the next day's celebration. I knew how much I had to be thankful for in the past year.

I took off Lindsey's sneakers, and once more pulled off my heeled suede boots. Placing both pairs in the corner, I turned to locate my place on the floor and got an immediate surprise.

The lethargic little boy had been replaced by an energetic child who was fascinated by me. He was standing in front of me, rocking back and forth on his toes, flapping his hands in small up-and-down autistic motions.

I reached out for him and as I settled on the floor, he knelt in front of me. As I'd done with Bobby, I cradled his left hand in mine and began to count out fingers. He was rapt with interest, as if nothing like this had ever happened to him before. Occasionally I'd break the pattern, trying to ensure that this didn't become yet another perseverating behavior. Touching his nose with my finger, I'd pull away fast, as if it was too hot to handle. I was certain to make the right *ouch* sounds as well. At times he would lean forward and hug me, as affectionate as if he were my own son. I'd keep my eyes on his, trying to hold direct contact for as long as he'd allow.

The session was supposed to last for thirty-five minutes. Then I was to return him to his classroom, unaccompanied by a staff person. We continued to play with each other, sometimes lapsing into quiet, impromptu games of stroking arms and pushing fingers. I had no sense of time, only that we were enjoying being with each other.

Lindsey was sitting in my lap, face to mine, legs wrapped around my waist and back. One moment he was active, interested, alert, and engaged in all that was happening. The next instant he was gone. It was as if someone had drawn a curtain over his inner self.

Fortunately I'd been watching as his face lost its softness and gathered hard lines of tension, stress, and tiredness. His eyes, so alive and alert, were now dead, lifeless, and without depth or sparkle. His legs relaxed, his fingers became limp, his torso stiffened, almost as if all the energy had been called back from the provinces of his extremities in order to support his central core. Lindsey was definitely no longer interactive, but when he had been, he had given it all he had.

I realized that his back had been to the camera during most of our encounter. It had never caught anything more than my facial reactions and responses to him.

The session was over. Even though there was still another ten minutes left, I decided it would be useless, as well as frustrating for us both, for me to try to push the interaction beyond his clearly defined limits.

I stood and took his flaccid hand in mine, gently tugging him toward our shoes. Kneeling down, I put his sneakers on him, then yanked my boots over my tired and swollen feet. No words passed between us now. We had become friends, and sometimes friends can say more by saying nothing.

As I passed the door leading to the hallway of two-way mirrors, it opened and I caught a glimpse of the director moving away from the one that had been facing the room I'd just vacated. I returned Lindsey to his class, gave him a last hug, and wished him a happy Thanksgiving. He barely acknowledged my departure. Still, we'd had a satisfying session together.

As I headed back to the office, the director called out my name. I turned and walked to him. He asked several questions about the encounter, mentioning that it had been difficult for him to follow some of the things that had happened. Our voices had been too low to be heard on the intercom, our positions had been too far away for him to see well. He apologized, telling me he had to leave shortly so he could get an early start home for the holiday. Almost as an afterthought, he asked, "Why did you end the session so early?"

I told him I hadn't, it was Lindsey who had stopped the interaction.

"Nonsense," he replied, "I watched as you stood up, put on his shoes, and left."

Trying to help him understand what had really occurred, I said, "But he had shut down. He'd stopped interacting. I watched him and he changed, so I abided by his wishes and aborted the session."

The director's answer was no longer gentle and polite. "I know what I saw. You, not Lindsey, ended the session early." And with that he wished me a safe trip home, a happy holiday, and a good afternoon. I'd been dismissed, and so had my response to him.

I left the school at 4 P.M., hoping to beat the traffic out of the city. Once I'd joined Interstate 95 in lower New Jersey, I popped a mindless instrumental tape into my tape deck, placed my brain on autodrive, and moved northward like all the other metal lemmings surrounding me.

I like long drives. They give me uninterrupted opportunities to cruise the corridors of my mind and my memory. I can slip into a stream of consciousness, review things I've done, how I've behaved. It allows me to conceptualize and plan for the future.

I began to review the events of the past two days. Overall, on a scale of one to ten, I'd rated the total sessions as a ten. Except for. Except for. I could sense that "except for" lurking in the shadows like a guilty feeling. I just couldn't locate what it was about.

If I was pleased with everything, then the problem didn't stem from something I might have forgotten to do, or something wrong I might have said or done. So then, what was it?

The elusiveness of the answer was starting to wear on me, interrupting my inner cruise control, and I was becoming frustrated.

I took a break at one of the rest stops. Calling home to my son, I made certain that all was well with him and that he knew I was on my way to him. I decided to relax and have a small snack to give me more energy until I returned home and could have a real meal. Standing in line with my tray in one hand and my money in another, I overheard a quiet little argument between a mother and her son.

"But Mom," the boy was protesting, "I didn't take the money." "Well, who did then?" she asked. It was her tone of voice. It reminded me of the director's during our last conversation. Incredulous, sarcastic, that tone said she knew everything, and the kid was too stupid to know the truth. Even when she might be wrong, she was THE MOTHER, so she couldn't be wrong. Suddenly I understood the "except for" I'd sensed earlier during my trip.

Sitting down in a booth, I began to scribble notes, hoping to put them together the next time I had some private quiet moments to myself. It was all so simple, so logical, like looking at a picture labeled "What Do You See Wrong Here?" I'd been seeing things from a limited perspective, trying to fit my discoveries into a normal, mainstream set of requirements for identification, testing, and measurement. I'd hoped that experts in the field of autism, as well as in marine mammology, would recognize the same things I had when I spoke to them about my work and my findings. I had also hoped they would understand the same degree of importance my discoveries in communication had for the children and the dolphins. One way I had attempted to do this was by trying to fit it all in under the preexisting paradigms for testing and measuring in a scientific manner. Accurate and useful as these rules might be, they were inoperative and ineffectual for my needs and those of the children and the dolphins.

The director had truly seen me put Lindsey's shoes on. The camera had recorded my standing up and taking his hands, apparently ending the session. Observation—the dispassionate, noninvolved tool for gathering data without inserting oneself into the scene—was the foundation for good research. When dealing with lower-order animals or inanimate subjects, observation, as well as the repeated testing and reproduction of those findings, could produce respectable data. Subjective studies would always be flawed, as even some objective ones might be. Usually they were considered interesting only as studies, inconclusive at best.

I'd witnessed what the camera had not caught, what the director had been too far away to see. I'd been so close to Lindsey, sharing so much a part of him, that I was sensitive and attuned to the most minute and immediate alterations in his being. The only way this could have happened was for me to have been subjectively involved with him.

I thought back to my interactions with other autistic children and with dolphins. In order to communicate, I'd had to have direct contact with both populations. I'd experienced numerous situations which would have defied examination under the scientific model. But I'd succeeded in communicating anyway.

I thought about the dolphins, trying to recall the information I'd read about their attention span. This conclusion was reached after many tests, as well as input from trainers. During all of my sessions, the animals had far exceeded the expected time frame for interaction and attention span.

I thought back to the worst job I'd ever had in my life. It had been in a pencil factory and had demanded constant repetition. The rewards were high pay, but I could feel my brain atrophying. There wasn't enough money in the world for me to have lasted more than two months.

What if progress, not repetition, was one of the answers to the problem of the lack of a lengthy attention span? Dolphins have quick and creative minds. How could they not lose interest in all the tests and training which had been designed to repeat findings rather than to progress and discover new ones?

I set up two imaginary models, using three subjects as prototypes—Spray, Beth, and myself. Could any one of us take part in a series of tests which would be the same day after day after day? No. Why? We all had hungry minds. We would become quickly bored and try to avoid testing at all costs.

If we held a job, would any one of us want to do the same task day after day after day? No. Why? Trainers know they must keep the dolphins fresh, not bored, or the show suffers. They are constantly trying to vary the sequence of behaviors in order to keep interest levels high. Unlike many mentally retarded individuals who work well at repetitious jobs, people with autism quickly lose interest in any and all tasks that they themselves don't perseverate on. As for me, I'd once made seventy-two pies from scratch in one day. Once. Having met the challenge to see how much I could produce, I then wanted to move on to more, or to something else.

Progress was important. It meant all three of us had achieved a certain level, understood, learned, mastered, or rejected it in our own personal ways. The one thing we had in common was that at some point we all lost interest and wanted to change or move on. We didn't want to keep doing the same thing repeatedly, regardless of the reward. I'd seen the same problem when I'd read about the subjects of the E.S.P. tests whose scores had dropped over a period of time and testing. Maybe I would have to rate my research on a scale of progress, showing that progress and improvement could be measured, even if on a nonconstant, day-by-day or moment-by-moment basis.

I noodled the thought around a bit more as I threw away my cup of coffee, unlocked my car, and continued my trip home. Having finally identified my feeling of uneasiness, I was free to examine my thoughts for the remainder of the trip, The settling darkness seemed to provide a cocoon for my active mind to metamorphose my long-dormant knowledge. From my perspective, my world of research turned upside down like the ship *Poseidon* on New Year's Eve.

When I was working with real subjects, on their turf, objective became subjective, subjective became objective. I asked myself what this meant, acting as both the formulator of the concept and as a curious listener needing further exposition on the matter.

Well, the director and the camera missed not only the obvious visual cues, but the intuitive ones as well. No one who stands on the sidelines will ever be able to experience the innate sense of knowing and the exchange of silent intent and understanding which can pass between the researcher and the subject. Unless the observer becomes involved. Which means he or she no longer qualifies as a dispassionate third party.

Conversely, I, as the involved, subjective researcher, am able to accumulate nontestable data which is very much an integral part of the life and behavior of the subject. It can only be categorized under "opinion," but so what? That doesn't necessarily invalidate what has been perceived.

Moreover, by admitting the existence of cognition and creativity in the subject, I, again as the researcher, am no longer bound to identify repetitive behaviors, but rather can focus on those that are positive and show progress. I wondered how I was going to be able to test or measure my research and its findings. Without the standard format, I'd have to find alternative methods.

I recalled Bob Peck's statements about the times when Scotty and Spray would behave differently when they were with me. I thought too about Bea's comments in regard to Beth's behavior when we were together. Then there were the favorable remarks made by other parents and by direct service staff workers when they'd watched me with autistics.

Here was the place to set my guidelines.

If parents, direct services people, medical support personnel, and dolphin trainers identified and commented upon positive differences, ones that showed progress and improvement when I was interacting with their children, clients, or dolphins, then I had a means of measurement. I would accept what they said as an approved commentary, leaving aside all that I felt was important but not commented upon for later consideration. This meant I might feel there were many more significant situations within an encounter than had been recognized by those observing us. I would give them importance, assign a value to them and to the additional information, and wait to see if it occurred again, either with the same person or dolphin, or with yet another person or dolphin. Even if this "unapproved" information was not recognized by others, I would give it deeper consideration from the standpoint of what I'd learned somewhere in my past.

How would I test? I wouldn't. Instead I'd look at my findings and see how they were utilized by my subjects, by myself, by those working with me, and by those who spent more time with the subjects. I'd even try to see whether or not the more basic findings were being altered to help individuals to succeed in communicating with each other.

If the value of the interactions and exchanges was increased, even minutely, by those who had the most to gain when using them, then this would be test enough. In other words, if an autistic child was willing to interact easily with a new person in a short space of time, and previously he or she wouldn't, then something must be happening between the two people. This "something" would then become the target of study, rather than the child.

I would also flip over my priorities. I would not seek any definitive findings, but rather would pursue those which seemed to meet the individual needs of those I had sessions with. It would be of no importance that I wanted the child to speak. Instead, if any form of communication was being exhibited, I would try to allow the child to develop the course of making him or herself understood. It would all be in the child's hands.

I realized that unless I could find others who would be willing to place all their attention upon one subject and record continuous, ongoing, and long-range research, I would be doomed to a career of publishing papers which were studies rather than reports. I could live with that. It meant I'd never be an expert, but only a person who lived on the outer perimeters of new knowledge. I could live with that too.

It also meant I'd have to be constantly on my guard against losing the edge of excitement which comes with quantum leaps. If I were to become swallowed up by one single aspect of my discoveries, I would lose the very qualities that had made it possible for me to make them. The willingness to be wrong, to pay for my errors, to not be an expert, to allow others to be in control, and to work for the betterment of others rather than myself requires a delicate balance of the body, mind, and spirit. Once lost, it requires great effort to repossess that balance, as I'd learned from experience.

Once again it appeared that the primal drive to survive was at the core of everything. I'd have to be willing to live and work in such a manner that I'd always have to be testing myself, my research, and my reasons for doing both. I'd never be able to feel that I was safe, the absolute master of all that was known on one topic, unassailable by my critics. Well, I could live with that, too.

By becoming too attached to being right, unable to admit being wrong and to take the responsibility for the error; by feeling I knew more than anyone else, including those I was working with; by caring too much about how I appeared to others and protecting my sense of expertise; and by having my own "career" as my goal, I would be looking for security rather than survival. This idea began to scare me more than anything I'd thought about during the entire ride home. I'd end up protecting all I had without allowing others to share it, and I'd spend too much time surrounding and clutching what little I had rather than seeking to find out what else existed.

I'd seen the same problem before, in a different context. Did I want to bake pies and make lots of money, or investigate communication and make a difference? I'd already made my choice, so it was easy to transfer the concept over to my new mind-set. I also knew I had never been, and still wasn't, interested in setting up a negative target or symbol of what I didn't want to be.

I certainly had no ax to grind, no grudges against science. My life and my vision had been given back to me because of science. I also didn't need to have a single person to resent, to accuse of stymieing my work.

I had many reasons to be thankful to the director of the school. It wasn't that he was jealous of his position and status. It was that he represented the system he'd succeeded in, a system which unfortunately made it almost impossible for new ideas, new ways of looking at things to receive enough light to grow.

The man had invited me to visit his school, to interact with his students, to meet and speak with his staff. He had taken me to lunch and been generous in many ways. In his own way, he'd taught me and I was grateful to him for the opportunities he'd provided. He'd made abundantly clear the problems I could expect if I continued to attempt to mainstream my work.

From that day I would continue to do my research as before, but now with a greater understanding of the manner in which I had to present it to the "experts" in any one field. For the time being, until something less ponderous came along, I labeled it Interactive Behavioral Communications Research. Like MID★POINT, I thought, the name spoke for itself.

Mine was a science that was like an art form. It was a work in progress. And progress, not repetition, would be its foundation.

# *Fourteen*

*O*NCE AGAIN my past brought me the means to propel my future. Although I hadn't taught a class in intuitive development in four years, I still liked to see what was new and what was being developed. I'd made a spur-of-the-moment decision to stop off at New Milford's Unicorn Bookstore, a thriving gathering place for people to pick up new ideas, a cup of hot tea, and the best collection of books on alternative thinking for miles around.

I'd known the owner, Barb Straub, for years, even before she'd taken a chance by going into her own business. Barb had always greeted me with bear hugs and cheery news of local happenings. Instead of being pontifical or fanatical in her beliefs, she was a beacon of light to others because she allowed them the right to share their opinions, while keeping her own to herself.

I'd dropped by just to visit and see what was new. As we were chatting, another customer came to the counter to check out some books. Barb introduced us and explained that Sue Sherman lived in a nearby town and had been sincerely interested in learning about intuitive development. We spoke for a while and then Sue asked me why I'd stopped teaching courses. I explained that I'd become too busy with my research to make any effort putting together classes. She asked if I'd be willing to teach a class if she recruited the students.

I silently studied her for a moment. She was about five-feet-six, stocky, with brownish blond hair and a serious expression. She was dressed casually and seemed to be sincere, not flaky.

I wasn't particularly eager to teach again, but Sue seemed to have the drive, the energy, and the realness necessary to put together people for a workshop. Besides, it would be good for me to review what I'd learned so long ago by teaching it to others.

I smiled and said I'd do it. I'd already accumulated a list of people who had expressed interest if I decided to teach again. I told her that I'd be willing to contact those folks and that I'd try to help out as much as possible. We'd do our best to work together and see what happened.

To my surprise and pleasure, I was scheduled within a month to do an intensive two-day workshop in intuitive development in my home.

I'd always loved teaching and since 1977 hadn't made a conscious effort to stop. It had just sort of happened. I hadn't missed the preparations and the labor-intensive hours I spent teaching the actual classes. As the years had stretched on, I would remember the teaching with fondness, but all the rest with relief that I wasn't doing it anymore.

The ten people who attended the workshop came from different states and very different backgrounds. Sitting in front of them, helping them to understand their own sensory perceptions and how to expand them, I realized how much I missed leading workshops. It was a warm and fulfilling feeling to be sharing my knowledge with these people.

I'd stopped when I began to feel like a sieve, with all of my energy draining away because I had been doing too many activities. The time had come to pull back and allow myself to regenerate, to place all my attention on what I wanted to do most. It was then I'd begun to focus entirely on working with dolphins and autistic children.

Doing this workshop was like walking into an attic with the intention of giving it a good cleaning. Pick up one item which has great meaning and suddenly you are reminiscing and forgetting your original purpose for being there.

When the course was over, I allowed the students to convince me to teach them the second level. We set a date for the next three-day intensive class, for the entire duration of which they would be required to live in my home. We had all worked together so well, I had no qualms about making such a commitment. And it was no small commitment, at that. I would have to teach three days, all day and some of the night, as well as prepare all the meals for eleven people.

Once again the weekend came and went with amazing speed, and once again I rediscovered how much pleasure I had in sharing information with the students.

The time spent with them was as fascinating for me as it had been for them. But it was so much work that I knew it would be a long time before I would agree to do another one.

Fredericka Cadmus had attended the first workshop because of Sue's recommendation. She'd taken the second one because she'd done so well at the first. Freddie was a dynamo, a walking illustration of the saying that good things come in small packages. The woman was incredibly small-boned and slim, probably not even one hundred pounds. She wore her short ash-blond hair in an easy-maintenance style. Her clothing was simple but at the same time tasteful. Inside her burned a candle of incredible brightness.

Freddie was a horsewoman, an expert on hunting and jumping, as well as an equestrian judge. Her body was strong and wiry, small-muscled but absolutely in shape from the years spent riding horses.

Freddie and Sue had met at a yoga retreat center in southwestern Massachusetts and had gone on to take many more courses together. They shared many of the same interests, including the more paranormal approach to health and healing.

In the 1970s, Freddie had been closely associated with the Transcendental Meditation movement and had lived in Europe, working for the organization. She'd met and befriended the future lieutenant governor of Pennsylvania, William Scranton, and his future wife, Coral. They were all young together and his work in politics was many years ahead of him.

Freddie had maintained close ties to the couple, and eventually became godmother to their three beautiful little girls. She had also moved to Harrisburg, Pennsylvania, to be close to them. Eventually she wound up working in the capital city for a state senator, making a difference for many minority groups and organizations.

At the close of the last workshop, after all the others had gone home, Sue, Freddie, and I cleaned the living room, then relaxed on the glider in the breezeway. We talked about what had transpired during the two workshops, about ourselves, and about what we each hoped to achieve in the future. As I gave a further explanation of what I'd done in researching communication with autistics and dolphins, as well as what I hoped to do, a look of deep concentration crossed Freddie's face, as if she were making a great decision.

In a soft voice, she said, "I have friends who might be interested in what you're doing. Would you be willing to come to Pennsylvania and work there if it was possible?

I was quiet for a moment, not knowing what to say. Finally I said I'd be happy to go there. I had no idea what she had in mind, but I was willing to try anything and go anywhere.

It was then that she explained her relationship with the Scrantons. She said the couple had had long-term involvements in the personal development field and she was sure they'd be interested in what I was doing and in helping some of their constituents as well.

Freddie returned home and after a series of phone calls back and forth, we set the date and the agenda for my first visit to Pennsylvania.

It was more than I could ever have hoped for.

Coral Scranton had offered to host a small luncheon. She felt that people who would not normally have given me the time of day would come because she had invited them. The guest list included people from diverse segments involved with autistic populations—among them parents, senior state government staff, the President of PennSac, and the director of the Developmental Center for Autistic Children. No wonder I was nervous.

Freddie had also taken the initiative to call a local television station and suggested they do a segment on my work. They agreed, but wanted to see me interacting with dolphins and autistic children. So sessions were scheduled for me with the dolphins at Hershey Park and then with an autistic boy. As if being filmed was not stressful enough, this would also be the first time I worked in front of others who were not directly related to my research. To make the day as nerve-wracking as possible, we *had* to be at Hershey Park no later than two o'clock or we'd miss our time slot. The dolphins were set to perform their regularly scheduled show at three.

Knowing how limited my funds were, Freddie had arranged for me to stay at the lieutenant governors' small guest house, across the street from his home. The entire property sits next to Fort Indiantown Gap, an Army Reserve training camp. It was like living in a potential war zone, with helicopters flying at all times of the day and night, and the sound of marching platoons drifting over the quiet hills even as the sun rose and set.

The guest house was divided into two separate apartments, and Coral had worked her decorating magic on the small bedroom I occupied. The white and flowered wallpaper gave a bright cheeriness to the room, while the white-covered four-poster bed and cherry furniture gave it warmth.

I decided I could easily live right there and never leave. I suppose this feeling was also a small recognition of the fear I felt growing inside me. My mind raced. What if I fail? What if they all laugh? I have no credentials, only experience. What if that's not enough? What if the dolphins won't come near me? What if the autistic boy won't interact? What if, what if. The "what if's" stretched on forever, like little demons let loose from my subconscious.

Well, I could always go back to baking pies. I decided to give it my best shot, and if I failed, so what. At least I'd tried. This made the "what if's" head for the hills—temporarily.

That momentous morning I dressed with enormous care and thought. Freddie had outlined a schedule that was both demanding and difficult, one which would require almost split-second timing to meet. At eleven-thirty, Freddie walked over to pick me up and go to the main house. She once again reviewed the day's agenda, warning me to do my best to keep everything moving.

As I sat on the couch in the living room, I could see the cars coming up the road to the house. In my left hand I tightly held a much-folded sheaf of papers. Bea had given

me copies of Beth's writing. With her permission, I was
going to allow the others to read the poetry and prose the
girl had produced.

One by one, the guests arrived, introduced themselves,
and took seats around the room. We made polite conversation and then the director of the school for autistic children began to ask more probing questions about my
research. I quickly explained my own personal background, then outlined my work with the dolphins, culminating with how I'd become involved in autism.

They all listened intently and with obvious interest.
Next to me sat Nancy Kenley. She was not only the
mother of a severely autistic teenage boy, but president of
the Pennsylvania Society for Autistic Children. She asked
me to clarify the relationship of dolphins to autistic children and I explained the basic nature of the research. At
this time, other than communication, I was the only link
between the two, but I was hoping to teach others the
same techniques and skills.

Nancy asked me whether I hoped to place the kids in
the water with the dolphins. I said I'd thought about it,
but had decided it wasn't part of my real goal. I supposed
I would eventually do this, but not in the near future. I
had no intention of using the animals as a therapeutic tool
or aid. I felt that would be one more way for humans to
avoid taking responsibility for enabling communication
bridges to be built. If there was ever to come a time when
I would put them together, then I intended to be in the
water as well, an equal one-third partner in whatever happened.

Nancy seemed satisfied with my answers, so I changed
the topic to my interactions with Beth. In telling the story,
I took great pains to obscure the true identity of the girl
and her mother. I described how we'd met, several of our
sessions, and then I reached behind me and produced the
pages Beth had written. Passing them around, I let them
know that with Bea's permission, I'd made copies for
them to keep.

Deep quiet descended upon the room as each person
began to read, then reread the papers.

The director spoke up. "Would this child's real name

be . . . ? And is her mother's name . . . ? Are they from . . . ?"

My answer to each question was yes. To this day I'll never know how the director knew who Bea and Beth were. I never gave any clue as to their identity.

The director went on to say he had met with the girl several years before. At that time she was not speaking, not writing, and not communicating in any way. He asked me how it came about that she was now writing, and I told them the story of the day Bea put a pencil in the girl's hand. Incredible as the tale might have seemed to everyone, it took on a deeper sense of honesty and validity because of the director's comments about Beth.

The ice had been broken and everyone began to bubble forth with polite but enthusiastic questions. I became so engrossed in the conversations, I hadn't realized the time was one o'clock. But Freddie had. Explaining my schedule, she got everyone up and we quickly moved to the porch, where a buffet lunch and a long, white-clothed table was set up for us. The questions and comments made for an animated meal, one that passed too quickly. Freddie gave me the five-minute signal and I finished up minor details and offered people my business card.

Nancy invited me to meet her son, Kevin, and I promised I would visit during a later trip to the Harrisburg area. The director asked me to visit his school in September, which I agreed to do. Making our apologies, Freddie and I said good-bye, then literally ran out the door to my car. Even with her help, I was still running ten minutes late. I'd have to really hustle when we arrived at the amusement park.

Once there, we spotted the television crew heading our way, introduced ourselves, grabbed my gear from the trunk, and hustled through the employees' entrance to the dolphin area. I was brought around to the back entrance of the pool area and told to wait for the trainer.

A man in his early twenties came up to me and introduced himself as John Fishback, the head trainer. His cooperation had made this visit possible. He'd cleared it through all the proper channels and made sure we would have enough time to accomplish our goals.

I was shown the shower room and hurriedly changed to my gray wetsuit with the three blue stripes running down the arms and torso. As I walked out to the platform, I wondered if I looked as conspicuous as I felt.

I climbed the steps to the show platform and was unsettled to see the tank. I'd never expected to see such a small pool. Circular, it had two tiny holding areas on either side. To my surprise I was told that there were not only three full-grown Atlantic Bottlenose dolphins in there, but a pair of sea lions as well. This was one densely populated tank.

Surrounding it, for almost three quarters of its circumference, was a large bank of rising bleachers. To the rear was strung a heavy wire, upon which periodically passed an alpine gondola, winding its way over the park for an aerial view. Tourists looking out the open grating would wave and call to the dolphins.

Over the center of the pool hung a large circular awning, from which loudspeakers were positioned. Guy wires held the awning taut and were firmly anchored behind the pool. Large bags of salt were piled to the right of the tank.

I'd never worked in an inland pool before, and unthinkingly asked what the bags were for. The salt was combined with chemicals and piped-in fresh water to create man-made seawater. This seemed fine, until I was to later witness one of the dolphins' favorite games.

The chlorine would be dissolved into a big bucket and one of the assistant trainers would slowly walk around the pool, pouring the concoction into the water. Unfortunately, the dolphins would swim under the bucket and enjoy a bath of fresh chlorine. I wondered if this was a good thing for their health, especially for their eyes, but chose not to say anything.

I'd already decided to ask the camera crew to do me a favor. I rounded them up and told them I knew time was short and that they really had to get their shots the first time. Would they please go along with a crazy request? Go over to the edge of the pool, put one hand in the water, and wait for a dolphin to show up. Once there, talk with the animal as if it were human. Tell the dolphin why they were there, what the camera was for, and that the equipment was not to be the center of attention.

I suppose they were accustomed to strange people, because with barely a shrug they agreed to do it. (Later, at dinner, all they could talk about was their amazement that the dolphins seemed to have listened and then never paid them any attention again until the taping was done. Later still, when the segment was shown, the narrators of the piece commented, for the audience to hear, that the crew had tried my techniques and they'd been successful. Well, whatever works, you know?)

John came up and gave me some background on the dolphins—their names, ages, and some of their behavioral history. Buddy was the oldest and the dominant male. Cooter was only seven, but he really wanted to take over from Buddy. Tessie was shy and hard to interact with unless she knew and trusted you.

Looking around, I asked him where the dolphins were housed in the winter. It didn't seem humane or possible for them to live there in cold weather. He explained that they were rented for the summer season from a large business in Gulfport, Mississippi. The animals were flown in and out every year. They were three of over thirty-five dolphins which were routinely shifted around the country to amusement parks too small to keep their own animals.

I asked him some additional questions, then gave him my now standard speech about who I was and what I did. Then I explained what I was going to do and how I would be doing it. When we were through talking, I signaled the camera crew to get ready.

I moved over to Freddie and asked her to help me with the rest of my gear, then sat down to compose myself. This accomplished, I walked to the edge of the deck.

Once more I was prone on a platform. I created my best school lunchroom mind-set and put all the people, noise, distractions, and demands out from my conscious mind. There was only me and the dolphins.

As I hung my hands in the water, Buddy glided over to investigate. I moved them up and down, then over each other. He opened his mouth wide, took my hands, jiggled them in the same way Scotty, Spray, and Rebel had, added an extra little shake, and moved back expectantly.

I turned to the camera and explained what had happened and told them what my next plans were.

Sitting upright, I put on my gloves, left off my weight belt and hood, then slid into the tank. The dolphins circled for a while, sending investigatory sonar signals throughout my body. Minutes were ticking away and I could sense the crew's growing impatience. Something had better happen, and soon.

Suddenly I realized that this was the worst possible attitude I could have. Hadn't I already prepared them for the fact that they might be wasting their time? Hadn't I told them I wasn't going to make anything happen, but would allow the animals to take the initiative? Well, then, why was I changing my mind and hoping to create a camera-worthy photo opportunity? I'd done my part. I was there. The rest was up to Buddy, Cooter, and Tessie.

As I allowed my needs to change, I saw Buddy coming in for some contact. By then I was lying prone on the water's surface, gently inhaling and exhaling through my snorkel hanging on the left side of my mask. Buddy swam in, stopped head-to-head, then grasped my right hand in his mouth. I became vertical and face-to-face with him. He pushed against my hand, moved in for the obligatory tow, and off we went. Cooter and Tessie swam on either side, but not within touching distance.

Again, I chose not to be totally passive, and so swam as well as I could while holding Buddy's dorsal fin. After one tour, we stopped and he drew back, then stared intently into my masked eyes. The water drops on the faceplate distorted the world, but I could see well enough to recognize his piercing stare. Like Spray, Buddy was not just looking at me; he was looking into me. While I didn't feel the same sense of connection I'd felt with her, there was a hint of unlimited intellect within his eyes.

I had to work with this dolphin again.

With a rising and sinking motion of his body, he broke the contact and swam away, joined by the other two animals. I watched them begin to swim purposefully and deliberately around the pool. I'd lost all sense of time during the session, but I could tell they hadn't. They were moving through the water like dancers limbering up before a performance, knowing that a few early ticket holders were there to look at them.

I saw by their movements—it was showtime, folks.

"Time!" John shouted. His call was more a confirmation than a reminder. I already knew what time it was, without even having to look at my watch.

I finned to the edge of the platform and kicked hard, lifting my body free of the water. As I twisted around, I saw that the three dolphins had come with me, as if providing me with an escort.

I toweled off, all the while being captured on tape. Warning that grave bodily damage and harm would come to the crew if they were to actually show footage of me exiting the water, I consented to a poolside review of what had happened.

John was kind enough to take a moment to give his insights as well, even though it was growing closer to performance time. His remarks, captured forever on tape, supported my appraisal of the uniqueness of the session.

"The dolphins," John said, "especially Buddy, rarely interact so swiftly with strangers. It usually takes them quite a while to build a rapport with them. Sometimes it never happens." Given the stressful conditions and the pressure on all of us, it was even more noteworthy. He was impressed.

To tell the truth, so was I.

Freddie, ever vigilant, drew me close and whispered, "You have to get changed right away. We still have to drive to Camp Hill to meet with the autistic boy."

I squished down the steps to the trainers' dressing room. Saying a waterlogged hello to the other trainer, I moved into the shower, wetsuit and all, and washed out the make-believe salt water and dolphin feces that clung to my entire body. Ten minutes later, dressed, made-up, hair dried, I decided that I might have the right stuff to work with television crews. For the sake of my sanity, I just didn't want to do it too often.

I joined Freddie and the others and asked them to hold on for a minute. Going to the platform, I called John over and thanked him. He issued an invitation for me to return in September when things would be more quiet, and I assured him I'd be back. Who could know then how much I would discover because of those next visits?

Giving him a warm hug, I said my good-byes and took off to join the rest of the group. As Freddie and I quickly walked through the gates and toward my car, the activities of the morning seemed to have happened weeks ago. It was almost impossible to believe we'd done so much in so short a time.

# Fifteen

CHRISTOPHER KRATZER was sitting on a swing, moving back and forth, making high-pitched shrieking sounds. Apparently oblivious to the commotion around him, he paid no attention to a neighbor's golden retriever, rock in mouth, frolicking next to him.

We had arrived at the home of Mary, David, and Chris Kratzer after getting lost on the way. The camera crew had followed us on our odyssey, making all the same mistakes. Eventually finding the right road, we pulled into the driveway at the end of a cul-de-sac, hoping this was the place.

Mary and David came out to greet us, accompanied by an older man who was introduced as the boy's grandfather. We were late and they were anxious, fearing we might have lost our way.

The crew unloaded their equipment from the van and began a polite search through the house for the best place to tape and set up their gear. Eventually they settled on a relaxed setting in the den.

As Freddie and I walked behind the house to the deck, we heard thin, high-pitched noises coming from the tree-covered back area. Mary explained that Chris loved to run around the woods, singing and making his noises. She said he was extremely hyperactive and almost never sat still for any length of time.

Chris whizzed by in a flurry of sound and motion. What little glimpses I caught of him were of a boy of ten with the ever present fragile, transparent porcelain look to his face. His hair was golden blond, and with his long arms and knobby knees, he looked as if he had just gone through a growth spurt. He was six months younger than my own son, also named Chris, which gave me some frame of reference for age-appropriate behavior.

I asked his parents not to tell me any information about

their son until I'd completed my session with him. I was concerned that if I knew too much, I might create expectations I couldn't—and he wouldn't—fulfill.

I'd again warned the camera crew not to expect anything. I had no idea how they were going to capture such subtle communication for others to see.

By now, after having spent so much time with autistic kids, I knew most of them disliked wearing shoes. In preparation for my interaction with Chris, I'd removed mine and was padding around the den, feeling we had to get started soon or we'd lose the moment.

Chris's parents and grandfather positioned themselves behind the cameras after David had firmly placed the boy in a comfortable plaid cushioned chair. Sitting all the way back in a corner of the chair, he looked tiny, as if he were being engulfed.

David had warned me that because of the boy's hyperactivity, his son might not stay in the chair for even a minute. I was prepared for the possibility and told him this session was to be designed by the wants and needs of his son. Not an easy thing to say when the house was packed with television people on a tight schedule.

A small round drum table stood to the right of the seat. Next to that was an upright piano. I settled down in front of the table and piano, with my legs off to my right side on the carpeted floor. As usual, I hoped to silently convey my intentions and attitudes toward Chris through my positioning and behavior.

I looked past him, allowing him the right to meet my eyes on his own. He grew curious about my sidelong glances and brought his gaze full front to meet my eyes.

I'd long ago chosen not to explore the possibility of telepathy in my communication techniques. I suspected it played some role, but a minor one. I was then and still am certain it is the total, overall package of what my thoughts create in my visibly detectable body which gives the clues and cues to the dolphins and the kids.

I'd also warned Chris's parents I might not speak at all during the session. As it turned out, I never said one word.

He leaned over to the drum table and removed from the

surface a label with a thin brown string hanging from a hole at the end of it. I watched as he kept running his hands over the label, touching, feeling, and moving it constantly. I had a sudden insight, an intuitive understanding of the information he was gathering from his efforts. I'd never perceived anything from this point of view in my entire life, had never even considered it. I had to assume that I was somehow tuned in to him.

The label was just a thing. He had no interest in its noun identification, or its purpose, or why the string was attached, or even in the fact that the string was called a string. He was only interested in feeling the item, in much the same way as Beth had wanted only to feel my blue jeans. Chris had no drive, no need, no desire to move beyond experiencing the label and thread in the way he chose to deal with it.

I couldn't help but compare this behavior to how dolphins identify objects and never give noun assignments to them.

Somehow what I had just experienced made sense to me. I understood his perceptual process, and thus why the autistic children and dolphins had such short attention spans. We communicated too slowly for them. With their holographic use of their sensory receptors, they'd already identified objects in a way that was meaningful to them. Anything else held little value.

What use would it serve for a dolphin to have a word for a glass? None. Why would a dolphin construct a syntax like ours, when the things that were important to them had no need for verbal identification?

Here was this little boy showing me the truth. The label and the string had no meaning for him. His interest extended no further than to the fact that he was interested. So why bother to learn sounds that would identify objects, or sit still to be told what function these things performed? I had no good reason to try to force a need upon him to know more than he already did. He had already gathered sufficient information for his own purposes.

He dropped the label, letting it fall to the carpet, and again turned his face to mine. Raising my left hand, I thought about asking him for permission to touch his fingers. Although no words were spoken, he immediately moved his hand forward and gave it a slight waggle, as if showing me his consent. I slowly moved my hand forward and gently stroked his right hand, in small circular motions. He kept his head toward mine, by now having established solid eye contact, and then with his left hand quietly lifted a lemonade-filled glass to his lips for a swallow.

I slid my hand back and away from his, not wanting to push the meeting too much. He switched the glass to his right hand and let it rest on the cushion.

I nonverbally composed a request. Could I have a sip from the glass? The tape shows him pushing it toward me and into my hand.

Lifting the glass to my lips, I took the smallest amount possible; then, without words, asked him if he would like it back again. He responded by opening his right hand, allowing me to return the glass back to him. As before, during this entire exchange his eyes never left mine.

It had been a long and peaceful interaction. I'd totally forgotten the eight people crowded to the rear of the den, all watching in fascinated silence.

As if he had suddenly become aware of their presence, Christ turned to look at them, let out a little shriek, moved out of the chair, brushed past everyone, and ran nimbly out the back door, into the safety of the swings and his world.

Freddie came up to me, beaming, and drew me aside. Cupping her hand, she whispered, "Chris's grandfather was crying as he watched you two interact. He told me the boy never behaves that way. It was the first time he'd ever seen his grandson give a glass to someone else. He was moved to tears."

The assigned host for the television segment, Susan Taylor, immediately set up an interview with Mary and David. I moved away to give them privacy, as well as the opportunity to make any comment they chose. It was only months later, at the end of October when the piece was shown, that I heard their appraisal for the first time.

They'd only discovered that Chris was autistic when he

was five years old. When they learned of the fourteen characteristics, they found that Chris had twelve.

David volunteered that it was unusual for his son to sit with someone he didn't know. "Something was definitely going on," he said.

Mary felt the key was my acceptance of Chris. "He could always pick up when someone was accepting of him," she remarked.

It had been a remarkable and educational session for me. None of us wanted this to be my last visit, so we exchanged the necessary information and promised to get together again. That was August 2.

The next time we met was nine months later, although we had maintained contact through letters and phone calls. By then, Freddie had arranged for me to be interviewed by a reporter from the *Philadelphia Inquirer* who would do double duty, having sold the article to *Woman's World* magazine as well.

The writer called me and told me in no uncertain terms that there would be no article without her having observed one session between me and an autistic child. My gut response was to tell her where to put her typewriter, but an inner voice, sounding much like Freddie, cautioned a less aggressive response. My initial desire stemmed from my feeling that she wanted to use a child for her purposes. My conflict came from the worry that I might be doing the same thing.

I truly understood her responsibility to have more to work with than what I told her. On the other hand, her demand also seemed to reduce the child to nothing more than a tool for guaranteeing the truth.

I've never been able to fully come to terms with this problem, feeling that my interactions between both kids and dolphins is a very private matter. Taping the television show had been a problem for me for this reason as well.

In a flat, unenthusiastic tone of voice, I told the reporter I knew someone who might be willing to allow such an observation. I would call the person, but if she said no, then the article would not be done.

The reporter agreed to this and I promised to call her back as soon as I found out. Then I dialed Freddie and steamed into her telephone ear. She felt I ought to give it a chance (perhaps she really *was* my inner voice), and so I called Mary. She agreed to the meeting and set an April afternoon date for the interview.

When the day arrived, it was my chore to pick up the reporter at the train station. Her appearance didn't quite match the description of herself she'd given me, and we walked past each other for half an hour before we figured out who was who.

We returned to my car where Freddie and Hedy were waiting. Hedy had come on this trip to take slides of my session with Chris.

It was a warm day, patience was already at a premium, and the reporter was in a hurry. She hadn't eaten lunch, but with any luck, she said, she could do the work and be back on an early train for Philly. Oh great. This was just the type of attitude Chris would need.

This time I found the house with no problem, and Mary met us in the driveway. Standing next to her was another woman. In a stressed voice, Mary introduced us to Chris's teacher. She was there not only because of her interest in my work, but because Chris had been having a terrible day. Mary had called and asked for her help in controlling her son.

Mary looked at me and said that if she'd been able to reach me, she would have canceled our visit. Chris had been totally out of control that morning. He'd been getting fifteen minutes of sleep, then jumping out of bed and running all over the house. One parent would have to be with him, to protect him and the items in the house from possible harm. Because David had to work, Mary was usually the one with little or no sleep.

Chris was so hyperactive that morning that he was running nonstop. He'd become violent and had been hitting his mother in his anger and frustration.

Instead of starting at zero. Chris was at minus ten. I'd have to reject the challenge this presented. Any sign in my attitude and behavior of a need to look good in the eyes of the reporter would mean instant negation of my work. I knew I'd have to totally put aside the desire to succeed.

I placed my arm around Mary and we walked into the house. I smiled and said that as long as we were there, we might as well try to work together. Freddie, the reporter, and Hedy walked behind us, talking with the teacher.

As we walked past the kitchen, I saw the dining table was set for a meal. Mary had thought we might not have had lunch and had gone to the trouble of making one for us. Since I am a diabetic and have to watch my food intake at all times, I was grateful to her.

The reporter was not as happy. She mumbled something about making it a "quick snack and let's get going."

Chris wandered in to see who was there. Nine months had passed since our first and only encounter, an eternity ago. Mary called David in, who had come home early from work to watch the session. We shook hands warmly, and I introduced the reporter and Hedy.

As we sat around the table, speaking rapidly, I tried not only to bring them up to date on what I'd been doing, but also to distract the reporter from her own needs. Chris would sit for a minute, eat something, then rise and wander around, eventually returning to sit in his chair for a scant moment.

We finally finished and moved into the den. After looking around at the furniture, the reporter decided the room would be fine for her purposes.

I took off my sneakers and began to mentally prepare myself for our session. Out of the corner of my eye I saw David and Mary move off to the kitchen. Only later did I learn from Hedy that the reporter had asked them to leave. It was just as well I didn't know then—my anger at the woman might have seriously affected the interaction.

David entered the room with Chris in his arms. He placed the boy in the chair, then returned to be with Mary. As before, I withheld my eye contact from him, but used my peripheral vision to keep track of his responses. At first he darted glances at me. Finally he looked directly toward me and I allowed my eyes to meet his. We sat this way for a few moments, then he suddenly let out a screech, jumped from the chair, and bolted out of the room.

His parents had been watching the interaction through slatted kitchen shutters. Now David rushed in and asked if he ought to go and get Chris. Vetoing this idea, I explained that the boy was in control of the session and I would wait for his return. Five minutes later he reappeared, this time clutching a bag of corn chips in one hand and a glass of lemonade in the other. Climbing back into the chair, he resumed eye contact with me while slouching back against the cushion. He allowed his legs to relax and positioned them in front of my hands.

I again asked him, without speaking, if I might touch his feet. He blinked once, lifted his right foot, and wiggled his toes. I picked up the foot and began to gently massage it, then allowed it to slide down and rest on my thigh. During the entire time, Chris maintained eye contact with me.

Seeing him sip his lemonade, I remembered the last visit and his grandfather's reaction to our sharing a drink. Again I nonverbally requested some, and again he pushed the glass forward into my hand.

Hedy had been sitting quietly on a sofa far from the action. She was carefully choosing her shots, trying not to interfere with our growing relationship. Her sensitivity to the situation allowed her to capture all of the high points of the encounter, actually making visible the invisible.

Shown in sequence, the photos reveal a ten-year-old boy slowly coming out of his autism for a short period of time. At first I'm sitting back from Chris, who is looking off to his right. He then turns to look directly at me, while I'm still using my peripheral vision to see him. The third photo shows him with his foot in my hand as I'm gently stroking his arch, then his calf muscles. Next he pushes the lemonade glass into my hand so I can take a little drink. It's the second time he's done this, so it's no longer a coincidence. It happens after my unspoken request.

I think of a joke that will please a ten-year-old, courtesy of my own Chris. Anything relating to body parts is fair game—especially disgusting sounds like belches and other bodily explosions. Smells are even better.

Lifting his sock-covered, formerly sneakered left foot, I grandly bring it to my face and perform the most courageous act of my life. I inhale deeply, allow a stunned look to come over my face, and then grimace.

No sound comes out, but my contorted eyes and lips say what my mind is shouting.

Your feet really stink! They really smell. Ugh. Ugh. Triple ugh!!!

For a moment he looks at me as if he has no understanding of what has happened. Then his lips begin to pull back, his eyes capture a light of awareness, his body shows involvement, and suddenly, without warning, he begins to laugh.

It's our joke, and we both know what has occurred between us. I can't believe what I'm hearing: real and appropriate laughter. Until that moment I'd never experienced this with any other autistic child.

The newspaper article reported what happened next; "Suddenly the boy looked at her, then started to giggle as she picked up his foot. She giggled too, rocked back on her heels, then reached up under his T-shirt to tickle his stomach. The boy curled up, shrieking in laughter. She extended her right hand palm out, and the boy met it with his left. They sat like this, watching each other as if in some kind of silent communion for several seconds. Abruptly the boy jumped up and scampered from the room."

The article went on: "Of all the specialists who have worked with Christopher—and there have been so many the Kratzers have virtually lost count—they say that Pat St.John, a 40 year old former teacher from Bridgewater, Conn., has been the most successful in actually reaching the boy.

" 'It may sound a little off the wall,' [acknowledged the Kratzers,] who watched breathlessly from the next room while St.John worked with their son, 'but it seems to work.' . . ." The reporter quotes Mary: " 'What happened in there—well to the untrained eye it wouldn't look like anything significant, but the fact that he sat down at all was significant. And to hear laughter—that was music to my ears. There has to be something special going on there."

Once again I understood how only those who truly knew the child intimately could judge accurately the success or failure of an interaction. What made this success all the more remarkable was how difficult Chris had been in the morning. The child I'd begun the session with that day was not in a good space, yet my behavior had positively affected his. In fact, better than having just an anecdote to recount, I now had sequential slides and the unbiased opinion of the reporter to substantiate what had happened.

Although nothing was able to stop or slow Chris's headlong descent into his autism, that afternoon and in subsequent sessions he had been willing to spend time in a nonautistic framework with me. And he'd also indicated his ability to decide just how autistic he would remain.

Clearly, this episode was not one of therapy, but of communication. It was tantalizing, much as those wispy paranormal events I'd experienced throughout my life had been, but better. Here I was dealing with an actual external reality, one where there was a true need for improved understanding and for intensive research. Once more I found myself deeply in love with what I was doing, with what I had come to think of as "my work." I loved being with autistic people. It was exciting, sometimes dangerous, always fascinating, neither better nor worse than working with dolphins. To the now familiar question, which do you like better, the autistic children or the dolphins?, my answer is, why there's no difference at all, they're the same to me.

The breakthroughs in communication, advancements in interaction, the skills and techniques to learn how to share all end in the same way. Once the sessions have ended, they leave me feeling a sense of awe, wonder, and a deep thankfulness that both dolphins and autistic children find me somewhat acceptable. Enough so we can cross lines and boundaries and begin to know each other.

Perhaps the better, more correct question to ask would be which part of my work I have come to love the most. Here, my answer would be different.

Learning. It's got to be the learning. I go into each experience like a starving person who is about to have her first meal in weeks. I want this, I need this, I must have this influx of unknown information in order to make each day worth living. It's what keeps the price high and the gift of life worth keeping.

To discover and understand what has been missing from the human experience, to use it to help others, is the supreme joy in life. At least in mine. To know there is so much I don't know, and to be learning, is the electricity that courses through my body and my mind.

Like an enormous game of cosmic hide-and-seek, the discoveries always seem to be hiding just around the next corner, the next tree, or the next dolphin pool, waiting to jump out and shout, "Here we are!" To my mind, there can be no better way to live than to be part of playing the game.

# Sixteen

*I*T WAS Labor Day weekend in September 1985, one month since I'd first met Buddy, Cooter, and Tessie. I had come back to Pennsylvania, joined by Jim and Judy, the American couple who had once helped me with my research in Bermuda. We were staying at the Scranton guest house, which was large enough for all three of us.

Freddie had arranged for me to speak to a local organization of parents of autistic children. I would meet with three of the kids and, hopefully, as a result greatly increase my knowledge of autistic behavior.

She'd arranged with head trainer John Fishback for me to return to the dolphinarium. She had also received permission for herself and Jim and Judy to enter the water.

Although comfortable with horses, Freddie had no experience with marine mammals. On the other hand, Jim, an ex-Marine and a scuba instructor, had met Rebel and Patrick in the water. At that time, his wife Judy, a U.S. Navy officer studying communications, had stood on the deck and watched, so she was as inexperienced as Freddie. As we sat together the first night in Pennsylvania I spoke nonstop about what they could expect and how to behave.

I outlined the basics for Freddie, but I went into greater detail and gave more specific instructions to the couple. I'd recognized Buddy's need to be totally in charge of females and was concerned that he might become aggressive toward Jim.

In the past, I'd witnessed an episode at Sealand when Scotty had literally attacked a man and his fiancée because the fellow had been territorial about his future wife. Once in the water, Scotty had beaten both of them with his tail, seriously endangering their safety, if not their lives.

Before they had gotten in with him, I'd told them to try not to show any relationship to each other, but the man couldn't resist. Only quick action by Bob Peck made it possible for the pair to get out of the water. He'd thrown a ball to Scotty and told him to retrieve it. The change in focus had allowed the couple to exit the pool in a hurry.

I'd liked Jim and Judy but knew little about them. They had arranged for vacation time in order to come to Pennsylvania and be with the dolphins, and had arrived a few days earlier from Bermuda to stay at my home. As I got to know them better, I grew to feel there might be some areas in their personalities which could cause problems with the dolphins. They were both superdedicated to the military, willing to take orders without thinking. This is fine in the Navy, but was too rigid a mind-set for interactions with dolphins, which might demand flexibility. They also clung to each other, never making a decision alone, always consulting each other. I was concerned that Jim might not be able to relinquish control of his wife to Buddy. This could create a major difficulty. Jim was an ex-Marine, but inside of him he was still in the service. He was strong, aggressive, and seemed to be eagerly waiting for a situation which might enable him to show how tough he really was.

Jim and Judy had come with their own wetsuits and equipment, including an underwater camera, but Freddie had rented a wetsuit for the occasion and would pick it up the day of the first session. I asked her to describe it, but all she could say was that it was black.

I explained why the suit was necessary. Even though it was early in the month, the past days had been cool and I knew the water would have given up much of its warmth. The next day we all met outside the employees' gate at the park.

After saying my hellos to John and his assistant, Michelle Abromitis, I went to the trainers' dressing room to change into my working outfit. As I came out, I suggested to the others that they put on their wetsuits as well. This way they'd be ready by the time I entered the tank.

Because there was no show to perform, I had time to spare. Seeing I was unoccupied, Michelle asked if I'd like to meet the other two residents of the pool. I'd never been up close and personal with a sea lion, so I eagerly agreed.

She opened the gate and released a small female, shining

and brown, with liquid eyes and wire whiskers. The animal slid over to Michelle on a magic carpet of water, stopping at her feet.

With the trainer's permission, I reached down to pet the sea lion. Her pelt was rougher than it looked and she smelled like the fish she was fed. I asked why the sea lions and the dolphins didn't share the pool, and Michelle explained that the sea lions were afraid of the dolphins. To illustrate, she signaled the female to enter the tank, which she did with all the speed of Mercury. In. Out. The dolphins hardly had a chance to know she was there.

Michelle then freed the biggest marine mammal I'd ever seen. The male, or bull, lumbered out of the opening and over to the deck. He wasn't overly fond of dolphins either. For some reason, he decided to include me on his least-wanted list.

Seeing me in my gray wetsuit (could I have looked like a dolphin to him?), his eyes flew open, his head reared back, he bared a set of huge brown teeth, and let out a roar. Then he dropped his head and, with a speed that belied his size, took off after me.

I never knew I could run down a set of stairs so quickly. I think I only touched one step in my hurry to escape. I don't even want to imagine what would have happened if I'd tripped or fallen, or been a slight bit slower. Thankfully, I hadn't and wasn't.

Michelle, recognizing my decision not to pet the behemoth, put both pinnipeds back in their enclosure.

Having just gone from zero to one hundred in two seconds flat, I decided to gather the shreds of my dignity and begin my session with the dolphins. Besides, I never said I was Dr. Doolittle.

I knelt down on the platform's edge and rapped my rings on the side of the pool. The three gray dolphins immediately headed toward me, lined up in front, and sent out chatters and sonaring signals. Reaching my hands out in front of me, I slowly undulated them in the now familiar up-and-down motion. Buddy separated from the others and came directly to my hands. Once again mouthing them, he returned my greeting through his body movements.

Backing up, he thrust his head high out of the water and began to toss mouthfuls of pool water in the air. Once again I recognized a behavior similar to that of one of the Bermuda dolphins.

I heard some voices behind me and turned on my side to see who was there. Jim, Judy, and Freddie had suited up and were now standing on the deck, anticipation showing in their eyes and their nervous pacing.

As I got a good look at them, I let out an involuntary groan. Freddie's wetsuit was indeed black, a throwback to the days of the Navy frogmen. It was thin, stubble-ridged all over, and created for any age or size of human other than a woman.

She was wearing only the top portion of the suit. I asked her why she wasn't in the bottoms and she pulled them from behind her back and held them up. They were three sizes too big for her. There was no way she could keep them on, much less wear them in the water. The top wasn't much better. It had wide gaps at the thighs which would allow a steady stream of water to pass over her torso and steal her body heat. This would totally defeat the purpose of renting the thing.

We decided that at the very least, the top would provide buoyancy and a small amount of warmth, so we agreed she should wear it in the pool.

I spent a few moments with Jim, Judy, and Freddie to identify which dolphin was which, and then took time to explain to Jim what he should do in order to get the best underwater photographs. Buddy glided to me, gave a direct look, and backed away to await my entry. It was almost as if he was asking what the holdup was and why I'd taken my attention away from him.

Twisting around and back into position, I slid off the deck and allowed my body to penetrate the surface, then adjusted to the water.

I was wrong about the temperature. It was way past being tepid; in fact it was much colder than I'd expected it to be. Dressed in full wetsuits, the other two would be fine, but Freddie was going to have a short, cold visit.

This time Buddy approached me immediately, pushed against my hand, and took me away for a tour of the tank.

To my left was Cooter, below Buddy swam Tessie. When we were done, Buddy moved away, turned in a tight little circle, and then stopped.

Coming to me a second time, he repeated the actions. His behavior indicated his seriousness, as if he was saying, *Watch what I'm up to. This is important. Keep your eyes open and remember what you see. There'll be a test later.*

Jim asked if he could join us and I suggested he follow my lead and lie on the deck with his hands extended. He did this, and Buddy left me to check him out. Within a few moments the dolphin had shifted his position to indicate his approval.

Jim slid in, holding his camera in front of his head. As I'd suggested, he began to explain what the camera would do, what its purpose was, and what he hoped to achieve. He asked Buddy to ignore him and allow him the freedom of movement necessary to capture the action.

As soon as he finished speaking, all the dolphins gathered around the camera with lots of clicking, buzzing, and bubbling sounds. Once done with their investigation, they moved away from Jim and had little to do with him until the session ended.

Now it was time for Freddie to join me, time for things to become serious.

I had her repeat the now familiar ritual with her body and hands. At my suggestion, she put on her mask and snorkel, then slid into the water. I could hear little chirps of dismay from Freddie as she felt the cold wetness flow through her top and around her body.

At first the dolphins kept their distance from her but then began to make swimming passes near her lower torso. Finally they crowded around her thighs. It was fascinating to watch how interested they seemed to be in her body.

Suddenly Buddy broke away from the others and swam directly toward me. Stopping, he became vertical in the water, stared directly at me, then righted himself, slowly opened his mouth and took my left hand in his jaws. Tugging gently, he guided me over to Freddie's feet, put my hand on her right heel, then removed his mouth. Once

again giving me his best *Pay attention* stare, he returned to
my hand, placed the bottom part of his lower jaw on my
left hand, and gave it slight pressure. Having done this, he
swam away over to Freddie's left thigh, where Tessie and
Cooter had already stationed themselves.

Buddy pushed against my friend's thigh muscle, sent
out a burst of sonaring sounds, then pushed again. He did
this two more times and then allowed the other dolphins
to follow suit.

Next, he moved down to her left calf. He looked at me
to see whether or not I was still holding on to Freddie's
heel. Seeing I was, he proceeded to push against her calf
muscles. I watched as he ran his rostrum from the top of
the area where the muscle met the knee, along the line of
the bone and down to the ankle. He did this twice again,
then once more allowed the others to follow his lead.

Then Buddy swam to me, chattered, lifted Freddie's
foot into a higher position, placed his rostrum on my hand
again, and pressed down firmly. He pulled away, looked
me in the eye, looked at where my hand was situated, and
returned to Freddie's calf.

I watched as he pushed and sonared the calf muscle,
following the sensory responses as they flowed down the
leg and to the feet. Several times he did the same movements, including the repositioning of my hands on her
legs, until it finally dawned on me what was happening.

The first thing I understood was that he wanted me to
keep Freddie's foot in one place, the position he'd put it
in. It was my job to hold the leg; I was the one with the
hands. The second discovery was his specific interest in
not just her legs, but how the energy flowed through the
muscles. His movements indicated that a definite and
well-delineated course of examination was being performed.

It started with the thigh muscles and stopped at the
upper knee. The next section began at the lower knee,
went down the calf, and stopped at the top of the ankle.
The last began at the bottom of the ankle and traveled
through the center of the foot and out to each toe.

I'd been watching carefully as the three dolphins pushed

and sonared Freddie's left thigh and calf muscles. They no longer needed to show me what to do. I was free to hold her feet and observe the situation.

Once done with articulating Freddie's leg into many different positions, Buddy came to me, again took my hand in his mouth, and moved me around to Freddie's right side. He placed my hand on her calf, pushed down, and immediately moved away to the ends of her feet. It was then I saw the dolphins touch and sonar her ankle, foot, and toes.

The series of slides shot by Jim show all of this as it happened. It would take me weeks to understand what I was seeing. It would take me years of observing the same behavior in other dolphins, whether in the United States, Sweden, Germany, or Russia, to recognize the universality of what they were doing and how it referred back to their interactions with humans.

The first concept was the role they'd assigned me. I was a human with the ability to steady their other human subject. Through repeated movements by Buddy, it was clear that he had given me a simple task to perform. I was also made part of a working team, which was to be an important factor in my next session with them.

The dolphins were picking up information from Freddie's body. They were specifically interested in her body, rather than mine or the bodies of others who had been in the water with them. What was different about Freddie?

She was very slim, with tight and well-formed leg muscles from years of riding horses. She had an absolute minimum of body fat. I had read in my initial research on dolphins that they had difficulty sonaring through fat cells, which seemed to distort their signal flow. I'd also been told by several trainers that their charges preferred people to enter their pool without a wetsuit because the rubber in the suits trapped air and confused the animals' ability to sonar humans. Perhaps the absence of any great amount of fat cells on Freddie's legs allowed the dolphins to have a clearer holographic picture of the inner workings of her system.

They listened in specific areas of the legs, only where the muscle met the bone. I theorized that they did this because the hollow bone area might be an additional magnifier of the information they were seeking.

They always went from the top of the muscles down toward the feet. Perhaps, like the flow of oxygenated blood from the heart, the sensory impulses stemming from the brain carried more information than those returning to the brain. If the human's neurological output was working correctly, perhaps it might be traced as it came from the brain and traveled through the body. I'd watched dolphins as they played with specific areas of my own legs and feet and had always wondered about their interest. I began to think that I was finally on to something important.

The course of my research was beginning to branch off into unexpected areas of development. Sometimes it was as if it had a mind of its own. But the concepts that were beginning to reveal themselves demanded more of my attention than I would have originally wanted to give.

I'd never been interested in massage therapy, unless I was the one getting the massage. Even now I rarely write longhand because the same medicine that injured my eye muscles also affected some of the muscles in my hands and legs. Too much use of my hands makes them ache and stiffen.

I was curious about those specific areas that the dolphins had shown such interest in. I also wondered why they always sonared down and along definite lines of the muscles. Perhaps this was the first proof I had that indeed, Freddie's minimal layer of body fat had allowed the dolphins closer inspection. I felt that this might be something to look at more closely.

Some weeks after that session, I was to spend an afternoon with Beth. She again had problems controlling her arm muscles. As I watched her, all of what I'd done, all of what I'd learned, and all of what I'd seen began to shape into an idea.

What if the dolphins had been testing Freddie's body for the proper neurological flow as it came from the brain and through the extremities? If this was so, then they would also be able to recognize when there were problems present in the brain.

Because the animals were constantly checking out each other's health status, they might be doing the same with humans. I wondered if it was possible for them to gather more accurate information by sonaring the muscles next to the bones and how they transported the energy that was emitted from the brain. If there were basic malfunctions at a neurological level, then those disabilities might be present and identifiable through testing other portions of the body.

Taking one more leap ahead, I wondered whether or not I could help Beth's arms to self-correct if I were to rub them in the same way I'd seen the dolphins work with Freddie's legs.

The final question in my mind came from left field. If all of the autistic kids I'd been with preferred not to have shoes, and sometimes socks, on their feet, was there an even greater connection through those feet? It might just be coincidence, but if the dolphins were interested in human feet, and the autistic children wanted theirs unshod, maybe there might be some kind of correlation. The least I could do was explore the idea.

I picked up Beth's arm and began to run one of my fingers down her muscle from her elbow to her wrist. It was easy to do and didn't create any strain for my hand.

She began to relax immediately. I did this with one arm and then lifted the other. With each stroke of my one finger, she seemed to be more in control of her own body.

I lifted her leg and, starting at the lower knee, traced a path along her calf muscle and down to her ankle, then from her ankle to her toes. Again there was a positive response, as if her body was finally receiving signals from the brain in a more normal manner.

Here were the roots of the same technique I was eventually to use on Bobby, the boy at the school in Philadelphia. It was this technique which was so helpful to him and his social worker.

For a long time I had no idea of what was happening and why it was of any importance. It wasn't until I'd given a lecture that I finally figured out why autistic children prefer not to wear shoes. I showed the audience the slides of my interaction with Chris and his response to massage.

I explained how successful massage had been for him and for his parents when they needed to calm him down. Putting it as a question, I wondered why he and the others preferred to be shoeless.

One of the men in the audience raised his hand and said he'd once heard that man's first step away from the other creatures of the earth came when he put shoes on. The shoes cut off his access to the information that was gathered from being in contact with the ground and forced him to use his other senses for survival.

I'll never know whether or not this is accurate, but it certainly seemed to fit.

I thought back to how much I'd had to rely upon senses other than my sight when I was a child. My entire survival depended upon how I evaluated everything around me. Regaining my vision allowed me to rely less upon those heightened perceptions, but they still continued to register and appraise everything and everyone around me.

If autistics were as sensorially aware as I'd come to suspect they might be, then they'd absolutely want to know what was happening in their environment by picking up the data through their pedal extremities.

I thought about the early Native Americans who would do the same thing. Wasn't this one of the benefits of their wearing soft moccasins which protected their feet but didn't cut them off from feeling the earth and recognizing the messages written upon it? Footprints in soft earth, broken twigs on a bush, still warm fecal droppings all spoke loudly of those who walked through the woods. I had often read of the skills of humans who could read the language of the earth and the "words" that the creatures who trod upon it had left for the educated to decipher.

Returning to my decision to work from an interactive level, I decided that my theories were fine; they made it easier for me to explain my findings to others. But my real goal was to help people, and this was where my efforts eventually proved to be worthwhile.

Time and again, I was to teach and use the same massage techniques to help autistics that I'd first seen that September day in the water with the three dolphins.

The intensive examination of Freddie's legs had happened so unexpectedly, so easily. Without the slides that Jim had taken to prove it had actually transpired and for me to review later, I might never have been able to support the discovery I'd witnessed. But Jim and Judy's presence added more than photographs to the body of knowledge.

Judy had not entered the water in the morning. After we left the pool for lunch, she asked if she could have a semiprivate session with the dolphins. She wanted to get into the water with Jim, but have me stay on the deck. I agreed to this, remembering how much I'd learned by observing Hedy with Rebel and Patrick. But I warned her a second time to be submissive to Buddy and to ignore her relationship to Jim. I went so far as to predict Buddy's physical response if she behaved incorrectly.

Freddie, having rented the wetsuit for just one day, asked if she could also get back in, and I said that would be fine.

Once back at poolside, the three of them lay prone on deck and performed the protocol movements. One by one they were admitted into the water.

The dolphins circled Freddie and resumed their sonaring of her legs, then stopped to swim over and investigate Judy. Jim had left his camera on the deck, hoping to have some contact without being separated by the camera lens.

Freddie didn't last very long, climbed out, wrapped a huge towel around herself, and stood next to the water's edge to watch Jim and Judy.

Buddy came over to Judy, sonared her, and then began to push her, gently at first, then with a little more force. She grew uncomfortable, even though I told her there was nothing to fear. Ignoring my words, she called Jim's name, asking him to come and help her. I knew that if he did this, it would be like waving a red flag in Buddy's face, so I yelled across the water and told Jim to stay where he was. He either didn't hear me or pretended not to and swam quickly to Judy's side.

Once next to his wife, he reached out and pulled her to him, holding her and stroking her affectionately. He was claiming his female and this was bound to cause problems.

I tried to keep my eyes on them and on Buddy at the same time.

Buddy had begun to circle, picking up speed with each rotation. His body movements plainly told what he was thinking, and he was not happy with the situation. He wanted Judy's undivided attention, and by golly he was going to get it. He finally came to the couple, stopped in front of them, then forced himself between them, using a slight body bump to push Judy farther away from Jim and closer to the far side of the pool.

By his third circle, he had managed to isolate Jim in the center of the pool. Buddy finned to a halt in front of the ex-Marine, sonared him for a moment, then moved forward toward Jim's chest. I heard a distinct *ooof* sound and watched in fearful fascination as Jim doubled over.

Buddy immediately swam away and waited for Jim to right himself in the water. He appeared to be making a decision, perhaps waiting to see whether or not Jim understood the message, which was *Get out of the tank.* When Jim resumed his previous position, making no move toward the water's edge, the dolphin approached him again.

This time Jim pushed out with his arms in an attempt to shove the dolphin away. It was a useless move, and Buddy hit him again, just a little harder, then swam away once more. The sound Jim had made was also louder, telling me how hard Buddy had hit him.

Standing next to a set of metal stairs, I took one of my weights from my belt and rapped the railing, hoping to get Jim's attention. At the same time, I called his name loudly.

"Jim, Jim. Swim slowly to the side of the pool and get out of the water."

I saw him turn to look at me, then shake his head from side to side, signaling no. Luckily Judy was more than willing to obey, grabbed the edge of the pool, and lifted herself out.

Once again Buddy came in to Jim, but this time he had increased the speed of his approach. *Oofff!* I heard this sound two more times and began to put on my swim fins and mask. If Jim didn't get out soon, I might have to call a paramedic to remove his body from the water. Buddy was angry and he meant business.

He had clearly and politely indicated his commands through his behavior. Each time Jim had refused to understand, the animal had "spoken" louder through his movements and body hits.

I took quick stock of the situation and came up with one last idea before entering the water. Jim had been a Marine, accustomed to taking orders. If I couched my request in the form of an order, perhaps he would respond without thinking.

"Jim!" I yelled authoritatively, at the top of my voice, "Get out of the water, NOW!!" To my astonishment, he turned, gave me a petulant look, and then finned to the pool's edge and pulled himself out.

I was angrier with him than I'd been with anyone in years. By not following my initial instructions, by not obeying my original commands, he had jeopardized the project, his life, and the animals. Too angry even to discuss it with him, I stormed off into the trainers' dressing room, took a shower, dressed, and then began to load the car. Freddie joined me, trying to calm me down, adding her insights as to what had just happened, agreeing with my evaluation of the encounter.

It was lucky for us that neither John nor Michelle had been there to see what had happened, or I might never have been allowed into the water again. As far as I was concerned, this would be Judy and Jim's last time with the Hershey dolphins.

We didn't talk about it for two days, until we were in the car returning to Connecticut. Finally, in a more civilized manner than I really felt, I outlined what they had done wrong.

I'm always willing to listen to explanations, and secretly I hoped Jim might have a good enough reason for his actions, one that might change my opinion of him and what had happened. He said he hadn't heeded my first warnings to get out of the pool because Buddy and he were just becoming friends. In his opinion, Buddy hadn't been attacking him. The animal had been increasing the strength of his body contacts because he was testing Jim

to see how strong he was and how much physical interaction he could take. I had misinterpreted a "mano-a-
mano" encounter which only males could understand. He
told me I had interrupted a special and private moment
between the two, that they were just beginning to really
get to know each other.

Even now, in retrospect, I am amazed at his appraisal of
the situation. I've never come up with a strong enough,
satisfactory enough explanation which would have been
able to cut through Jim's incorrect observation. He was
forever convinced that his understanding had been correct
and mine wrong. On the other hand, I hadn't wanted him
to be injured or die for his error.

I did try to tell him that dolphins don't physically test
people, they are direct in their communication, and Buddy
was clearly telling him to get out of the pool. Jim never
would believe me.

From this episode I learned to be even more cautious in
selecting who would actually take part in our research. It
was too dangerous to accept help from anyone who offered. Desire and good intentions would never be a good
enough reason to admit outsiders into our small circle of
hardworking volunteers. We would have to create methods by which to pick the right people. Anyone coming
with us would have to exhibit the willingness to accurately
appraise and use the proper protocols for dolphin interaction.

There was never any doubt that Hedy was one of those
special people, and in view of how aggressive and dangerous an animal Buddy could be when he chose to be, my
next set of interactions took on even greater importance.

# Seventeen

S TING'S MUSIC fell from the overhead sound system, enveloping the dolphins as well as myself. It was John's cassette and he'd put it on to relieve the silence that rose from the empty amusement park. The tape had played through the first side and was now on the first cut on the second. I'd never heard the song before, but the steady, swaying rhythm of "We Work the Black Seam," from the rock musician's *Dream of the Blue Turtle* album, caught my body in its web and I began to weave across the deck in time with it.

I heard the sound of water being broken and looked to the tank. Buddy, Tessie, and Cooter had moved to the center. They'd lifted their heads high out of the water, as if straining to better hear the music, then had begun to do what can only be described as a dance.

I'd seen them do a controlled version of this behavior when John had given them the proper cue, but he wasn't there and the dolphins were doing this on their own. I watched in fascination as they moved within the small circle they formed, dipping, touching, sliding around each other, weaving like cobras to the tune of a piper, swaying to the directions of some unseen choreographer.

John was in the back doing paperwork. Michelle had gone to lunch. This was the second day of my visit and I had arrived alone, having left Jim and Judy at the guest house to sleep late. This display was performed by three, watched by one. I stood on the platform, hardly daring to breathe, afraid my slightest movement would interrupt the spontaneous joy of the moment.

They stayed there, performing their sinuous dance, until the last notes of the song faded into the surrounding seats and off into the cocoa–laden air. In the seconds of silence that followed, they returned to their normal swimming patterns.

The air fairly dripped with the smell of hot chocolate. Humidity had trapped escaping odors from the nearby Hershey factory, and the desire for brown gold was inevitably aroused. It was nature's way of giving free advertising.

I called to John, asking him when I could begin my work. Trusting me now, he yelled back, "Anytime you want. I'll be here in the back if you need me."

I prepared my equipment and laid it all out on the edge of the deck. I didn't want to get out of the tank if I needed anything later in the session.

Doing a quick protocol series, I entered the pool and quickly acclimated myself. This time all the dolphins rapidly approached me.

Buddy took me off on a trip around the pool, again completing the behavior by going to the center. This time he sped up as he circled, forcing me into a tighter spin. Once my body had done this, he moved away to face me. Staring intently, he sent out a sequence of chatters, as if to ask if I understood what had just happened.

Over the years I'd learned to cope with the problems relating to my lack of depth perception. My tendency to rapidly become seasick in a dolphin pool had increased since my earlier days at Sealand, and my mobility in the water would always be something I'd have to deal with. Simply stated, I can be horizontal or I can be vertical in the water, but when I begin to mix the two, it's time for a Scopolomine patch, or Scop, to handle the problem.

Buddy approached me for another spin around the pool. Each time he'd made me complete the circle in the center; it was now becoming a pattern of behavior. A pattern of behavior? How could I have not seen it before? Once again I was being shown a sequence of behaviors which, when strung together, formed some sort of communication.

If I had this right, I should begin by grasping his dorsal fin, then move with him around the pool. After a complete circle, I should then stop in the center and make one full turn of my body. This had to be it.

The test of whether or not I was right would have to wait until after I'd eaten lunch. I hadn't expected so much activity and was beginning to feel uncomfortable. I needed to attach a Scop patch behind my ear and allow it enough time to work through my system.

As I climbed up and out of the pool, I called back over my shoulder to John that I'd be back.

It's too difficult to force a body back into a wet wetsuit, so I'd come prepared. I quickly stuck a Scop patch behind my left ear, slipped an extra large pair of jeans over my legs and a huge sweatshirt over my head, climbed into my car, and went off for a taste of Pizza Hut's finest. I'd chosen that restaurant because of their plastic seats, as much as for their speed in service. I didn't want to lose one minute of precious time with the dolphins, but I also didn't want to leave a wet surprise for some unsuspecting customer sitting on a cloth seat.

When I returned, I checked with John and found he had also given the animals their lunch. Now we were all in good shape to work. I entered the water and Buddy immediately picked up where we'd left off. Now, however, when we had finished the lap around the tank, I left him, swam to the center, and made a watery pirouette by myself. The Scop patch had worked and I felt only a slight wooziness.

Buddy instantly responded to what I'd done by increasing the pitch and rate of his chatter. He then came directly to my face and stared into my eyes. He pushed his flank toward my hand, waited for me to attach the flat of my palm to his side, and slowly began to move forward.

When dolphin trainers teach the animals their show behaviors, they create a sequence of actions which all end with a whistle, or what is called a "bridge." The whistle tells the dolphin it has successfully completed the action and it's time to move to the next one. But first comes a fish reward to show approval for the correct behavior.

It seemed to me that Scotty and Spray had done the same with me. Now Buddy was also doing it. It also appeared that the circling behavior was to indicate the end of a sequence of action.

Buddy swam to me, slid to my right side, moved gently past my right hand, paused, and once again solicited the placement of my left palm on his right flank. As we slowly moved around the circle of the pool, I realized the situation had somehow changed.

I was no longer an intruder in the pool, but rather a part of the team. Tessie was no longer shy around me, and continued to swim beneath me. Cooter, who was supposed to love to bite, took my hand in his mouth and gently rubbed my fingers. He also joined us as we swam, having placed his left flank along my right palm.

Around and around we went, all four of us in a tightly knit mini-pod of mammals. Buddy and Cooter stayed at the surface, respecting my limited ability to surface dive, while Tessie would usually move under the water, beneath me.

I suddenly became aware of what had happened. I'd somehow broken through the barrier separating human from cetacean. We had both crossed the midpoint and now were bonding together. The silent voices of my attitude and behavior had made it possible for me to speak eloquently of my purpose. I needed no words, no sounds to make myself known to them. The animals had responded in kind, through their behavior toward me. Yes, there had to be other forms of communication going on between them, but they'd found one way that would work for all of us.

We had begun circling in the center of the pool as I was thinking about what was occurring right then. The excitement I felt building inside of me was more than I could control. As Buddy began a slow surface dive, with my hand still attached to his flank, I started to breathe heavily, out of control. Like a runaway freight train, my breath picked up speed. I couldn't hold in air as I descended and had to release myself from Buddy's side and head for the surface, gasping wildly as I broke through.

Even as I'd succeeded, I'd failed. For the first time in all my years of doing research, I'd allowed myself to lose control of my thoughts, my attitude, and my body responses. It was, to use an old-fashioned term, unseemly behavior.

The three dolphins gathered around me, sending out signals to detect the state of my body. Staying just outside of my reach, they patrolled around me, patiently waiting for me to become calmer. Properly chastened, I retreated to the area close to the deck, allowed my body to become horizontal in the water, lying on my back to collect myself and locate my sense of inner peace and calm. The animals kept their distance while I did this.

Once in control and able to continue, I became vertical in the water, extended both hands, and hoped Buddy and Cooter would accept my motions as a sign of readiness. Within seconds, I watched as Buddy's large gray shape slipped past me on my left and Cooter's drew in to my right. I reached out and gently touched their flanks while Tessie came in to her place below us, and off we went for our swim together.

This time I kept a tight mental rein on my emotions, and once in the center again I took in a full measure of air, then fluidly flippered down to the bottom of the tank with my compatriots. Time and time again we did this, until I totally lost track of the number of revolutions we'd made. We eventually stopped, but only after the dolphins had lost interest in what we had been doing.

My body hadn't complained during the entire time we were moving. It was only after we stopped that my thighs, calves, and feet began to revolt by going into cramps. It was time for me to leave the water.

I raised myself up and out, then turned and pulled off my flippers and booties. Laying them beside me, I dipped my bare feet back into the pool.

I didn't want to end the session quite yet. I wouldn't be able to return until the following week. My heavy schedule required that I meet with the parents of some autistic children, drive back to Connecticut for a lecture and a meeting, drop off Jim and Judy, pick up Hedy and Sue Sherman, then loop back to Hershey. By the end of eight days, my little car would have traveled over two thousand miles.

The day's interactions had occurred in what felt like a bubble of time. Even the cool, humid weather had dampened and dulled the transmission of sound, giving the environment a feel of pale velvet. Everything that happened that day seemed to have been filmed through a soft-focus filter.

As I inserted my feet back into the chilly pool, I hoped to be able to pick up on a pattern of behavior surrounding the dolphins' interest in my extremities. Where would they touch, how much pressure would be exerted when they pushed, was there a specific place of primary interest?

In years to come I would sit on platforms and pool ledges in Cape Cod, Florida, Sweden, Russia, the Bahamas, and Bermuda, watching as dolphins repeated what I was now seeing in the tiny tank in Hershey. This was more than a game, more than casual interest on the part of the animals. They were repeatedly interested in specific areas. Clearly, their selection of body areas wasn't random. I watched the dolphins so intently my eyes began to ache as I tried to memorize what I was seeing and feeling. I would have to write all of this down as soon as possible so I wouldn't lose it.

As the sunlight began to fade from the September sky, I realized I could no longer sit on the deck. Even with the help of the wetsuit, I was losing too much body warmth. My feet were beyond pruney and my ability to feel anything was greatly reduced and fading fast.

I pulled my feet from the water, threw a cheery goodbye in the dolphins' direction, and stood up. Gathering my equipment, I headed for the showers, meeting up with John. We spent a few moments talking until he noticed I was shivering and sent me to get warmed up.

He wanted to let me know he wouldn't be there when I returned. He'd accepted a job at another dolphinarium in Hawaii and was leaving within the next two days. He told me Michelle would be in charge and she'd agreed to allow me to continue my work there.

After I'd showered and dressed, I found John, thanked him, gave him a gigantic hug, and wished him well. His willingness to observe and comment on my sessions had been of enormous help, and we would remain friends for years after. Eventually he would leave his new job in Hawaii, unable to abide the militaristic manner in which the dolphins were trained and maintained, and would return to college to get his degree.

In the days that followed, I met with three children of different ages and varying degrees of autism. I learned much from each of the boys, as well as from their parents. I had no doubt I was uncovering needed tools for making communication possible for all parties.

The five-hour drive back to Connecticut seemed to take sixty minutes. Except for brief, strained conversations between myself and Judy and Jim, most of the time was spent in silence. My mind tried to make sense of all I'd seen and experienced. Everything was coming in at lightning speed, almost too much and too fast for me to be able to review.

I dropped the couple at La Guardia Airport in New York City, then drove north for my next commitments and home.

The night at home allowed me the privilege of doing the laundry and repacking fresh clothes for the remainder of the week. It also gave me a chance to be with my son and enjoy his company.

The twin pulls of child and research were beginning to take their toll. Over the years, regardless of where I was or what country I was in, I always knew when it was three o'clock at home. That was when Chris would be there and I could call and speak with him.

Coming home, regardless of the wonders that would await me in my travels, always made leaving so difficult. But had I known what was to come, I probably would have lit out from home like a human Viking probe, exploring unknown universes, witnessing things unreported and unbelievable in their scope.

# Eighteen

$\mathcal{H}$EDY AND SUE arrived at my home the next morning and we loaded all of our things into my stalwart little car. With her genius for packing, Hedy was assigned the job of making it all fit together.

I filled the five-hour return to Hershey with accounts of all that had happened during the previous week. I was excited about what might take place in the next few days, hoping it would be at least as successful for them as it had been for me.

Like Freddie, Sue had decided to rent a wetsuit from a dive shop, although hers was in Connecticut. Her suit was just as archaic as Freddie's had been and I wondered how well it would fit. At least I now knew where old wetsuits went when they were no longer in style.

By the time we arrived back at the Scrantons' guest house, I had completed the story of how I'd placed my hands on Buddy's flank. Hedy said she hoped the same thing might happen to her. This would be her first interaction with dolphins since our trip in February.

We went out for dinner and then to sleep, wanting to be rested for the next day's session at the park.

The morning dawned bright, clear, and warm. It was a typical Indian summer day, a short period of deceptive heat which had followed a few days of deep frost. It was winter hiding in summer's clothing. But I'd take any heat we could get.

Because the park was closed for the week, I was able to drive my car inside and right up to the gates of the dolphinarium. At least we wouldn't have to lug all our gear like packhorses.

Michelle hadn't arrived yet and I didn't want to do anything that would compromise her position. It would have been a betrayal of her trust to get on the deck without her reiterated permission. We left everything in the car, walked over to the tank, keeping off the platform, and just stood together by the outer rim.

The dolphins came over to us, eager to see who we were and what we might want. I dipped my hand into the water and murmured Buddy's name. He came up with a *whoosh* sound from his exhalation through his blowhole, turned on his side, and gave me a long stare of recognition.

As Cooter and Tessie approached, I began to introduce the women with me.

"This is Sue Sherman and she's a friend of Freddie's. And this is Hedy, not only my friend but also here to take photographs of you. Please treat them as you would treat me."

The three dolphins "spy hopped"—held their heads above water—for a few seconds. It was as if they were imprinting the appearance of the women in order to re-member them later.

Buddy took off to the opposite side of the pool and, taking a striped ball in his mouth, dove down and popped up in front of us. He shoved the ball at Hedy, who took it and tossed it toward the center of the pool. Buddy imme-diately swam and retrieved it, bringing it back for another toss.

There were three balls, three dolphins, and three women. It began to look like a jugglers' convention with balls flying in the air and people and animals tossing them back and forth.

Suddenly Buddy stopped playing. In a firm motion, he flung his ball high into the air, over and out of the tank. The first time he did this we thought it was a mistake on his part. Walking around the pool, we found the ball be-neath a bleacher seat and tossed it back to him.

But once again, with an exaggerated toss of his head, he threw the ball not only out of the tank, but into an area we could not enter. Then he rounded up the other two balls and did the same with them. That certainly put an end to our little game.

Michelle appeared a few minutes later, explaining her tardiness and adding that the dolphins were accustomed to being fed at this time in the morning. It wasn't the first

time I'd seen animals that were impatient for their breakfast. In fact I'd made it a standing rule never to begin an
in-water session until the dolphins had been given their
morning vitamin fish. They were always hungry in the
a.m., and trainers would stuff vitamins and supplements
into one fish for each animal in order to support their good
health. They were always eaten if the dolphin felt well.

Now I understood Buddy's behavior better. He was
saying, *OK. We've played. Now where's the food?*

The three of us returned to the car and began unpacking
everything. I showed Hedy and Sue where to stow everything and went to change in the dressing room. They
followed me in and we once more rehearsed our game
plan. I was to go in first, Sue would follow, Hedy would
be last. She would shoot photos of the intitial interactions,
then get underwater shots.

I eagerly walked out to the deck and set my gear in
placc.

Prone on the platform, I sped through the protocols,
anxious to see if the dolphins would remember our interactions from the week before. As soon as possible, and
with my antiseasickness patch firmly in place, I spun
around and dipped into the water, too interested in my
work to feel how chilly it was. Each day brought the
temperature lower than the day before.

Face down, snorkel hanging from my mask, arms extended outward like a crucified diver, I waited for the
animals' response. I didn't have to wait too long.

Buddy immediately moved into position to my left,
Cooter to my right, and Tessie below. They had remembered. It was as if I'd never left. We swam together in
harmony, performing all the correct movements in the
proper manner, testing one another to see if there were
any gaps in recall.

Once we'd become sure of each other, I turned to see if
Sue was ready. Hedy was on the right side of the deck,
camera raised to her eye and hand moving the focus on
the lens. Sue was sitting on the edge of the platform, feet
crossed in a yogalike position. She'd been carefully watching what had gone on in the water.

Finning over to her, I called out and said it was time to get ready. She put on her wetsuit top, then her booties, and turned to lie prone on the platform.

Following my instructions, she placed her hands together in the prayer position and made the proper signals. The dolphins surrounded me and Buddy came forward to mouth her hands, then slid backward, awaiting her entry.

Sue donned her flippers, then eased her body into the cool water. I waited a few moments for the liquid to edge around her skin and for her to acclimate herself to her surroundings. Once I felt she was ready, I reached out with my right hand and took hold of her left one. I wanted to allow my left hand the freedom to touch Buddy, rather than Cooter. Leader to leader, rather than leader to follower. Protocol was always present in some form in our interactions.

As Sue and I began to slowly fin around the tank, Buddy moved in and under the palm of my left hand. I peeked out of the corner of my mask and watched as Cooter came to Sue's right hand and flattened his flank to touch her palm.

She slowly reached out to complete the contact and we continued our watery stroll. By this time, Tessie had joined us in her customary bottom position.

We made two complete circles, then stopped in front of the deck. As the dolphins swam away, I pulled the snorkel from my mouth and chattered wildly about what had just happened. The animals had actually accepted Sue, a total stranger, because of her relationship to me. They'd even allowed her to have the identical pattern of touch and movement. I couldn't help but assume the reason was because of the sessions we'd had before, my leader's dominance as well as the animals' trust in me.

This was thrilling, but I desperately wanted Hedy to be a part of this whole thing. I looked up toward the platform and she was nowhere to be seen. Where the heck was she? Why hadn't she photographed what had just happened?

I called out to her but there was no answer. Pulling myself halfway up the side of the tank, I rested on my arms and increased the volume of my voice and called her name.

A quavery answer floated out from behind the platform stage. "I'm here, in the dressing room. I'll be out in a minute."

Accepting her answer, I dropped back into the water, took Sue's hand, gathered up the rest of the pod, and went for another turn around the tank.

It was all so wonderful, so exciting. For a short time I'd crossed the boundaries between research and total participation. For a few minutes I also was able to just enjoy the very "beingness" of the situation, not standing back, evaluating and critiquing. It was my very first time in this role, and to my surprise it was pleasing, enjoyable.

Grudgingly I let the moment slip away. The professional side of me wouldn't allow too much playtime, and so I kept a sharp eye out for Hedy's appearance on the platform.

After what seemed to be years, she finally came up the stairs and onto the deck. She had her camera in her hand, and had I been less concerned with myself and my desire to share the dolphins with her, I might have also noticed how pale and drawn her face was. But I didn't.

I called eagerly to her, pushing her to gear up, do the protocols, and join us in the water. This she did, but there was a slight edge of reluctance in all of her movements.

After she finished the final protocol motions in her first interaction with Buddy, she turned and slowly dipped her body into the tank. As she became totally immersed, Cooter swam to us and yattered insistently. I turned my head trying to locate Sue and saw that she was face-to-face with Buddy on the other side of the pool, and so well taken care of. I clearly remember thinking, Well, if Cooter, who is a dolphin, wants us to join hands and swim, then it must be all right to do so. After all, he must be able to tell whether or not we're ready.

So I reached out, literally grabbed Hedy's hand, tugged her next to me, and took off with her and the dolphin for a swim. I was excited for Hedy, for her to finally have a special interaction with these gregarious and cooperative animals. I wanted it to make up for the difficult sessions we'd had in Bermuda.

Suddenly Buddy was in front of us. He'd arrived at high

speed, so fast I hadn't even realized he was coming. He stopped dead in the water, faced Hedy, and began to jabber quickly, in a high pitch. Then he moved forward and shoved her repeatedly toward the edge of the tank. We weren't even near the deck, but he wanted her out of the water, and he wanted her out NOW!

She quickly figured out what the message was and pulled herself up the edge, over and out of the pool.

Once that was done, Buddy turned to Cooter, then to me, and picked up where he'd left off. I felt like I was being scolded by my father for having made some grave and dangerous mistake, but I couldn't figure out what I'd done wrong. To make matters worse, Cooter was somehow involved in this whole thing.

Lunch! When in doubt, call a lunch break!

I headed for the platform, hauled my very puzzled self out, called over to Sue, and told her of my decision to stop the session. She swam to the very place I'd always exited, put her hands on the lip, and tried to lift out. After repeated attempts, she just couldn't get enough momentum to use that area.

I looked around and found a spot with a lower edge. Pointing it out to her, I suggested she try to get out there. She finned over, placed her hands on the concrete, and with great effort was able to come up and out of the water.

I handed her a towel and explained what had just happened. It was now close to noon, and cold water can sharpen even the dullest of appetites, so she readily agreed to my proposal.

We all donned our oversized clothing and headed off for pizza. The silence was intense in the car as I drove. Each of us was doing a mental review of what we'd done and what we'd experienced that morning.

We must have looked like a scruffy group to the people in the restaurant, because we drew more than our fair share of stares. After giving our orders, I began to explain to Hedy what had happened between the dolphins, myself, and eventually Sue. I told her how excited I had been, how smoothly things had been going, and then why I had pushed her to hurry and join us.

She listened quietly, nodding her head in agreement to

most of what I was saying. Once I'd finished, she began speaking in a halting and subdued voice. She explained how she'd been taking photographs of the first interactions. After Sue entered the pool, Hedy had run out of film. She quickly rewound the roll, but in her excitement must have moved the winder too rapidly. The film was stuck.

Fearing she'd lose everything, she went into the dressing room with some towels. She'd hoped to correct the problem by working beneath the covers and thus cutting out any light. Her film changer was back in Connecticut and she was trying to work with this makeshift emergency setup.

I'd begun to call to her and she'd tried to yell back and let me know the problem, but the distance was too great and her words had floated away, unheard, except for the last few sentences which she had screamed out.

Once she'd managed to extract the troublemaking roll, she'd quickly reloaded and come out to see what I wanted. She was already shaking from the stress of the situation and not in a clear frame of mind. It was then I had given her rapid-fire instructions and hauled her into the water. She said she'd trusted my judgment and hoped everything would work out all right.

Once she was in, I hadn't done for her what I had for Sue. I'd never given her a chance to acclimate her body to the coldness of the water, but just grabbed her hand, mumbled some unintelligible instructions through my snorkel, and taken her for a swim around the pool. Cooter had been on my left side, Hedy on my right, and she'd never even realized that the dolphin was with us.

Hedy said she'd begun to hyperventilate and gasp for air, feeling the toll of the stress from the film, the coldness of the water, and the insecurity about what she was supposed to be doing. She was rapidly losing her survival base. It was when her reactions worsened that Buddy had come up and bawled us out, sending her out of the tank and me away for lunch. She said she was certain he'd done this because of her distress.

This was the first time I was to see how my misguided efforts at leadership could affect those who trusted me, although other than during our trip to Bermuda and my years as a teacher, I'd never looked at myself as a leader. Now I would have to seriously consider the effect my decisions would have on the safety, even the lives, of those who worked with me. I'd never thought about it when I'd made the right choices, but the realization of what it meant to make the wrong ones suddenly became a reality. There might be room for mistakes when I was working alone, but never when I was responsible for other people.

I had to start reviewing my errors with the same intense consideration as I did my successes. I had made no attempt to see if things were all right with Hedy. While I'd been helpful and thoughtful of Sue when she'd first entered the water, I hadn't given Hedy the same courtesy. Worse than that, I'd placed my trust in Cooter rather than Buddy, expecting that he would be a better judge of our readiness to interact.

I had lots of apologizing to do, to humans and to dolphins.

We returned to the dolphinarium two hours later, having given everyone a chance to think things out. Sue decided not to reenter the pool, saying she'd become too chilled to be able to stand a second session that day. Hedy indicated she was ready, in fact eager, to go for another interaction.

After the proper protocol movements, made to a receptive Cooter and a distant Buddy, I once again slipped into the water. As I looked toward Cooter, I saw Buddy come to him and begin to chatter in a tone and manner reminiscent of a stern teacher. Then Cooter altered his behavior through his movements and sound. It appeared to be a dolphin's version of an apology to his superior.

I decided that this might very well be what I was seeing, and because I was just a transient student guest in Buddy's environment, perhaps I had better offer my own regrets. I slowly swam to him, stopped, and then began to explain what I'd learned at lunch. "I was wrong in my actions. I was wrong in my decisions. I'm sorry." He moved back a bit, then eyed me with a hard-boiled look.

Buddy made the dolphin equivalent to a harrumph,

moved his head up and down, and seemed to be only marginally mollified. I knew I'd made the right choice in offering the apology. Now I had to figure out what it would take to get back into his good graces.

I turned to Hedy and suggested she get ready to enter the water. As she leaned over the edge of the deck, Buddy came directly to her, mouthed her gloved hands, then moved back in expectation.

She dropped into the water and wisely took a moment to let her body adjust to the water temperature. Buddy came to her and she asked me what to do next. This time I knew it would be all right for her to reach out for a dorsal ride, which she did. Off they went, and I wasn't to see them again for quite a while.

Cooter came to me and pressed his flank to my palm. I moved into the familiar position and we went off for a few trips around the tank. Each time we stopped, he would open wide his mouth and with my bare hands, I would play with his tongue and around his teeth. I'd done this with Scotty and thought, correctly as it turned out, that Cooter wanted me to do the same.

I somehow understood that Buddy had relegated me to working with Cooter as a demotion for my less than correct behavior. Still, I was learning quite a lot even from this interaction.

Time can pass like quicksilver when I'm in the water with dolphins. I don't know how long it was before Buddy came to me next. I just know that the shadows had shifted and deepened, so I suspect it was at least forty-five minutes later when he moved Cooter away from my palm and led me across the pool to Hedy.

She and I were both prone, but she lifted her head up and back and spoke through her snorkel. "Buddy has been trying to show me something, but I don't understand what he wants. He keeps coming to me, taking my hand, then my arm, shaking them and moving back. When I don't respond, he begins to shake all over. What should I do?"

I fully understood the shaking of a frustrated dolphin body. I'd watched Scotty do that long ago in Cape Cod.

Buddy, this male, dominant dolphin, was trying to get a point across, but the communication gap was too broad. What could I do to help?

I decided to take Hedy's right arm and hand into my left one. Perhaps if we were joined together, Buddy might try the same movements again with our joined hands and I might be able to figure it out. Once I'd melded with Hedy, I turned to look Buddy in the eyes. Adjusting my attitude, I let him know I was ready.

Only after I'd done all this did Buddy move forward. He glided in, opened his mouth, took our joined hands, and gently put pressure on them. Then he moved down to my arm and pulled it toward him.

Well, that certainly didn't mean anything to me, and I let him know as much.

Once again he repeated the movements; once again I had no idea what they meant. He finned backward and began to exchange a barrage of sounds with Cooter.

Once more he came to me, this time with a greatly exaggerated set of motions, and repeated the sequence. Again I was lost. I turned to him and explained that he would have to be more overt in his actions for me to understand.

Thinking back on that moment, I realize how strange it was that I'd chosen to use the word "overt." For crying out loud, who says "overt" to a dolphin? But it was my best word at the moment. It set my mind on a clear and concise path. The dolphin had to make his actions even simpler, more understandable, and coherent for me to recognize his intent.

Once I'd made the statement, the two animals swam off to a further section of the pool for a conference. Hedy and I righted ourselves and watched as Buddy chattered in a distinctively high "voice" and Cooter responded in a lower register. They *dee-dee-dee*ed and *che-diete-che-diete*d back and forth, and then became quiet again.

I softly suggested to Hedy that we swim over to them as a team. I hoped she still had some more curiosity and courage left in her little bag of qualities. Would she ever have the opportunity just to enjoy an interaction? I was beginning to think not.

She agreed to go and we finned toward the pair of dolphins. By now Hedy was on my right side. As we approached, Buddy was facing Hedy, Cooter faced me. We came to a stop and allowed our bodies to become vertical, but still kept our arms and hands together. Buddy made a long string of sounds, looked at Hedy, then at me, finally at Cooter. Translation could have been, *Now pay attention, for crying out loud, and see if you can figure this simple movement out.*

Cooter pressed against my side, drawing my attention, and I looked at him. Winking his large eye at me, he slowly moved forward, opened his mouth, and placed his teeth on my fingers. Then he released the pressure, save for one tooth, which he began to draw backward and away to the tip of my finger. As he pulled, he left one slim little white line as evidence of his presence.

I'd spent many days with my hand in his mouth, even during the last hour, and he had never once tried to bite my hand. Now, with great deliberation, concentration, delicacy, and awareness, he had created this mark on my index finger. I was suddenly filled with an absolute, no-questions-asked "knowing" about what he wanted.

I turned to Hedy and said, "He wants you to take off your reef gloves."

She looked at me in surprise. "But you've always told me that I had to wear gloves to protect the dolphins from being cut by my nails."

"Yes," I answered, "but that's what I want. It's clear that Buddy wants you to take them off so you can feel his flank with your skin. So do it. Now!"

Reluctantly, Hedy pulled off her thin gloves, protesting how uncomfortable she felt by doing this. I asked her for them, crunched them into a ball, and threw them onto the far back corner of the deck. I wanted to be certain that she didn't put them on again—more out of desire to please the dolphin than distrust in her behavior.

I took Hedy's two hands and covered them with my lone right one, then told her I'd stay with her through whatever happened. I added that when the time was right, I would leave her alone with Buddy.

As soon as I finished speaking, Buddy moved forward,

opened his mouth, and engulfed the three hands. Hedy was still not thrilled with this, but I explained that it was his way of showing dominance and I had come to trust him. Then, slowly pulling my hand from the top of hers, I allowed Buddy direct contact with her skin.

I stayed by her side as she became accustomed to and comfortable with his mouth around her hands, whispering words of encouragement to both. Then Buddy pulled back.

At some signal, not seen or heard by me, Cooter moved forward and pressed his flank commandingly next to my left palm. I placed my hand on his side and moved forward, between Hedy and Buddy. As we passed, I called to Hedy and asked her if she was comfortable. With her "Yes" hanging in my ears, I felt free to move farther away with Cooter and leave her alone with Buddy.

Round and round we went. Each time we made a complete circle of the pool before we stopped in front of the platform. Then we stopped, faced each other, interacted in a variety of ways, such as my stroking his body or his opening his mouth for a tongue rub, then moved off again for another "stroll."

At one point, before we'd completed yet another circle, I began to think about Hedy and realized I hadn't seen either her or Buddy in quite some time. I wondered where they were and whether or not Hedy had left the tank. In a flash, as if he had read my thoughts, Cooter changed our direction and for the first time, cut the pool and took me into the center. He stopped, maneuvered my body in the opposite direction, then made a *che-dee* sound.

Lifting my head up and out of the water, I saw Buddy swimming around the edge of the tank. Firmly attached to his flank by her palm was Hedy. I knew how much she'd hoped to have this happen, remembering her words when I'd finished telling about the first time it had happened to me. I realized how special a moment this was for both the dolphin and my friend.

My curiosity satisfied, I was ready to resume our swim. Cooter pushed against my hand and immediately picked up where he'd left off.

A few minutes later we had stopped at the opposite side

of the pool, facing the platform. I was beginning to tire and chill and needed a short rest. I heard a *sploosh* from near the deck and looked in that direction. There were Buddy and Hedy, facing each other. I watched as he took her hands in his mouth, then moved his head up and backward, flipping her hands up, away, and into the air. I'd seen this motion before, earlier in the day, but when?

Suddenly I knew that he was telling her that he wanted her out of the pool. I opened my mouth to say that this was what he wanted, and just as quickly closed it again. It was her first chance to experience the rush of amazement that came with bridging the communication gap. Let it all be hers.

Without hesitation, Hedy turned and lifted herself out of the pool. When I asked her about it later, she said she'd recognized Buddy's head toss from the early morning when he'd thrown the balls clear of the pool. She figured out that he was doing the same behavior with her hands and this might be what he wanted from her as well.

With Cooter swimming next to me, I paddled to the same spot and turned to look at Buddy. I made a watery obeisance, turned to Cooter and did the same, and then exited.

By now I was a frozen Popsicle, too cold to take in the incredible events that had happened that day. It was only later in the evening, as we sat together and discussed everything, that we understood.

The dolphins, through their behavior, had taught us, shared their desires with us, made themselves known to us. They'd been willing to interact with all three of us because of my previous sessions with them. We, in turn, had been stupid enough to have made major errors, yet intelligent enough to have rectified many of them. Through keen observation on our part, we had been able to perform correctly, and successful interactions were our rewards. Most and best of all, I had witnessed, for the first time in my research, events that were sequential and totally related to each other, to the dolphins, and to us as humans.

Buddy had wanted to interact with Hedy so badly that he had figured out a way to communicate. While I was working with my partner, he was working with his. The result was that we four were able to understand each other. It was so remarkable that it made my discoveries about the importance of legs look like a minor breakthrough.

Actions most definitely had spoken more loudly than words. And if this day that had just passed was not proof enough of the incredible abilities of our cousins the dolphins, the next day was to cement our appreciation.

The night had been cool and the water temperature had continued to drop. Hedy was once again setting up her camera equipment and I had asked Sue to enter the water after me. She joined me in the tank and took a minute to get cool. Then Cooter took her off for a swim, dropping her near the platform.

Buddy approached Sue and began to sonar her vigorously, up, down, across, then with sharp jabs to her abdomen. He abruptly ceased his investigation and began to prod her, first gently, then with increasing strength.

With each jab, he shoved her closer to the area where she, alone, had exited the pool the day before. Once at the exact spot, he began to jam her into the side of the wall. *Get out. Get out, now!* was what his behavior seemed to say.

Taking no chances, Sue climbed out of the water, walked to the platform, and sat pouting in a puddle on the deck. Neither of us had a clue as to why Buddy had acted this way. Sue hadn't made any wrong moves. She hadn't had time to.

In less than five minutes, my attention was drawn to a wailing sound coming from the deck. It was Sue, doubled over in pain, unable to straighten up. She remained this way for a few minutes, until the throbbing ache in her abdomen lessened and she was able to control herself. She left the area and went to the dressing room to take a hot shower, change, and put on warm clothes.

Later, we studied the situation. She did not have her menstrual period. She had felt fine when she'd entered the water, but she had forgotten about her tendency toward arthritis, which was activated by extreme cold. Sue felt certain that the chill of the water had brought on a totally unexpected arthritic attack accompanied by great pain.

We all knew there was no way we could have ever gotten her out of the water if the attack had come while she was still in the tank. The water was too deep for Hedy and me to have been able to hoist her out. It was highly probable that Sue might have drowned had she not already been safely sitting on the deck.

We also knew that it was because Buddy must have picked up on this incipient life-threatening problem that he guided Sue over to her own area of exit, and probably saved her life.

A human can feel quite humble under such circumstances.

When we left Hershey Amusement Park for the last time that year, we had high hopes for what we would learn during our sessions in 1986. But this was not to be, and all because I had decided to write a thank-you note.

Freddie had called me to ask whether or not she should find out when the animals would be arriving from Mississippi in the spring. I told her I wanted to thank the officials of the park for having allowed us to work with the dolphins the year before, and tell them how much they'd enabled us to learn. I never received a response from them in writing, but the repercussions were powerful.

I was sent a letter from the director of the organization which owned Buddy, Cooter, Tessie, and many other dolphins. They didn't want me to interact with their animals unless I received permission from federal authorities. I called the director, solicited a detailed list of what I would have to do, which included sending him a proposal, then met all of his requirements. It was all a smokescreen, designed to send me on a wild paper chase and to ensure that I never again had contact with any of their dolphins, much less the remarkable Buddy.

One year later, under what was something like a military escort and after many telephone calls to the office down South, I was allowed a few well-guarded moments of lying on the deck. There, I did what I felt was the proper and polite thing to do. Thanking all three dolphins for their cooperation and for their willingness to work with me, I put a closure upon that segment of my research and my life.

It was the only time I ever allowed myself to feel the pain of leaving a dolphin in a tank. I didn't want to make a habit of repeating a mistake.

I'd originally learned how wrenching an attachment to a dolphin could be when I'd been told that my first teacher, Spray, had died. Somehow, I'd thought of her as always being there. The death of such a vibrant, special animal was not anything I'd ever considered.

Perhaps, subtly, I too had been drawn into the myth of these miraculous marine mammals. So filled with life, they seemed to be eternal.

# Nineteen

*S*ERENDIPITY is the playground of the inquisitive mind. It forces you to look back, reread through your mental files, and see how interconnected are the smallest actions of our lives.

Meeting a group of able-bodied and non-able-bodied divers in Massachusetts resulted in my becoming a professional speaker, which all began because I sang in a local amateur group in Connecticut.

I believe everything we do touches the world in some fashion. Even if I didn't, the events that I'm about to describe would have altered my beliefs.

In 1984, I was a soprano in a New Milford choral society which offered two performances each year. We did everything from Handel, to Bach, to Mozart, to more modern composers like Orff. It was a fun way to spend time with other people and stretch my limited singing ability. I've always thought of myself as an alto who tried hard in the higher ranges. I had to be a soprano because they usually carried the parts I could hear. I'd never learned how to read music, so I had to memorize it. Instant soprano!

Joan, one of the other sopranos, returned home to Michigan for a wedding for the first time in twenty years. At the reunion, she met Kathy Taylor, an old friend whom she hadn't heard from in at least as long. They talked, catching up on the years. Kathy said she'd become a scuba instructor, and Joan immediately responded that the only diver she knew was a woman with whom she sang. This person swam with dolphins.

Kathy jumped at the word "dolphin." It had been a dream of hers (as it is, it seems, for most of the civilized world) to swim with dolphins. Could she have my name and number?

When my singing mate returned, she warned me that I

might be receiving a call from her old friend. But it was too late—I'd already spoken with her three times.

Kathy was an older woman with a grown family. She sounded serious and well-grounded, not like what I termed an airy-fairy person, one who "just loooved dolphins." I let her know I was usually pretty standoffish and guarded about working with unknown people, especially because of my experience with Jim and Judy. She understood, agreed with my reticence, then offered an incentive.

She had friends in Boston, members of a unique diving club. Perhaps we could combine our trip to Cape Cod with a slide presentation for the group. While they wouldn't pay me, they would cover my expenses.

She explained how she'd gone on a trip with the Moray Wheels, a play on the name "moray eels," which was an adaptive scuba association. This meant it was a group of divers who had adapted scuba equipment to meet their specialized physical needs. She had provided diving support when the group made a short documentary film in Bonaire, an island near Venezuela, which is a popular place to scuba dive.

She had met Rusty Murray, a scuba instructor who'd become involved in a research program testing the positive effects of diving on disabled individuals, most of whom were wheelchair-bound. In the beginning days of the project, the early 1980s, the thought of teaching the disabled how to dive was an unheard-of goal. The program began working with and testing both quadriplegics and paraplegics. When the study was over, the participants were so keen on continuing that they formed their own nonprofit organization, which is still going strong.

Like the time that I had contacted Spiritual Frontiers Fellowship because I thought they would have parents of autistics who might be open to new ideas and concepts, I wondered whether or not a member of the "Wheels" might consider joining me in the water with a dolphin. After all, who was better to work with than a person who was already comfortable in the water and willing to dive?

If I was ever going to place an autistic child in a pool with a dolphin, then I'd first want to be certain dolphins would have the proper caretaking responses. Perhaps it would be helpful to set up an interaction between a dolphin and a physically disabled person and see what would happen.

I agreed to Kathy's offer and told her I'd call Sealand and set up a date for us to go there in early January. She said she'd make the necessary arrangements to come to Connecticut as well as for the Boston meeting.

I called Bob Peck to secure a date and was stunned when he informed me of Spray's death. He wasn't too clear as to the cause, but was willing to have me come back to the Cape. The only warning he had was that Scotty had become even more aggressive with humans since his tank mate had died.

Both my parents had had a history of medical problems. They had heart disease, diabetes, high blood pressure, and a myriad of minor but health-threatening difficulties. I was no stranger to late-night telephone calls which would send me to either the local hospital or to their house to await the arrival of an ambulance.

When my seventy-nine-year-old father died in February of 1983, it was after moving a cord of wood, to prove to himself he was still strong. The next day, after he complained of chest pains, I'd taken him to the hospital, where he succumbed to a massive heart attack.

My mother died in October 1984, after having spent a glorious weekend leaf-peeping through the hills of Vermont on a bus with other senior citizens. Her 2 A.M. phone call, telling me to get there quickly came too late for me to save her by the time I arrived twenty minutes later. Although I knew CPR, her coloration clearly indicated that she was beyond restoration.

I had grown close to both of them over the years and would miss being able to casually call them during the day. But I had known since I was a teenager that they were alive only because of the miracle of modern medicine. Their tenuous hold on life made it easy for me to know and accept the inevitability of their death.

I'd never applied the same ideas to dolphins. As when I'd overlooked how many teeth they had, I'd also passed over the issue of their mortality.

When I ended the phone conversation with Bob Peck, I walked into my bedroom and lay down. I couldn't believe the tremendous sense of loss I felt about Spray's death. Unlike my parents' passing, I had been totally unprepared for hers.

One week later, Kathy arrived and we set about getting to know each other. Although we found we had much in common, we never broke through the natural reserve which we each possessed. We became more associates than friends, but we also each admired what we'd achieved in life and had no difficulty in working together.

The long five-hour trip to Brewster was uneventful but filled with talk and music tapes.

Our sessions with Scotty weren't much more than simple swims in which Kathy made his acquaintance and Scotty and I renewed ours. Later, the only item of possible interest I could find in my notes was his willingness to interact without the aggression Bob had warned me about.

Three days later we traveled two hours north to a motel on the outskirts of Boston. As we checked in, we were concerned about contacting someone who had directions to the home where I would show my fifteen slides. This was in January of 1985, just before Hedy joined me in Bermuda, so I would have to fill in the gaps with stories of my work, allowing words to form pictures which would illustrate my efforts.

Kathy finally reached her contact and we were told to meet at a home outside Boston. It was owned by the parents of Betsy Pillsbury, a paraplegic member of the group.

We showered, changed, and found a fast-food restaurant for dinner, then drove into the dark winter's night, hoping to find our destination. We had no difficulty until the very end, when we cruised the streets like the lost ghost ship the *Flying Dutchman* in search of our home port. The streets were narrow, unlit, and poorly marked. We discovered the house only when Kathy called out that she'd recognized one of the cars.

We were not quite late, but I had lost lead time for setting up my slide projector and screen. Hurrying in, I introduced myself to Betsy but I barely saw the other people sitting and waiting for us. All I wanted to do was set up and have a few moments to catch my breath.

The day had begun with a session in the dolphin pool, then a long ride to an unfamiliar area. Now it was ending with a slide show. I was fast learning how to manage my energy so I could do my best at all times. But all that activity was also draining, and being something of a perfectionist, I hoped to give a good slide presentation.

It must have gone well enough because once I'd finished, I received an invitation to speak at the Boston Sea Rovers Clinic—whatever that was. I assumed it was a small group of divers who would like me to give them a nice night's entertainment. I had no idea of how special, remarkable, and famous the organization was.

It was made up of divers who had loved the sport from its early days in the 1950s. They'd wanted to educate people about the marine environment and about diving. They were the first volunteer group to offer a day's worth of slides, films, lectures, and workshops on the subject.

The main club was made up of local members who did all of the unpaid work needed to put on such a major endeavor. Later an honorary membership was created, including such luminaries as Dr. Eugenie Clark (who does shark research), Captain Jacques-Yves Cousteau, Dr. Bob Ballard (who located the *Titanic* and the *Bismark*), underwater cinematographers Stan Waterman and the late Jack McKenney, as well as many other underwater notables.

I felt truly uneducated not to have known that the Sea Rovers was not just a little club. No one had told me there was so much more to diving than breathing compressed air and getting wet. But because of their enfolding acceptance of my work, I was at last, after three years of solitary effort, to find a family that was eager to provide emotional support.

It had been a difficult, solo journey those three years. Without peers to critique my work, without feedback, I was almost like a tomato grown in a hothouse environment. I needed more than sun, soil, and water to continue to grow.

Among men and women who had fallen in love with

the sea and its occupants, I was able to learn how to become a professional speaker, how to judge our slides for
presentation, and how to communicate with large and
small audiences. My schooling would have been incom-
plete without their help, my life sorely lacking without
their friendship. Before any others, these people who
cherished and honored the ocean environment saw and
understood what I was doing.

I first spoke for the Sea Rovers during their March
Clinic and discovered the high energy and excitement of
being surrounded by folks with similar interests and dedicated attitudes. Even now, after so many years, I fairly
tremble with enthusiasm when I'm able to spend a few
precious hours with my friends, the professional gypsies
of the sea. The kinetic energy of the conferences is sometimes what keeps me going throughout the entire year.

Speaking at a scuba conference not only educates the
public, but allows those of us out there on the edge an
opportunity to relax and learn from each other. The giant
fish stories told by these people are no fairy tales, even
when they include encounters with Great White Sharks,
giant manta rays, three-mile-long underwater caves, and
long-lost shipwrecks.

It was at my first Sea Rovers Clinic that I met Butch
Hendrick, a pioneer in lifesaving and rescue techniques
whose work has enabled firemen, police, and many other
organizations and individuals to save lives. He approached
me after my pitiful fifteen-slide presentation and offered
to help me create more electric, more vibrant, more
professional shows. All I'd need was more slides. Thank
God for Hedy and her fine eye for action.

I saw Rusty Murray and Betsy Pillsbury at the clinic,
behind their booth, and was again struck by Betsy's radiant sense of life and willingness to try new ideas. We
stole a few minutes of private time so we could learn more
about each other.

After trading the usual information, we became serious.
I asked her about her disability and she was more than
willing to explain. She was now in her thirties, but it had
happened when she was seventeen. She had been sitting

on a second-story railing, talking with her sister. Blacking out, she fell over backward, landed on a log, and broke her back. She'd been bound to a wheelchair ever since, having undergone many operations over the years. She was employed full-time and served the Massachusetts Barrier Board, an organization which seeks to rid public places of barriers to access by disabled people.

Betsy had been diving for years and had also had one pool in-water interaction with a dolphin in California. She was more than willing to take part in getting wet with me and Scotty. Because our schedules were so heavy, we agreed to wait until the summer before setting a date.

The months sped by and I contacted her in late June. She hadn't forgotten my invitation and was ready anytime I was. I called the ever cooperative and generous Bob Peck, set a day for mid-July, and phoned her with the news.

I agreed to her request to bring along two other people as assistants. The first was Gwen MacDonald, who had originated the study which gave birth to the "Wheels." The other was Patrick Kilbride, a third-generation scuba diver from a well-known diving family based in the Virgin Islands. He would be in the Massachusetts area, having won a second-place award from the Our World-Underwater Scholarship based in Chicago. (Who would have ever guessed that because of Pat's wonderful sense of humor and absolute cooperation, I would one day willingly accept the offer to become an area coordinator and a sponsor for this nonprofit scholarship? Because of his contribution to our sessions, I was to eventually bring young people with us all over the world.)

We agreed to meet at Rusty Murray's home in Nahant, Massachusetts, then drive in a two-car caravan down to the Cape. During that short stay I was put through the hot tub ceremony which entitles only a few truly courageous individuals to become official Moray Wheels.

Rusty's openhearted and open-home approach to life makes being with her an adventure anytime. Her selfless energies on behalf of disabled diving programs have opened the world to people once sentenced to a lifetime confined to wheelchairs. As things turned out, we were to share responsibilities for coordinating the scuba scholarship.

Once in Brewster, we split up for a short time. Betsy and Gwen had decided to stay at a different hotel than mine because of the wheelchair access provided at their place. It was the beginning of my growing awareness of how little thought is given when buildings are planned to those who are physically disabled. I had been thinking only along the lines of the barriers society had created to lock out mentally and emotionally disabled persons. Now I was seeing an entirely new area of discrimination. I'd only expected to have learned from the dolphins on that trip, but Betsy truly opened my eyes forever.

That first afternoon we met with Bob Peck. He had wanted to interview the trio to ensure that they understood his rules about interacting with Scotty. I suspect he also wanted to be certain Betsy would be able to survive the sessions.

He told us our first interaction would take place that evening. Scotty had more shows to perform during the summer months and he would need some extra time to relax before having us in the water. We agreed to begin after dinner.

Knowing how cold the water could be, even in the warmer months, I had rented a drysuit. Although I'd been in the tank during the summer the year before, I hadn't done a night session at the time. I was looking forward to a situation similar to the one in Bermuda.

With the glass doors opened wide and the spectator section unsealed, the night air and sounds were free to flow through the enclosure. It promised to be a special encounter—but it was to be more than I ever expected.

We ate dinner, then drove to Sealand, parking next to the gate which bypassed the main entrance. It would be easier to lug our gear to the site from this location. As we made our way back and forth, I could hear Humphrey the Camel chewing his food. I couldn't help wondering what he was thinking when he saw us.

The night was still breezeless, the air filled with sounds

of the neighboring marsh. It seemed like the perfect setting in which to work.

Gwen and Betsy disappeared into the marine biologist's office to change. I took the ladies' room and Patrick suited up in the men's.

I wore the top half of my rented drysuit down around my waist. Women have the tendency to overheat more rapidly than men, and I intended to finish dressing only at the last possible minute. Besides, this was an especially thick and buoyant suit and it would hamper easy movement if I brought it up any higher.

We all met in the dolphinarium, near the end where the platform was. Bob pulled out a can of industrial-strength bug spray and offhandedly told us to feel free to use it anytime. I didn't want to be distracted by a few pesky mosquitoes and jumped at the chance to spray my head and upper body. Everyone else decided to take advantage of the spray too, and the air became a dense cloud from the spray and the smell of the stuff. It was enough to repel us, let alone anything that flew.

Once Betsy was ready, she gave the signal. Bob and Patrick lifted her up and out of her chair, then high enough to bring her over the railing and onto the platform.

We settled her in a sitting position, legs hanging over the deck, then I sat down next to her, on her left side. Scotty immediately surfaced in front of us to check things out.

A phone rang in the distance and Bob ran off to answer it, yelling over his shoulder that we could start without him. His departure also freed us to work more naturally and in a relaxed manner.

I'd already explained during dinner that I wasn't certain what I was looking for, but I'd know it when—and if—I saw it. I'd also said I would take full responsibility for Betsy's safety, which later would prove to be a key concept.

Now, with Scotty facing us, I had to play a delicate game of seesaw, watching and evaluating even his most minute movements and changes. While I had made my mistakes, as well as my correct calls, with Hedy, she had been physically able to protect herself. I didn't have that little leeway here, and I hoped I was worthy of Betsy's trust.

Leaning forward, I verbally explained to the dolphin who each person was, why they were there, and what their roles were, saving Betsy for last. I told Scotty of her disability and how I had agreed to be responsible for her safety and well-being. I would be her partner and her protector. I expected him to be on his best behavior when she was in the water.

I showed him her wheelchair, explained its purpose and that it belonged to Betsy. Then I repeated my request for his cooperation and understanding when we were in the water, reinforcing that I hoped he would modify his movements when interacting with Betsy.

He moved forward and opened his mouth. At the same time I leaned over the water, extending my left hand toward him, still holding on to Betsy with my right. Scotty gently held my hand, moved it up and down, then retreated and swam in a circle. He came back, opened his mouth, and took Betsy's right foot. We could all hear his loud sonaring sounds as he tried to jiggle her unresponsive foot and force it to move.

Again and again he did the same thing. Was he trying to perform a protocol movement, but with her foot? It certainly seemed that way. It was the month before my discoveries about legs with the Hershey dolphins, so I had no idea what I was looking at. If this was so, and my guess about the protocol was correct, then what could I do to simplify the situation?

Explaining to Betsy what I hoped to do and why, I inched even closer to her, then gently slid my right foot on top of her left one. Scotty came forward, took them both in his mouth, and tried to move them together. I could see I'd made an error in judgment in positioning my foot. With mine on top, there still wasn't any mobility.

Removing it, I put it under hers, providing it both support and movement. Scotty again came to us, and once more engulfed our two joined feet. Up, then down. Up, then down. He stopped and waited.

I moved our feet up, then down, doing it once again. We must have done it right, because he moved backward with a flurry of sounds. Then he came to us again, making us repeat the motions, as if to check that we really understood what had happened.

By now, Gwen had become so fascinated with the events that she'd drawn closer to the side of the pool. Finding that the wheelchair was keeping her from coming closer, she had settled into it rather than move it.

Scotty came over to her, raised his head out of the water, sonared her, and began to push against her arm. Push, push, push harder. What was he doing? I'd watched him perform many shows and had never seen him do this to any person by the railing.

Suddenly it dawned on me. Even though it was a totally off-the-wall idea, what if he was trying to get Gwen out of the chair because I'd designated it as belonging to Betsy?

I asked her to get up and stand near the railing. As soon as she did, Scotty stopped pushing and allowed her to touch his melon. Checking to see if this was just a coincidence, I asked Gwen to again sit in the wheelchair. The dolphin immediately came over and pushed her with increasing force.

Once she'd again left the chair and gone to the railing, Scotty gentled his behavior. It was not a scientific experiment and the conditions were less than perfect, but the signs were all there anyway. The dolphin had behaved as if he knew the chair was Betsy's and Gwen didn't belong in it.

By this time I had begun to sweat. The warmth of the suit, my own ability to exude great amounts of heat, the lack of cooling breezes, and the physical effort I was putting out on the platform all caused my pores to work profusely, totally overriding the bug spray. I was the only one who was creating such a luscious situation for the bugs. The others were just mildly annoyed by their presence.

I had just begun to slide Betsy into the water. She needed to become acclimated to her surroundings, and I was lying prone on the deck, holding tightly to her right arm. At first I was too engrossed in my activities to even hear the little flying teeth, but soon they arrived in greater numbers. Then I suddenly heard them, like a chorus singing one-note Gregorian chants, a steady *hummmmmmmm*.

I called to Patrick to come and take Betsy's arm while I solved my problem. He rushed over, took hold of Betsy, and allowed me to dash over the railing and to the bug spray.

I let the cloud of aerosol protection hang over my head, but it was too late. My own body was nulling the beneficial effects and I was still surrounded by mosquitoes.

There was only one thing I could do. I quickly pulled the rest of the drysuit over my shoulders, catching a few hungry insects and holding them prisoner inside the suit. They greedily bit me in places I couldn't scratch, making me even more uncomfortable.

But it was my head that was the worst. The sound of their whirring wings was breaking my concentration. I couldn't put the bugs out of my consciousness. The only thing I could do was pull the thick neoprene hood over the top of my head. This would trap the heat even more, preventing it from exiting through my hair. The finishing touch was the mask and snorkel, which I put on so I could keep the bugs out of my eyes and mouth.

I climbed over the railing, relieving Patrick of his responsibility. Scotty hadn't come near Betsy during the entire time I had been combatting the flying creatures. He'd only been interested in watching what I was doing. No wonder he was smiling.

Once settled back into position, we waited for him to join us again. He swam over, then made passing movements all over Betsy's body. It took him fifteen minutes to satisfy his curiosity, but when he was done, he moved backward again, seemingly waiting for me to enter the pool.

By this time I was melting with heat. Still holding on to Betsy, I used my right hand to wipe what little showed of my forehead. I moved my hand under the hood and drew it back, totally soaked with perspiration. This was more than my system could bear. I started to lift the hood from my head when I realized that it felt more cushioned than it ought to be.

I called Patrick over and as he approached, he stopped, staring at me in horror. Trying to remain calm and under control, he spoke in a low, commanding voice, ordering me not to remove my hood. It was moving, alive with thousands of frustrated mosquitoes that were also clinging to my back and shoulders. He feared I might freak out if I pulled off the hood and allowed the bugs to assemble in my hair. He was right.

My upper body was the mosquito equivalent of a bee swarm, every inch aquiver with bloodthirsty bugs. This was utterly, completely disgusting. (That night I won the *Guinness Book of World Records* award for the longest skeeve in history. A "skeeve" is that involuntary shudder and shiver one experiences when one is totally grossed out. Let me tell you, I skeeved for ten minutes.)

If I couldn't take my hood off and if I was beginning to have serious problems with heat exhaustion, then I'd have to find another solution. Now!

It was time to get into the water.

Telling Betsy that I was about to enter, I asked her if she would be able to float unassisted for a few seconds. I wanted to duck my writhing head and shoulders under the salt water and remove my living blanket.

It was no problem for her, so I made the fastest entry in my career and ducked down and under. When I surfaced, I watched what must have been thousands of mosquitoes float away on top of the water. It was a truly revolting sight, and I remember thinking we would have to be back the next evening to work again.

Turning my attention back to Betsy, I saw that she was comfortable but could lose her balance at any moment. Finning my body toward her, I moved into a position which would allow me to hold her in my arms. My right hand supported her upper back, my left held her beneath her knees.

Scotty swam to us with his ball in his mouth. He tossed it up into the air and to me. I tried to catch it with my left hand, but it bounced off and back to him.

He did this a few times, finally realizing it wouldn't work. As he swam away, still holding the ball in his mouth, I could hear him "talking" to himself. When the sounds stopped, he turned and came back to us.

Moving in toward Betsy, he placed the ball in her free-floating right hand.

"What should I do?" she asked me.

"Throw it," I said.

She tossed it as far as she could and he took off to get it. He did this several times, obviously having altered his behavior in order to accommodate Betsy and my restrictions.

When he lost interest in this game, he came over to us, submerged, and began to sonar her spine. She said he also placed his rostrum directly on the spine, as if sending in signals to sense how she was constructed. There was a lot of metal holding her fused spine in place. He spent a long time working with her body, covering as much of it as possible. He had never exhibited as much interest in mine or anyone else's I'd been with. His actions were definitely skewed in regards to Betsy's body. He would only swim away for one reason.

The aquarium personnel had placed a large loggerhead turtle in the water with Scotty. They hoped having a tank mate would alleviate his loneliness and boredom, even if it was another species.

Each time the turtle swam near us, the dolphin would leave. He would chase the poor creature away from us, never allowing it to approach. Whether he was protecting us from possible danger or jealous of losing all the attention we never could determine.

By now, Betsy was getting cold from lack of movement. She asked to be placed back on the deck, so I called Gwen and Patrick over and they assisted her up and out of the water. I steadied her from my position below, ready to cushion her if she fell back into the water.

I had hoped to spend a few private moments with Scotty. I must have had a foreboding feeling about him, or perhaps I was still sensitive to Spray's passing. As it turned out, I was only to see him a few times more the next year before he died.

Swimming over to him, I readied myself for whatever form of play he wanted to engage in. He came up, spy-hopped to look at Betsy, now seated on the edge of the deck, then looked back at me. Making a song of complex sounds, he moved forward, then pushed me to Betsy's legs. I took them in my hands for a moment, not sure what he wanted me to do. When there was no action on his part, I again finned to the center of the pool and waited.

Once more he came to me, sang his song, then pushed me over to Betsy. What was he saying? And why was he behaving in such a strange way?

I decided it must have something to do with Betsy, because he kept pushing me toward her. The more I thought about it, the more I realized what I'd said to him when I was first on the deck. Betsy and I were together. We were a team. She was disabled and I would accept responsibility for her well-being. So if she was sitting on the deck, then why was I still in the water?

Bingo!

I had taken the human approach to the situation. I knew she was safe with Patrick and Gwen. There was an entire set of unspoken clauses in my willingness to accept the role of Betsy's protector. But to a dolphin, there were no such codicils. Responsibility was . . . well, it was responsibility. There were no exceptions.

It was suddenly crystal clear. As long as Betsy and I were in the same area, Scotty would never interact with me as a single person. It was the two of us or nothing.

By now I was cooled down enough to risk exiting the water. I'd also taken the opportunity of being in the water to pull the hood back off my head. This allowed the cool water to reduce my body temperature via my scalp. I was salty, but not from sweat. But I was also too enervated to get out by myself. I called Gwen and Patrick over and explained my problem. With much grunting and straining, they were able to pull me from the water.

I straightened myself up, then sat next to Betsy's right side, once again putting my foot under hers. Scotty swam to us, mouthed our joined feet, moved back, stared directly at us and hummed a few bars of the dolphin version of "Good Night, Ladies," then dismissed us for the night. We knew this because he went to the center of the pool and just floated there, every so often letting out a *ploosh* to show he was breathing.

It had been an incredibly eye-opening and educational session. Once again I had discovered how little I knew, how much I had to learn, and how lacking in social awareness and responsibility I was. I had gained a larger insight into the mechanisms of social responsibility, something I knew next to nothing about. My poor training was not to be laid at the feet of my parents, but rather in the lap of humankind.

I could see how far we humans had gone from the simple structures of basic societies where individuals depended upon one another for survival. We had amended and weakened those basics with clauses which said, "It's all right to pledge eternal support, and it's all right to select just when that support is needed. Maybe now, maybe not. Excuse me if I make an error in judgment, even if it adversely affects you. If you live through my mistakes, I won't mess up again."

For the dolphin, living in an environment of constant predation, there might never be a second chance. Eternal support means eternal vigilance, as well as a code of behavior which can be totally depended upon.

I was rapidly learning to change my life in such a way that when I promised support, I meant it, regardless of what it might cost me. If I didn't want to go the full limit, then I would also have to place restrictions on my promises as they were being made, not after.

I was also shown, in relation to Betsy's disability, just how in control Scotty could be of his behavior. He was fascinating, educational, even instructional to observe. Once more I came away from a session with Scotty feeling that for all I thought I had learned, I had only begun to scratch the surface of what these animals had to teach humans.

This information amazed me. It was so simple, so uncomplicated, so right for helping autistic children and adults.

To me it was clear that by now what I had learned was beyond theory. In order for me to ever move further in my research and use it to help others, I would have to restructure myself. Though my work was research, I would have to place it entirely in the realm of reality. Even if what I was learning was untested and untried, I would have to respect it as having value, without knowing exactly what that value might be other than continued survival. This would place my mind, my brain, and my body in a similar state to that of the dolphin—always vigilant, always alert, always seeking, sensing, and sifting incoming data.

All those years I had been looking for a way to use my heightened perceptions for real situations. Now I fully understood the scope of that reality. It all came down to survival and how a society is structured. Does a society evolve in such a way that it protects only its own kind? Or does it grow to envelop and include other species as well?

For humans and dolphins, the answer was the latter. But in growing so quickly, with such ethnic and geographic differences, humans had forgotten the basics. One of them was that we are all humans, regardless of any other circumstances.

Dolphins assist other dolphins in need. Sometimes they have even helped people. Humans long ago lost the ability to blur the lines of their differences in favor of enabling one another to survive. Instead, they had set about further entrenching those dissimilarities. Instead, they had set about further widening the gaps that separated them from their own species. They created reasons to hate, maim, and kill other humans totally based upon differences in color, religion, nationalities, and beliefs.

I'd never given much thought to this concept, but here, in the water with a dolphin and a disabled woman, I finally understood. This was no theory. If we were ever to communicate with our species, much less others, we would first have to learn to support each other in our survival. Everything else would then follow and fall into place.

Perhaps the last vestige of a more basic bonding of Homo sapiens today lives within the word "diplomacy." Diplomacy is more than people trying to free hostages, more than folks hoping to forestall war. A loose and free society such as ours in the West is faced with interacting with more restrictive ones. Diplomacy is the bottom line in protocol. It says, I respect you, your people, your society, your land, your environment, and your values. Even if they aren't the same as mine. And I expect the same behavior from you.

I would have to learn how to live as a diplomat for the rest of my life if I was ever to achieve success for my work, let alone for myself.

The rest of the sessions with Betsy were much the same, with Scotty reinforcing my understanding of accepting responsibility for the safety of others. We were lucky that the next two evenings were too windy for mosquitoes to be a bother again.

We spent the next day repairing seining nets, putting them over our toes and catching crabs, eels, and other fish in tidal rivers for exhibition in Sealand's small aquarium. Patrick, Gwen, and I would lift Betsy's wheelchair and park it where she could see and take part in our adventure. During a wild ride, trying to catch up to Bob's speeding car, Patrick sent us into fits of laughter with his version of a famous French marine explorer. His right-on satire was all the more hilarious because he knew the man personally. The warmth of the days was chilly in comparison to what we felt as we came to know each other and learned to work together.

The night after our final session with the dolphin, everyone, including Bob, let out all the stops. We ate dinner, then played in the hotel pool until 2 A.M., oblivious to anything but how much fun it was to be together. If it hadn't been for Scotty, this might never have been possible.

My work had begun with Scotty, had grown with Scotty, and was about to come full circle and end a cycle with Scotty.

Once more, serendipity, which brought me a diving community, the Moray Wheels, Betsy Pillsbury, and a crucial understanding of the most basic nature of my work, was to play a major role in bringing together all I'd discovered and done.

# Twenty

$\mathcal{A}$S IF TO forever bind my work together, a major chapter in my life that began with the eyes of a dolphin, ended with them as well.

Bea and Beth loved to vacation on Cape Cod. It was their tradition to leave for the Cape in mid-September, when prices were lower and tourists were scarce. The area they usually stayed in was within five miles of Sealand.

Bea asked her daughter if she would like to go and watch Scotty perform. After all, it was almost as if they knew him because of my connection with both Beth and the animal. Beth agreed and so they made their first visit. Once they'd returned, Bea had called to tell me about the experience.

Her daughter had come away from the dolphinarium with feelings of anger and sadness. She had hated the enclosure where Scotty lived, and was angry at his captivity.

In September 1985, she wrote a poem about her feelings. She titled it "A Sea Verse In Sea Rhythm."

> A sea angry sea season
> Wanders on with desperate reason
> To and fro and come and go
> Sea only knows. I don't know
> Why a sea rage went enraged
> And we decide a dead season saved
> Every dolphin and seal we caged
> To words decided some work to wish
> I am deciding a dedicated fish
> To reward with. In winter I
> No longer cry about such animals' plight
> As angry gales protect the whales
> From dedicated tourists who argue right
> Words but gesticulate
> Too much and laugh and cheer

> At every trick. I terribly fear
> We do them harm.
> I am doing all I can
> To save them and declare them won.

The captivity of dolphins was a subject I'd long ago had to reconcile myself to. Having worked with them, I felt I understood their situation better than most people. I also saw it from an entirely different perspective than did the owners and trainers, as well as environmentalists. This was no black-and-white problem, and Bea asked me to write to Beth about my feelings and thoughts on the matter.

It was time to put it all down on paper, to commit my opinions for anyone to see.

I realized it was difficult for me to dislike either side, and found myself speaking out in support of both, beginning with captivity. When done correctly, intelligently, and with care, by professional trainers and not just young kids cutting fish and taking low wages, captivity for dolphins is not as bad as we would think. When done incorrectly, it can be worse than any nightmare we might imagine.

The shows themselves are the reason why so many people have gained a high awareness of marine mammals. It's my guess that the moratorium on whales might have come much too late if an entire generation hadn't learned the truth about these enormous, remarkable animals from having watched the many "Shamus" perform in Sea Worlds around the United States. Even the dreadful television show "Flipper" brought a heightened understanding of the dolphin into our own homes.

These days the trend in marine shows is toward education. Trainers eventually discovered they were reaping the negative benefits of an uneducated public, most of which was their fault because of how they marketed the animals. Putting dolphins and Killer Whales through behaviors in shows which were narrated with inane story lines only made people think of dolphins as a cross between oceangoing Lassies and circus clowns. By 1986, administrators of dolphinariums began to see the awful thing they'd done and started to create shows that were more educationlly accurate and informative.

Breeding programs for captive dolphins have enabled the animals to reproduce. Captivity allowed veterinarians to perform long-term observations and tests. They were able to learn how to create a healthy environment for their patients, how to treat medical problems and how to avoid them. When dolphins began to strand in increasing numbers, what had been learned from captive animals served to help those living in the wild.

Should we ever reach the point of no return in our diminishment of dolphin pods, the knowledge that has come from successful breeding programs may eventually be the key to preserving the species and returning animals to the sea to increase their numbers. I think of those programs as savings accounts for the future, to be used only when necessary. Hopefully that will never be the case.

Captivity is a paradoxical situation. The very ability of the public to experience dolphins close up has created a movement toward freeing them.

Where the right line of defense should be drawn is not a simple decision. In my years of research, I have witnessed some of the all-time best dolphinariums as well as the absolute worst. Whether or not the animal is happy doesn't seem to be the question. The dolphins all appeared to be interested in interaction and communication, but they were all totally involved with their survival. As long as they were fed, they would find ways to survive in their own situation.

The one place that we saw a great difference in how captive dolphins behave with humans was in a certain swim program in Florida. We would interact with the animals in between their paid sessions with up to thirty people a day. The dolphins were jaded, as if they'd lost their ability to relate to people in a normal manner. Although they eventually began to behave with us as all the other dolphins had, it took them a long time to shed their "professional" personalities and relax enough to really be themselves.

They were immediately "on" the moment a human entered their water space. They never relaxed and were just dolphins unless they were alone without humans. It was as if they'd been robbed of the very thing that made them what they were.

In their place were animals who were supposed to fulfill everyone's fantasy of what a dolphin ought to be. Allowing themselves to be handled constantly seemed to lessen the very specialness of that contact. If I were ever to state a firm opinion on captivity, I suppose I least like swim programs. They educate many people, but the cost is too high for the animal.

One place even runs meditation workshops where people swim with the dolphins, then learn how to breathe in the same way. Of course they never will, because it is physically impossible, but the idea brings in willing participants who fork over thousands of dollars for the experience. Unfortuantely, some of the dolphins become overly aggressive, even sexual with people. Then they shove, push, and manipulate their victims so that the swimmers often exit the water with gigantic bruises.

One of the workshop leaders I met had this happen to her. She admitted feeling that this wasn't quite what she had expected the encounter to be. She must have adjusted her thoughts on this subject later, since she now speaks glowingly of having been selected by the dolphins as being special—an honor.

I once read an article by a psychologist who had totally bought this idea. She wrote of dancing with the "sea snakes," a cutesy reference to the elongated and limber dolphin penis. She told of being overly rubbed, of her bruises and her fear. But she concluded that it had been an honor to have been chosen to dance in this way. I've always wondered if she would have reacted in the same manner if her partner had been a male human or another species of animal.

Perhaps these women think in terms of dolphins as not being truly sexual beings, just perpetually smiling, benign and nonaggressive. They don't seem to accept that the animals' interest is nothing other than a desire for copulation and control.

One of my more amusing memories happened at the same location where people pay to meditate. I was sup-

posed to have met a woman, a friend of an acquaintance
of mine, at this open-air dolphinarium.

I arrived in the area, checked in to my motel, then drove
over to wait for her arrival. Walking in, I said hello to one
of the owners, a man I'd known for two years, then
strolled over to the edge of the enclosure to watch what
was going on in the water.

There was a woman, stark naked, hanging on to the
twin dorsal fins of two male dolphins. She was being
towed for a ride and was poised high above the dolphins'
backs, like a figure out of mythology. You could see she
was engrossed in her own fantasy come true for all to see
—and they did see all. Although I was embarrassed for
her, I couldn't help watching the spectacle happening in
front of me.

This continued for a few more minutes, and then the
animals dropped her in search of their fish reward. I
moved over to the owner, an older man, and asked him if
this was unusual. "Nope," he said, "I see women do it all
the time." No wonder he loves his job.

The mermaid eventually retrieved her suit and put it on
in the water. Then she lifted herself onto the floating dock,
climbed the ladder up the side, and came over to me. She
introduced herself as the woman for whom I was waiting.

Great. Didn't Allen Funt once ask what you would say
to a naked lady? Well, at least I could try to find out why
she had been undressed with the dolphins.

"Oh," she said, "when I held on to their dorsal fins, the
top of my bathing suit came down. I knew they were
trying to tell me that they wanted me to be as free and
uncovered as they were. I had to join them in my natural
state of being. It was an exhilarating experience having
bonded with the dolphins in this way."

Continuing, she proudly announced, "I'm going to
write a book all about communicating with dolphins."

I suddenly understood why so many trainers felt that
perhaps I was one of those "crazies." I was instantly em-
pathetic with them. I supposed they'd heard it all before,
especially from people who were going to write THE
book about communication. In spite of my normally
open-minded approach, I couldn't help but label this

woman as less than knowledgeable about her subject, although she did say she knew so much because the dolphins had channeled the information to her during their ride.

So many people think that because they've experienced the presence of the dolphin, they know and understand the essence of the animal. What they lack in education, they most certainly make up for with imagination. It's their vision of free dolphins which forms their mind-set.

The dolphin in the wild is an especially beautiful creature. Free and fast, it will sometimes choose to slow down and be with humans. I've experienced my fair share of wild encounters. These animals seem more ghostly, more ethereal than those trapped in tanks. They possess the very spirit of unfettered existence. Knowing that they don't have to spend time with you makes the interaction sweeter.

Watching them race on bow waves of boats, surf on the crest of white foam, stroke each other, and leap out of the water, twisting and turning in the bright sunlight makes the human spirit soar. It's like being on the bottom end of a kite string. You can feel the tug of the elements but you are firmly planted to the ground, never to possess that total freedom.

I suppose captivity to a dolphin is the same as being reeled in like a kite attached to a thousand feet of string. It's just that one is inanimate and the other possesses an exuberant attachment to living life fully.

My heart has always said that dolphins ought to be free. Yet in view of mankind's willingness to destroy the ocean environment and those creatures which live in it, my head must support the concept of benign captivity, whatever that may mean.

If it hadn't been for captive animals, with nothing else to do but spend the time teaching me how to behave properly, I might never have learned as much as I have, as quickly as I have.

Twice, I made attempts to exchange information with a gentleman who does research only with wild populations of cetaceans. Twice he wrote back, disdainful of my work, claiming it had absolutely no validity because it was gathered through interactions with captive dolphins.

Yet all that I've learned from these animals has proved
to be helpful and accurate when applied to those dolphins
living in the wild, as well as with autistic children. Can
anyone afford to disallow what is learned from creatures
willing to teach, regardless of the state of their freedom? I
like to think not.

This was what I wrote to Beth in answer to her poem,
ending by explaining that life is imperfect. We must all
make sacrifices in order to live. A captive dolphin may die
for many reasons, but a free one dies too. The difference
is that the captive animal serves to remind us of the treasures that live in the sea and provides us with the knowledge of how to protect them.

Willingly or not, some humans have sacrificed their
freedom for the betterment of their fellow beings. Perhaps
the same could be said of dolphins like Scotty and Spray.
Reasoning thus was the only way I could accept the prem-
ise of captivity and continue to do my work.

Beth's first visit to Sealand had been in 1985. Her
mother said they would return to visit Scotty the next
year. She later told me how much better her daughter felt
about his captivity once she'd read my heartfelt reply. I
suspect I felt better as well for having finally come to grips
with my own feelings.

Over the years, Beth continued her writing, and eventually coauthored a book with her mother and one of her
at-home teachers. The subject of how each of them perceived her autism was a fascinating concept.

Here is her poem entitled "Christmas 1986":

> *To try is to fail, so I am served by neither,*
> *Only appeased for the moment by my*
> > *lessened madness*
> *In some leaning towards an ordinary show*
> > *of what's expected.*
> *You want a normal performance.*
> *Well, I find the task prisons me*
> *Behind bars of mighty opinions righteously*
> > *ordained by*
> > *word wielding others*
> *Who dare to declare boundaries.*

*I try but little does nothing.*
*I drain lesions of their poisons—*
*Today is lanced of putrid yesterdays*
                    *and swelling tomorrows.*
*I foster fighting. I test my health*
*By more longing, not to open hands*
                    *take and hold*
*But loneliness recognize on each nodding*
                    *yes hiding needy*
                    *don't do mortal prison.*
*I generally fight. I test my other*
*By less longing, more to close hands*
                    *take and hold*
*And sense experience in each nodding yes.*

In the summer of 1990, Beth and I went to my local YMCA, together with Hedy, Bea and Cindy Cornett-Stendig, one of MID★POINT's volunteers. Beth and I had never been in the water with each other, and I felt that if the time ever came for us to swim together with a dolphin, I'd better begin building the bonds of respect and trust between us.

I had visited with her earlier in the year and asked if she would like to be with me and a dolphin. She'd written back "YES" in big letters.

Just before the session at the Y, she had come home from the school she was attending for a ten-day visit and was not in a good humor. She'd already had a difficult time for two weeks before she'd returned home. Now she was into twenty-four straight days of difficulty.

Bea met us at the Y and warned us that there might be problems, even no interaction at all. She also explained that Beth didn't like being in the water, didn't swim, and wasn't comfortable in a pool.

I walked over to Beth and gently took her hands in mine. Telling her I'd be there to support and protect her, I also let her know she was in control and didn't have to go in the water if she preferred not to.

Then we all began to walk slowly toward the entrance.

I have a deep sense of privacy about my work with

autistics and usually try to keep the sessions between the child, myself, and an absolute minimum of people. This was the first time Hedy had met Beth, although Hedy and I had worked together for five years. She was there to capture our session on film, while Cindy was to provide any assistance necessary in the event of a problem.

We entered the building and went through the necessary paperwork. While the others took care of signing in, I walked Beth over to the twin windows which faced the larger pool and the therapeutic one.

Her body began to vibrate with fear, and I could see it in her eyes. She pulled me to her and firmly placed her lips on mine. Even there I could feel the tension coursing through her body.

I drew away from her but kept our eyes locked together. I said to her, "If you don't want to do this, it's fine with me. I don't mind and we can leave right now. But if you choose to continue, I'll be there every step of the way."

She pressed her lips to mine again, this time with a barely perceptible lessening of stress. I let her see the pools again, explaining what we would be doing, then took her hand and led her back to the desk.

Bea asked her daughter if she wanted to continue, and Beth began to walk toward the entrance of the pool. We all followed her in and went to the dressing room.

Once we'd changed, we walked into the pool area, past the main pool, and over to the therapeutic pool. The lifeguard said we could have ten minutes before it was to be used by a class of little children, and so we all went into the area.

Here the water was a bathtub-warm 92 degrees. It was a great place to begin, because Bea had said that her daughter hated cold water. Placing our towels on a bench, I took Beth's hand and began to walk backward down the steps, into the water.

At first she looked apprehensive, but as the warm water moved around her legs, she relaxed. I didn't want to urge or pull her in, but time was slipping by and so I moved ahead of her, gently tugging her forward at her mother's suggestion.

A look of concern passed over the girl's face, but she moved forward with me and farther into the water. She occasionally pressed her lips over mine, always checking and testing.

As she became more accustomed to our being together, I began to move around in the three-foot depth. Her body relaxed; we were comfortable with each other and where we were. I could have stayed there for hours. Unfortunately, our time was soon up.

Gathering our things, we moved the few feet over to the Olympic-sized pool in the main room. It was family swim time and we wouldn't be interrupting the more serious folks who were locked into their laps. I knew what that was like, having gone there almost every morning for years to do the same.

Backing down the stairs at the shallow end, I held tightly on to the railings, trying to put off being totally immersed. Because I'd first been in the warmer pool, the water felt twice as cold as its 82 degrees. I knew Beth wouldn't appreciate this, because I sure didn't.

Bea knelt behind her daughter while I stood in front, holding on to her arms to keep her from going face first into the water. Her grimacing face mirrored my feelings.

Once in, she turned to me, her body stiff with fear, concern, and coldness, and alternated between holding my lips to hers and looking in my eyes. Softly, without words, I told her she didn't have to do this, but if she wanted to, I would be there to protect her the entire time. By now, after all of my years of work, I could be certain that I understood the true nature of my promise. I meant that if necessary, I would be there at the expense of my own life. I would never allow her to place her life in danger.

My mind slipped back to the past for a microsecond, to my first session with Betsy and Scotty. I realized how far I'd come in understanding the nature of any promise I might make. Sending a silent thank-you to the long-deceased dolphin, as well as nod of my head to Betsy, I turned my full awareness back to Beth.

She had calmed down, even though gigantic tremors brought on by the cold water coursed through her body.

She was as relaxed as possible, staring me in the eye, resting her arms on mine.

The water in the pool is kept cool at the request of those doing laps. It's cold when you first enter, but by the time you've done six laps, your elevated body temperature can't feel that of the water. Once you stop, the cold creeps up on your body again. If you don't move at all, you just become colder.

I could see this was the case, so mercifully suggested we move over to a third pool, the hot tub. There the water was well over 110 degrees, and maximum time in is supposed to be fifteen minutes.

I walked in first, then guided Beth in after me. The change in her was immediate, almost miraculous. She quickly responded to the heat and moved into my arms.

Cradling her like a baby, I felt her entire body totally relax. She hung in my arms as if she could stay there forever. I watched as her legs began to bob in the jets of bubbles merrily moving out of the spigots all around the pool.

The longer we sat there, the more relaxed she became. As for me, the perspiration began to ooze from my forehead and every now and then I'd get a taste of chlorine and sweat-salted water on my tongue. The hotter I became, the redder my skin grew. I looked at Beth, who was as fresh as if she'd stepped from an air-conditioned room. The longer we stayed, the looser and happier she grew.

Finally, unable to stand it one second more, I ended the session and moved out of the tub. Jumping up onto the side, I helped hoist her out and sat her next to me. Hedy's slides show me redder than a lobster, looking as if I'm about to faint, sitting next to a slightly pinkish Beth.

A few days later I received a poster with two dolphins on the front, mouths open, forever smiling at the camera. On the back was a note in Beth's bold handwriting which said:

Dear Pat,
We pooh pooh the widely held idea yonder wide ocean would want to dry up one day. Worlds of won-

derful vanishing home water creatures wane the
thought. Words we want to amaze world disbelief.
War words would have no meaning oodles on water
wonder animals. We hooray amare (Bea explained
that amare means love) wammo dolphins who woo
us with woman more wonderwater and under water
good work. Words we amaze you with but you
amaze me.

    Love, Beth

Bea called later and said her daughter's behavior had
completely turned around from the moment we left each
other. The remainder of her visit was enjoyable and they
both were able to make the most of the time spent with
each other. She felt the change was directly related to our
in-water session together.

Why had Beth been so willing to go with me, to push
herself beyond her own comfort, to try something that
might have been unpleasant? Why would she write "YES"
when asked if she wanted to someday be in the water with
a dolphin? To me, the answer was obvious. Its seed had
been planted in September of 1986. Back then, unknown
to me, Beth was about to help me finally decide to dedi-
cate my entire life, my total being to my research.

She had returned to Cape Cod for her vacation. Bea had
asked if they might visit Sealand and Beth agreed. At the
dolphinarium, they had stood beside the pool as Scotty
performed alone. The crowd was small, most people not
having chosen to vacation so late in the season.

As the sparse group of spectators slipped away in search
of other things to see, Beth had stepped closer to the railing. Scotty swam around for a few minutes, then approached the women waiting to see him. Gregarious as
ever, he found his ball, then tossed it to them for a quick
game of catch. Bea helped her daughter throw it back.
They did this a few times, then Scotty lost interest.

He swam in front of them, stopped, then directed an
intense stare at Beth. Eye-to-eye, the two individuals with
whom I'd shared so much, learned so much, were at last
in touch with each other. What passed between them only
they will ever know.

Then the spell was broken by the entrance of the trainer carrying a bucket of fish for a training session. He called the dolphin to him, and Beth was again alone with her mother.

They walked out of the building and over to the central one where the ladies' room was. Bea had brought Beth there to take care of her needs. It was while they were alone together in the small room that an incredible event happened.

The next week I received a simple postcard from Beth. On the front was a photo of Scotty leaping out of the water, touching a miniature basketball held by the owner of Sealand. Spectators line the railing, watching the animal perform. On the back, in bold print, she had written:

> Dear Pat,
> Today we saw Scotty again. He gave to me a big inspiration—and I spoke. You faded out too—meaning I address my thanks to both you and Scotty. I am about to emerge. Love, Beth.

She spoke? She *spoke?* What did she say? What had happened? How had it happened? And why did she think I had anything to do with it? Until they came home again, I would have to wait another week to find out the answers.

When I called Bea, she told me of the visit and the eye contact. Then she said they'd gone into the ladies' room. Turning to her, Beth had looked her in the eye, then loudly and clearly said, "Good."

That was it. One word, intelligible and loud. "Good."

I always buy special dolphin gifts for Beth as Christmas presents. It was late September, but I couldn't wait three months, wanting to congratulate her on her breakthrough. I wrapped up the glass hologram necklace of a dolphin and put it in a box along with a second necklace of a small gold dolphin swimming next to its larger, silver mother. How appropriate it was, under the circumstances. Then I wrote Beth a long letter of praise and congratulations and mailed it off to her.

Her answer epitomized all of the work I'd done, all of the sacrifices I'd made, all that I'd discovered and learned.

It brought into sharp focus the true reasons why I'd sought to listen to the silent voices of communication beyond words.

Dear Pat,

I am dearly so delighted with your exquisite gift— and even more by your letter which I am admiring not so much because of the wonderful feelings actually expressed as the actual feelings you inspire in me. I am going to say more than "good!" That was a beginning only.

I good am saying but am agitating to say wonderful. I love the dolphin necklaces—a golden holographic fish is long in beauty and the silver dolphin and child are long in durability. Beauty and durability —ancient words which you know the currency of. You are a direct descendent of oracular healers.

I am good and new again—fish out of water is swimming again.

Thank you. We are more than wordless—we are fortunate. Beyond madness lies delight and love in all lessons of life.

Love,
Beth

I could feel my heartbeat in the pounding in my chest and the pulsing in my head. It was as if I had been overcome with understanding, as if the final veil had been removed from my eyes. There it was, simple, beautiful, and eloquently explained, an idea I had chosen to avoid examining for so long.

My hand trembling, I placed Beth's letter on my lap, closed my eyes, and took a deep breath, finally allowing myself the freedom to examine the last important piece of the puzzle. I had thought of myself as a detective, tracking down the clues that would solve a mystery. I had told myself that I had maintained a proper, somewhat impersonal, even dispassionate distance from what I had sought to identify. But I had only been hiding the truth from myself.

Ironically, it took Beth's ability to communicate through her writing to show me that the circle was complete, not only because of what I'd learned from both dolphins and autistic children. It was also because of the quiet bonds of respect, appreciation, and mutual understanding we had built together that I had grown to be interwoven into the fabric of their lives and they into mine.

Without my realizing it, by frequently slipping over to their point of view, their side of awareness, perception, and appreciation of life, I had actually become the midpoint myself. I had stopped observing and begun to experience what was important to them, which ultimately became equally important to me.

The circle had become a triangle. No longer was the equation simply dolphins and autistic individuals. Through Beth's eyes, and the eyes of so many dolphins, I now recognized that I had quietly bridged the barriers of communication. We had all learned from one another, had all grown better because of each other, had closed the gap by defining the lines of our similarities, as well as accepting the right to maintain our differences.

The answer to the question, the mystery of what dolphins and autistic children have in common had finally been revealed. By Beth's including me, I realized that all of us, working together toward the same goals, create the necessary components for successful survival and interaction. Each of us not only held a piece of the larger puzzle, we were pieces ourselves. By giving equal value to one another, we had made it possible for all of us to communicate with and understand each other.

# Epilogue

$I$T WOULD BE wonderful if everything always ended happily ever after. But that only happen in fairy tales, and this is a story about events that really happened.

"Good" was the only word Beth ever spoke. Whatever her reasons may be, all her communications since her encounter with Scotty have been through written words and our silent interactions. As I told her, life is imperfect. We all make our own choices, then must try to live with them.

With or without words, she is an incredible young woman, and happily, I continue to learn from her and her mother.

I know the fate of Scotty and Spray, she having died a full year before he did. I have no idea whether or not Cooter, Tessie, and the redoubtable Buddy are still alive and performing. I never saw them again after that last time in 1986 when I lay prone on the platform in front of them, guarded by two women trainers ready to eject me at a moment's notice should I suddenly become crazed and try to leap into the pool. At least that was what their attitude seemed to convey.

Sealand is no more. Bob Peck, with others, eventually bought it and it's now named Cape Cod Aquarium.

Under the original ownership, Sealand permanently lost its permit to keep cetaceans, although for a time it successfully housed a large young pilot whale which had stranded on a nearby beach. The animal can now be seen at the Miami Seaquarium.

While it was still Sealand, Bob, ever the educator, improved and enlarged the Underwater Education Program, where divers of any age would come to the location and swim with the dolphin, observe the seals, learn about the aquarium, assist in gathering local specimens for display, do a scuba dive on a wreck, and take marsh walks to learn about the local ecology. He also employed well-informed naturalists who taught the course. It was well thought-out and a fine example of what good swim programs could become.

As for me, I continue to feel as if every day holds a miracle. When I began, I'd never expected my initial curiosity about my heightened perceptions would have led me on such an incredible journey. What had started as a search for a better understanding of my own sensitivity and how to improve and use it eventually evolved into an ever-branching tree of knowledge.

As the years have sped by, I've discovered a great deal more about communications, about interacting in communal situations, as well as about myself. I've also gained more than I've lost, even though most of what is gone was only possessions to sell and some innocence to lose. I'm sure I never owned them anyway, they were just on loan.

I've lived with this book inside me for many years. Of all those who knew that it would inevitably be written, I was the only one who hadn't known I could do it. But here it is.

I rediscovered memories I'd forgotten, came to see more clearly the way the research progressed, realized why it developed as it did, and recognized how what Hedy and I and eventually our volunteers at MID★POINT have done was even more deeply rooted in my past than I'd thought.

Since 1985, we have had too many adventures and learned too much to be able to include it all within this book. I hope the future will yield yet another one. Most certainly the quest has continued, at least enough so that I was elected a Fellow of the Explorers Club for my efforts. Me, an Explorer. I never would have thought that possible.

More than this, I've become a risk taker—a remarkable achievement considering my formative years. I amaze even myself sometimes—but what else, other than my life, have I got to lose? After all, I'm only an "exspurt."

Yes, I found myself at the core of my work, but I sure wasn't looking for me.

Having come from a family which was so self-centered,

I was initially uncomfortable with my discovery. Eventually I grew to accept the role I played within my own work. Luckily, this growth of self moved me ahead and into a far better position to continue doing the research. It also allowed me to reject and refuse to ever accept emotional abuse again.

The process, similar to all of my work, was a simple and basic one. It went something like, "Well, OK. I know I'm at the center of what I'm discovering. That's nice. If I know it, then I don't have to convince anyone else of the same thing. I'm free now. So let's get busy with something else." And I did.

I would develop the skills and techniques through which workshops and lectures would be shared with so may others. MID★POINT would enable many more people to do the same thing I have done.

No longer would it be "the work." It wouldn't be "my work." Instead, it would become "our work." Besides, sharing is so much more enjoyable than trying to protect some little thing you've learned. And it was a truer reflection of the social structure of a dolphin pod.

Our differences don't need to separate us from each other, creating barriers to communication. What is native to each one of us will be forever, and we should honor and respect it. I will always see things my way because of who and what I am, you will see them your way.

That doesn't mean I can't learn to appreciate your point of view, nor you mine, or that I can't learn from you. As long as we agree we each have a piece of life's puzzle, a clue to solving the mystery, then we can work together toward common goals. As long as we accept and respect each other for our divergent beliefs and ways of living, then we have a way to communicate.

The autistic children I've met in the United States, the dolphins I interacted with in so many pools, the friends I've made from around the world, all know.

Words aren't necessary to make us understand each other. No matter what our species, we all speak the same secret language. Steeped in silence, in voices that tell stories hidden to the ears but not the eyes and our other heightened perceptions, we create subtle bridges of com-

munication, built through the recognition of our most basic universal forms of self-expression.

Attitude.

And behavior.